D1448746

WITHDRAWN

# THE COLOR
# OF FREEDOM

SUNY series in Afro-American Studies
John R. Howard and Robert C. Smith, Editors

# THE COLOR
# OF FREEDOM

## Race and Contemporary
## American Liberalism

DAVID CARROLL COCHRAN

State University
of New York
Press

Published by
State University of New York Press, Albany

© 1999  State University of New York

All rights reserved

Production by Susan Geraghty
Marketing by Dana Yanulavich

Printed in the United States of America

No part of this book may be used or reproduced in any manner whatsoever
without written permission. No part of this book may be stored in a retrieval
system or transmitted in any form or by any means including electronic,
electrostatic, magnetic tape, mechanical, photocopying, recording, or otherwise
without the prior permission in writing of the publisher.

For information, address State University of New York
Press, State University Plaza, Albany, N.Y., 12246

**Library of Congress Cataloging-in-Publication Data**

Cochran, David Carroll.
      The color of freedom : race and contemporary
American liberalism / David Carroll Cochran.
          p.     cm. — (SUNY series in Afro-American
studies)
      Includes bibliographical references and index.
      ISBN 0-7914-4185-7 (hardcover : alk. paper). — ISBN
0-7914-4186-5 (pbk. : alk. paper)
      1. United States—Race relations—Political aspects-
-History—20th century. 2. Racism—Political aspects-
-United States—History—20th century. 3. Race
discrimination—Political aspects—United States-
-History—20th century. 4 Liberalism—United States-
-History—20th century. 5. Afro-Americans—Civil
rights—History—20th century. 6. Civil society-
-United States—History—20th century. I. Title.
II. Series.
E185.615.C634  1999
305.8′00973—dc21                                               98-30115
                                                                              CIP

10  9  8  7  6  5  4  3  2  1

*To My Mother and Father*

# CONTENTS

# ACKNOWLEDGMENTS

I could not have written this book without the advice, criticism, and support of colleagues, friends, and family. I owe my thanks in particular to Ronald Terchek, Mark Graber, Ollie Johnson, Melissa Matthes, William Galston, Clarke Cochran, David Cantor, Jonathan Olsen, Mary Beth Melchoir, Fred Morton, Issa Khalaf, Guy Deweever, Connie Hill, and Tara Santmire. My wife, Christine, was the first person I spoke to about the original ideas for this book, and her encouragement, as well as her hours of help with editing, during its long course has been nothing short of remarkable. She could write a book on how to deal with a spouse who is writing a book. Christine also joins my friends Scott Stefanski and Craig Price in pulling me out of the house on occasion to remind me that there are things in life far more valuable than working on, in Craig's words, "your little project."

# CHAPTER 1

# *Introduction*

Black and white. It is perhaps the deepest cleavage in American life, and from the beginning the question of freedom has been at its heart. At its founding, the United States was both the freest country on earth, a land where people came to escape the stifling constraints of Europe and its feudal legacy, and the least free, a land where people brought in chains from Africa endured the brutality of chattel slavery. The division between white and black Americans has its roots in the institution of slavery, in the starkest possible division between those who are free and those who are not. As a land "conceived in liberty," freedom has always been the cardinal virtue of the United States, and so its deepest and most persistent public problem has always centered on its history of either obliterating or subverting the freedom of black Americans and on their efforts to overcome this history. Slavery and the legacy of segregation, discrimination, and exploitation that followed it insured that the abiding struggle for African Americans in the United States would be one of moving from subjugation to liberation. It is a struggle that did not end with emancipation or with the fall of Jim Crow, but one that continues today. Black and white Americans still constitute two groups that experience the promise of freedom very differently.

This essential link between race and the ideal of freedom shows how questions of race are inescapably moral ones. The phenomenon of race is always bound up with a complex web of normative categories that shape its meaning in American life. Throughout American history, arguments for such things as natural black inferiority, the beneficent paternalism of slave owners, abolitionism, racial equality, civil rights, and black nationalism have all relied on deep and evolving moral assumptions for their power. In this way, race always exists against shifting and contested background understandings of its moral meaning and significance. By background understandings, I mean those sets of normative categories that people draw upon to make sense of and form opinions about issues in public life. Capitalism, for example, relies on a background understanding that establishes the moral value of categories such as individual initiative and choice, deserved inequalities, and rational self-interest. Communism, on the other hand, relies on a background understanding that gives categories like economic exploitation, alienation, and collective responsibility their normative force. People have very different moral reactions to economic issues depending on which understanding they draw upon. These kinds of normative understandings supply people with the moral language they need to make sense of, think about, and take positions on the world around them, and this is why they are so important in shaping public life. They provide the normative context in which particular issues are framed in particular ways and the moral ground upon which people struggle over them. So anyone examining issues in public life must be aware of how such issues are framed and their resolution shaped by particular normative understandings. Race is no different. Mapping and critically examining the normative understandings that Americans use to make sense of, think about, and take positions on issues tied to race is critical to any meaningful exploration of it. If we are to come to grips with the profoundly complex phenomenon of race in American life, then it is vitally important not only that we think about race, but also that we think about how we think about it—that is, that we examine the normative understandings we draw upon when doing so.

Perhaps the most important source of the normative understandings Americans rely on to shape their reactions to issues and events in public life is the political and moral tradition of liberalism. Liberalism provides Americans with the moral language they use to articulate their core political values—things like individual liberty and equality, the rule of law, rights, the free market, and so on. Liberalism's categories, therefore, have a powerful influence on how issues of race are framed in public life and on how Americans react to them. This is particularly true when we look at the relationship between race and freedom, since freedom is itself a normative ideal so central to the liberal tradition in the United States. Liberalism, in short, is one of the most important influences on contemporary understandings of race, freedom, and their relationship to each other. It provides the moral ground upon which questions of race and freedom intersect, and my aim in this book is to explore this ground. In it I offer a critical examination of contemporary American liberalism's normative understanding of race, one that centers on the role played by the concept of freedom.

I examine an understanding of race within American liberalism that has been profoundly influential since the Second World War. This understanding is that of color-blind liberalism. Color-blind liberalism claims that race is a morally arbitrary trait that should make no difference to one's prospects in life. People should be free to live their own lives as they individually choose with no restrictions or barriers raised against them because of their race. An individual's race should make no difference to his or her freedom, and so practices such as segregation and discrimination, which block an individual's choices and restrict his or her freedom due to race, are unjust and should be eliminated. This understanding represents a powerful strand of liberal thought and practice in the postwar United States. Indeed, both the right and left sides of the American political spectrum have come to embrace some version of it, even while each accuses the other of forsaking it. This color-blind paradigm, in short, has become the dominant public philosophy of race in the United States, the normative ground upon which most of our contemporary political struggles about race unfold.

Color-blind liberalism has proven itself a very effective paradigm in the fight to end de jure segregation, to reduce the most blatant forms of discrimination, and to extend basic civil and political rights to black citizens. It also remains a powerful foundation for efforts to address many forms of continuing discrimination and to open up more social and economic opportunities to African Americans. But color-blind liberalism also suffers from severe shortcomings that prevent it from offering a full and compelling understanding of race in American life. In its excessive individualism, it overlooks the profound importance of culture, of membership in cultural groups, and of the influence these factors have within the institutions, practices, and meanings of civil society. Color-blind liberalism's understanding of race is not completely wrong, but it is seriously incomplete and therefore inadequate.

This does not, however, mean liberalism is without hope. Indeed, it has the resources to overcome the shortcomings of its current understanding of race by expanding its view of freedom to include those elements ignored by the color-blind paradigm. Liberalism can do this by taking a closer look at its core commitment to individual autonomy, or the ability of people to make decisions about and control the course of their own lives. Autonomy is an ideal closely related to freedom, but it is a richer concept than the notion of freedom generally celebrated in liberalism, especially the American variety. It turns out that autonomy hinges on the very things color-blind liberalism overlooks—things like culture, membership in cultural groups, and the institutions, practices, and meanings of civil society. By focusing on these kinds of factors, autonomy provides a way for liberalism to expand its understanding of race and provide a richer and more compelling account of the relationship between race and freedom.

An expanded liberal understanding of race in American life recognizes that the individualistic categories of the color-blind paradigm are appropriate in some areas, but that in other areas, we need to pay attention to the importance of culture and cultural group membership to individual autonomy, factors too often minimized or completely ignored in liberal approaches to race. This means taking an explicitly group-conscious view much of the time, especially when it comes to civil society, though this does not include endorsing a notion of formal group-rights as some scholars and activists have suggested. Rather, it means accounting for the critical role black civil society plays in providing the cultural, social, economic, and political resources necessary for the autonomy of African Americans as members of a historically oppressed and marginalized cultural group. It also means expanding the liberal approach to public policy to include efforts to strengthen institutions within black civil society and to give African Americans as a group more control over state institutions such as schools and police forces that have a direct impact on their communities.

In short, my goal in this book is to develop an argument about how contemporary American liberalism understands race, what is inadequate about this understanding, and how it can formulate a better one. I do this by paying particular attention to the value of freedom and its requirements within liberalism, especially for African Americans as a cultural group in a land that, from slavery to the present, has been less than accommodating when it comes to the promise of freedom. I argue that if liberalism is to fully grasp and help contribute to the continuing struggle by black men and women to secure the promise of freedom in the United States, then it must recognize that African Americans have always experienced and continue to experience the ideal of autonomy very differently. This is a unique experience with autonomy that has two closely related dimensions. First, black Americans have always faced and continue to face distinct barriers to autonomy given their membership in a historically subordinated and exploited cultural minority. Second, this membership frequently means they must draw the kinds of resources needed to construct an autonomous life, as well as to overcome threats to it, from the distinct and unique space of black civil society, a network of institutions, practices, and meanings defined and dominated by African Americans themselves. In both of these ways, then, the autonomy of African Americans hinges on a complex and unique set of cultural, social, economic, and political factors, and American liberalism must recognize and account for this fact in trying to come to grips with the continuing struggle for freedom by black men and women in American life. Using the issue of race and freedom in this way, then, my argument examines, challenges, and expands American liberalism's normative understanding of race, and it is my hope that doing so will help open up the liberal dialogue on race to include factors we have spent too little time talking about in the past.

## LOCATING THE ARGUMENT

Too often political theory is simply the realm of constructing, refining, and deconstructing abstract principles and concepts, just as the realm of political practice is too often focused exclusively on strategic questions or cost-benefit analyses. We rarely spend much time at the intersection of the two. We either refine our theoretical paradigms with an occasional aside about the need for political action, or we loosely mention a few concepts like freedom or equality before turning to the nuts and bolts of policy debates. Spending some time at the intersection of theory and practice means thinking about how our normative ideals and commitments translate into political action, and about how the institutions and practices of public life embody certain moral assumptions and values. If theory is to have any relevance, we have to think about how it can guide action, and if political practice is to have any coherence, we have to think about what normative principles are at stake. It is not that people who study political matters do not see the important relationship between theory and practice; it is simply that they usually focus predominately on one or the other. My argument tries to keep one foot in either camp, engaging them both and exploring their relationship. It is an exercise in applied political theory, one based on the idea that looking at specific political contexts is one of the best ways to explore difficult problems of abstract theory, as well as the idea that political philosophy is most valuable when it can lead us toward new and more fruitful approaches to seemingly intractable political dilemmas like that of race in the United States. The intersection of theory and practice is where students of abstract political philosophy on the one hand and political activists, researchers, and policy analysts on the other have something to offer each other. My goal here is just such an exchange. With this in mind and before turning to the argument itself, I should say a few things about where it sits in the contemporary philosophical and political landscape, what some of its specific philosophical and political aims are, and how it utilizes some of its central concepts.

### Liberalism

Liberalism is a broad tradition of political thought and practice in the West running from the middle of the seventeenth century through the present, a tradition that has been particularly influential in the United States. Liberalism has many different strands and internal differences, but it is a coherent tradition built around several common themes (Gray 1986). It assumes the equal moral worth and basic rational capacity of individuals, claims that each person has a basic set of moral rights and duties that flow from this equality and rationality, and argues that this means individuals should remain as free to live their own lives as possible, so long as they refrain from harming others. Liberalism's traditional concern is with limiting the power of political leaders to abuse their subjects' liberty. In this quest, it generally supports constitutional government, the rule of law, and representative political institutions. It is committed to a wide sphere of individual privacy protected by strong civil and political rights; it includes a tradition of tolerating political, philosophical, and religious differences among individuals; and it generally supports private property rights and some form of market economy. Liberalism rests on a moral dedication to individual freedom. It tries to give people the room to frame their own plans of life, develop their own talents, and act on their own preferences with as little external interference as possible. In short, it tries to give individuals the space to be their own masters, to rule themselves as far as they are able. This is why the principle of individual autonomy is so central to the liberal project and why it plays such an important role in the argument to follow.

I engage three debates within contemporary liberal theory. The first is the liberal-communitarian debate that began in the years following the publication of John Rawls's *A Theory of Justice* (1971), reached full strength in the 1980s, and has continued in one form or another until the present. While some communitarians reject liberalism altogether, many others consider the communitarian critique a corrective to some of liberalism's excesses, a way to strengthen liberalism from within. My argument supports this position, claiming that the shortcomings of color-blind liberalism can be overcome, at least in part, through a more communitarian reading of liberalism. The second debate is over liberalism's relationship to social difference. Many political theorists criticize liberalism for contributing to the subordination of certain groups based on differences such as gender, ethnicity, race, sexual preference, age, disability, and so on. Some of these critics consider liberalism irreconcilably hostile to a truly emancipatory politics of difference, while others think liberalism has the internal resources to solve its problems with difference. My argument takes the second position, claiming that American liberalism can overcome its current problems with race-based differences.

The third debate is a narrower one that draws on both the communitarian and politics-of-difference exchanges and centers on the question of how liberalism should respond to the problem of cultural pluralism in ethnically or racially diverse states. The most influential writer on this issue is Will Kymlicka (1989; 1995a), who argues that contemporary liberalism does not properly account for the particular group interests of cultural minorities in its excessive focus on the uniform and universal rights of individuals. In response to this oversight, Kymlicka claims that liberalism should make room for certain types of group-specific rights that protect some kinds of cultural minorities in multicultural states. My argument engages Kymlicka's work in several places and considers how it might apply to African Americans in the United States. Ultimately, I find Kymlicka only partially helpful. His diagnosis of contemporary liberalism is often correct, but his prescriptions are not appropriate in the specific case of race and American liberalism, a fact he himself seems to acknowledge. In this way, the argument is partially an attempt to develop an alternative answer to the broad problem Kymlicka identifies in his work.

The communitarian, politics-of-difference, and multiculturalism debates within liberalism usually come in rather abstract formulations. While theoretical contributions of this kind are certainly important, there is also a real need for work on the implications such debates have in more concrete political settings. Without this kind of work, such debates often become stuck in the abstract realm with partisans fine tuning elegant but increasingly ungrounded arguments like mechanics endlessly laboring over race cars without ever rolling them out of the garage to see how they actually do on the track. The communitarian, politics-of-difference, and multiculturalism debates within liberal political theory are increasingly in danger of becoming stuck at the abstract level. It is time to spend more time and effort looking at how they work themselves out in more specific political contexts. As an exercise in applied political theory, my argument is such an effort. It tries to pull these debates out of the garage to see how they fare on the track, and a rather difficult one at that. The specific issue of race in the postwar United States provides an excellent opportunity to see what implications these kinds of debates have in a unique applied setting.

Liberalism has been particularly influential in the United States. It is not the hegemonic ideology that Hartz (1955) took it to be, but it is the country's principal political language. This is why contemporary political labels such as *liberal* and *conservative* can be misleading. What we call liberal and conservative positions today are generally different interpretations of the same broad liberal tradition. Unlike many other countries, where conservatives challenge the central tenets of liberalism itself, conservatives in the United States generally support a classical, laissez-faire version of liberalism with its emphasis on property rights and a strictly limited state, while those labeled liberals tend to support a modern reformist or activist version more compatible with today's welfare state. To avoid confusion, I use the terms *liberal* and *liberalism* in this book in their more general sense to indicate the broad intellectual and political tradition of liberalism I described above, the tradition most

Americans across the political spectrum identify with in one form or another. To refer to more specific positions along the contemporary American political spectrum, I use the terms *left* and *right*. Furthermore, by left and right, unless otherwise indicated, I do not refer to the political extremes—white separatists, militia groups, American communists, and so on. Rather, these terms correspond to those on either side of the broad political mainstream in the United States—positions we would expect left-leaning progressive Democrats and right-leaning conservative Republicans to take. To illustrate using the issue of race, I use the term left to refer to the typical views and policies advocated by such individuals and groups as Jesse Jackson, Ted Kennedy, Carol Moseley-Braun, Charles Rangel, the NAACP, the ACLU, and the Urban League. The left generally includes those who tend to favor such things as affirmative action policies, stronger antidiscrimination enforcement, and more programs to fight poverty and unemployment. The term right, on the other hand, refers to the typical views and policies advocated by such individuals and groups as Newt Gingrich, Clarence Thomas, Trent Lott, J. C. Watts, Pat Buchanan, the Christian Coalition, and the Heritage Foundation. The right generally includes those who tend to favor such things as ending affirmative action, dismantling or devolving to the states responsibility for antipoverty programs, and resisting diversity-based changes in school curriculums that conform with what they see as excessive "political correctness."

One of my central arguments in this book is that, while these mainstream left and right positions in the United States differ in many important ways when it comes to issues of race, they have both embraced the paradigm of color-blind liberalism in the last several decades, though they have done so in very different ways with very different policy implications. In the next chapter, for example, I show how debates over policies such as busing and affirmative action are defined by the underlying normative assumptions of the color-blind paradigm, assumptions both sides of these debates endorse. This is why color-blind liberalism has become the dominant public understanding of race; both the left and right sides of the mainstream political spectrum in the United States have adopted some version of it, and so its categories now frame the way most issues of race unfold in American life.

The centrality of the liberal tradition in the United States, however, does not mean that nonliberal traditions do not play significant roles as well, especially when it comes to race. First, the language of ascriptive hierarchy has had a critical impact on the history of race in this country (Smith 1993), and the reactionary and racist right continues to employ the rhetoric of overt racism, black inferiority, and segregation. There are still a significant number of Americans who oppose the extension of basic civil and political rights and fundamental equality under the law to black citizens. This language, however, is no longer part of the political mainstream, and to the extent that its ideas do find mainstream support, they must do so by avoiding explicit expression and instead rely on code words and implicit appeals. The political mainstream has at least rhetorically embraced the language of color-blind liberalism. Second, and more importantly for my argument here, many on the radical left have always pushed for alternatives to America's liberal political order, though they have generally had little real success as the history of the United States has been one of liberal reform rather than radical revolution. This radical left tradition, however, has always been an important strand of thought and practice when it comes to race, and it has had particular appeal to African Americans given liberalism's often dismal record on racial justice. Throughout American history and continuing today, challenges to the country's dominant liberal ideology in the radical tradition have come from African American intellectuals, activists, revolutionaries, labor organizers, communists, legal theorists, theologians, cultural critics, and social scientists. These include people like Nat Turner, Harriet Tubman, Ida Wells, W. E. B. DuBois, A. Philip Randolph, Angela Davis, bell hooks, Cornel West, Gayraud Wilmore, James Cone, Manning Marable, Patricia Williams, Derrick Bell, and James Jennings. A distinct but often closely related nationalist tradition among black Americans has also developed a radical critique of the American liberal order through such people as Martin Delany, Marcus Garvey, Elijah Muhammad, Huey Newton, Malcolm X, Harold Cruse, Stokely Carmichael, and Molefi Kete Asante.[1] These radical and nationalist traditions within black political thought and practice step outside the reformist tradition of mainstream liberalism to encourage black group unity, autonomy, and self-help; to focus on white supremacy as a pervasive cultural, social, and economic force in American life; and to press for the fundamental and radical reorganization of the social and economic foundations of American life.

My argument attempts to bring many of the factors emphasized by these radical and nationalist traditions into the mainstream liberal understanding of race. I try to open up the liberal dialogue to include these kinds of concerns, arguing that much of what these traditions uncover is not in conflict with liberalism at all, but rather necessary to a liberal understanding of race that is genuinely concerned with individual autonomy. Doing so can help produce an expanded understanding of race within American liberalism, one that retains the strengths of the color-blind paradigm while, at the same time, going beyond its limits. In moving beyond the cramped confines of the color-blind paradigm, where most contemporary debates over race are stuck, such an approach draws on parts of the radical and nationalist traditions for its strength, but it remains thoroughly liberal itself, meaning that it is still able to make its appeals within the broad language of mainstream American politics.

This kind of effort is particularly important if we are to see the reemergence of the left on issues of race in the United States. Following the accomplishments of the civil rights movement by the mid-1960s, the left lost much of its power to lead on issues of race. It quickly fragmented as many activists embraced or returned to radical or nationalist positions and many white supporters either lost interest in issues of race or drifted rightward and eventually became neoconservatives or Reagan Democrats. I think the left has seen its vigor and influence on issues of race decline in the last several decades, at least in part, because it continues to rely on a cramped and incomplete view of race, something many on the left acknowledge but have difficulty responding to in an innovative and politically compelling way. The expanded approach I develop can help revitalize the left's influence on issues of race by broadening its appeal. It offers a more coherent and comprehensive approach that combines a strong focus on structural factors like discrimination and economic disadvantage with attention to things the left has had difficulty accounting for, things like moral standards, group values, and strong families, neighborhoods, and religious institutions. The time is certainly ripe for the left to embrace such an approach, given the growing movement in political discourse, coming from both the Democratic and Republican parties, toward a focus on issues like the strength of civil society, the importance of moral values, and the need to revitalize a sense of community and civic responsibility in America. So, in short, the notion of autonomy found in liberal political theory provides a way to broaden the mainstream liberal dialogue on race to consider factors too often overlooked, and it can do so in such a way that helps revitalize the American left by giving it the basis for a much more comprehensive and influential approach to issues of race. In this way, my aim is not only to use the specific issue of race to contribute to debates within liberal political theory, but also to use liberal political theory to develop a more compelling approach to the persistent dilemma of race in American public life.

## Race

Race is not an essential characteristic; it has no fixed biological or genetic nature. It is instead a social construct that a race-conscious society uses to mark off certain groups and to structure certain power relations. It relies on a set of cultural meanings forged in particular historical and social contexts and attached to particular bodies (Omi and Winant 1994; Fields 1990; Smedley 1993). With no essential nature, race is an arbitrary, shifting, and contestable construct, but this does not mean it is any less real. Its existence may not be a biological or genetic fact, but it certainly is a cultural, social, and political fact, and so it makes sense to talk about its existence and importance in American life. Unlike many other countries, the United States historically deploys a very rigid division between black and white, with little room for a mixed-race category between the two. The American model is bifurcated rather than graduated; it relies on a culturally and often politically enforced "one drop rule" that classifies anyone with discernable black features—skin, hair, nose, lips—or a known black ancestor as black (Russell, Wilson, and Hall 1993, 74–79; Smedley 1993, 9).

This way of dividing people insures that race is not the same as ethnicity. Race transcends and cuts across ethnic lines, leaving wide ethnic differences within broader racial categories, a fact readily acknowledged when it comes to white Americans but rarely so when it comes to black Americans. This is why it is not accurate to consider African Americans just another ethnic group. Not only is there significant ethnic variation among black people in this country, but their experience as a subordinated racial group is also much different than that of most traditional, especially European, ethnic groups. As a racially defined group, African Americans have faced forced immigration; enslavement; and systematic, institutionalized, and state-sponsored violence, intimidation, segregation, and discrimination like no European ethnic group. They have faced a racial hierarchy built into the very structure of American society that white ethnic groups have not (Takaki 1987a). Indeed, it is the very existence of a racial hierarchy that has allowed various ethnic groups to enter this country and adopt the identity of white Americans; the racial caste system has provided a floor above which these white ethnics struggle to find their place in American society.[2] So we cannot collapse race into ethnicity. It is a distinct social construct in the United States with its own meanings and significance, and my argument examines this construct's place in contemporary American liberalism.

This book, then, is not intended to be a general theory of American multiculturalism. Instead, it examines the relationship of one minority group, black Americans, to the dominant group in the United States, white Americans, and the importance of this relationship for liberalism and its core value of freedom. The United States is a country of remarkable ethnic diversity, which exists within and across racial categories. There are also other groups defined by racial categories in addition to black and white Americans, groups like Asian Americans and indigenous Americans. Finally, there are groups such as Hispanic Americans that are defined using both ethnic and racial categories. Any comprehensive view of American multiculturalism must account for all these different kinds of groups, but it is also important for us to examine specific parts of this broader phenomenon, because different dynamics are at work in the relations between different groups. This is particularly true of African Americans, a group that has much in common with the experience of other ethnic and racial minorities, but one that has also faced a unique experience in the United States. We might think of this as the reality of African American exceptionalism; the African American experience has its own distinct history and dynamics and must be explored on its own terms. So rather than addressing the larger phenomenon of American ethnic and racial pluralism, I examine only one aspect of it, the line separating black from white Americans. While this line does not represent the whole of American multiculturalism, or even the entire story of race in the United States, it does represent a profoundly important dimension of American life and a critical issue within American liberalism. I mention other racial and ethnic groups along the way, but only as they relate to my central concern with black and white Americans.

## Culture, Cultural Groups, and Civil Society

The closely related concepts of culture, cultural groups, and civil society play a key role in my argument, so it might be helpful to explain how I use these concepts from the start. Culture is a notoriously slippery concept. On its most basic level it refers to the symbolic meanings shared by a people—meanings expressed in their language, stories, rituals, songs, expressive styles, works of art, and so on. These meanings provide the basic norms, habits, values, assumptions, and expectations that make everyday social interaction possible. They shape the way people understand the world around them and relate to each other within it. My argument here, however, takes a broader view of culture, one more often found among anthropologists than sociologists, that goes beyond the realm of social meanings alone to tie culture to the character of social structures as well.[3] According to this view, culture influences the entire range of ways people organize their collective life together, both symbolically and structurally. This certainly includes the realm of social meanings, but it includes the web of social institutions, networks, and practices surrounding people as well, because all of these are indelibly formed by culture. It is what determines their character, breathes life into them, makes them real and meaningful. The cultural and the social are inescapably intertwined, because we are at the same time cultural as well as social beings. Culture, in short, is what shapes the deep symbolic and structural background against which everyday social relations take place. It does this, however, only through the mediating roles played by groups and by civil society.

Culture is necessarily a collective phenomenon. Without social interaction and dialogue, culture cannot exist, and so it is something individuals must participate in with others in public life. In the words of Clifford Geertz, "Culture is public because meaning is" (1973, 12). Culture, therefore, only exists within groups. Such groups can come in many forms, they can overlap considerably, and we can belong to many of them. Americans, for example, participate in a common culture defined by certain meanings, institutions, and practices. But Jewish Americans, Hispanic Americans, and Mormons may also participate in different subcultures defined in the same way. Even the members of the U.S. Navy, a street gang in Detroit, or a software development division at Microsoft share in common subcultures defined by particular meanings, institutions, and practices. What this means is that an individual's relationship to a whole host of culturally defined meanings and social structures is mediated by the various groups to which he or she belongs, either voluntarily or involuntarily. Group memberships of one kind or another, therefore, are vital to the way culture shapes a person's social existence. Among such groups in the United States, ones marked off by race and ethnicity have always been among the most important, and it is the role played by this kind of cultural group that I examine here. My particular concern is with the importance of white and black Americans as distinct cultural groups.

The realm through which the influence of culture and cultural groups is most deeply felt is civil society. It is the collection of institutions, practices, and meanings around which our public life is built, but which are not tied directly to the state. It is the public space that lies between the formal realm of the state and our purely private lives. Civil society includes institutions such as churches, synagogues, and mosques; professional and neighborhood associations; trade unions; social clubs and sports teams; corporations, firms, and small businesses; colleges and universities; museums and galleries; the press; the entertainment industry; and hospitals and child care centers. In short, it encompasses the complex web of non-state social networks and institutional arrangements—as well as the practices, norms, and assumptions that structure them—in which we live out our lives. In this way, civil society provides the social space in which culture and cultural groups operate, the ground in which they come embedded. The institutions, practices, and meanings of civil society are where culture and the groups that mediate it find concrete expression, take on particular forms, and exercise their influence. All this means that an individual's life in civil society is deeply rooted in the role of culture and cultural groups in shaping the particular form and content of the institutions, practices, and meanings of civil society.

As we can see, the concepts of culture, cultural groups, and civil society are complex and intertwined, and I flesh out their meaning, relationship, and importance along the way. Essentially, I argue that all three concepts are critical to an understanding of race in the United States, but that color-blind liberalism has little or no room for them. The ideal of individual autonomy, however, provides an excellent way to open up the liberal understanding of race to just these very concepts.

## THE ARGUMENT'S OUTLINE

Chapter 2 describes color-blind liberalism, reviewing its central assumptions and categories. It then looks at its sources in the postwar era. These include the broad tradition of American liberalism, academic political theory, intellectuals and social scientists, the civil rights movement, the courts, political elites, and public attitudes. The chapter then explores how the color-blind paradigm now frames most debates over race in American life, and it concludes by discussing the view of freedom employed by color-blind liberalism. Chapter 3 considers the strengths of color-blind liberalism and reviews efforts by the left to respond to issues of race in the last several decades following the zenith of the civil rights movement. It then discusses the critical shortcomings of the color-blind paradigm, shortcomings that prevent it from offering a complete and compelling understanding of race in American life.

Chapter 4 explores the concept of autonomy and its role in the liberal project. Drawing on the work of political theorists like John Stuart Mill, Joseph Raz, and Charles Taylor, it argues that autonomy demands that liberals pay attention to the very things color-blind liberalism overlooks—things like culture, cultural group membership, and civil society. Autonomy, therefore, provides liberalism with a fruitful way to address issues of multiculturalism in states containing a variety of cultural groups. Chapter 5 outlines how a liberalism informed by autonomy can develop a richer and more compelling understanding of race in the United States. It centers on how the strengths of the color-blind paradigm can be retained, but only in an expanded approach to race that also considers the issues color-blind liberalism alone overlooks. It rejects, however, proposals to do this through a theory of formal group rights. The chapter goes on to focus on the shape of American civil society and how the institutions, practices, and meanings of black civil society provide African Americans with the cultural, social, economic, and political resources necessary for autonomy. The black church serves as a particularly important example of an institution that works to provide these kinds of resources. The chapter concludes by looking at how black communities also continually struggle to overcome those forces that threaten autonomy within the space of black civil society itself.

Chapter 6 describes how the expanded understanding developed in the previous chapter can serve as a better guide to public policy on issues of race. It pays particular attention to the intersection of the state and civil society as an area in which public policy can help African Americans in their struggle to secure the resources necessary for autonomy. The chapter's discussion considers policy issues in the areas of civil rights, the safety net and economic policy, social welfare spending and black civil society, economic development, education, and police protection. It concludes with a caveat about the limits of public policy and final remarks on the book's central argument.

This book is a work of synthesis. In it I attempt to integrate theory and practice, issues of race with concepts of freedom, the liberal tradition with the contributions of radicals and black nationalists, and individualistic color-blind principles with group-conscious ones. Along the way I draw on the work of many different kinds of writers, scholars, and activists—from those who never once mention race to those who seem to mention it in every sentence, from black Marxist Christians to white liberal atheists, and from those focusing on the theoretical intricacies of hypothetical veils of ignorance to those focusing on the very real intricacies of education policies designed to eliminate ignorance. Not every writer I rely on could possibly agree with the entire argument, and indeed it is quite possible none of them would. But that is not my goal. Instead, my aim is to weave together an original and challenging argument about race, freedom, and American liberalism, one that depends heavily upon the insights of many others who have explored these topics before, but one that also makes important connections not made before. If the argument as a whole says something new and ultimately useful about these issues upon which so much has already been written, then it has done its job. It is to this job that I now turn.

# CHAPTER 2

# Color-Blind Liberalism

To say the United States is a nation divided by race is not to make a particularly profound observation. Race has always been at the center of our most intense public conflicts. However, the ground upon which Americans think and argue about race has shifted considerably over the years. Few people still seriously debate the moral merits of chattel slavery, and even the far more recent reign of legally mandated apartheid has few public defenders left. Debates over race have shifted to new ground in the wake of the modern civil rights movement and its judicial and legislative accomplishments. While there are still those who deny that black Americans are entitled to the same set of basic civil and political rights as white Americans, their view is no longer dominant. The postwar United States has seen the fall of de jure segregation and the rise of a new public philosophy of race. This is the philosophy of color-blind liberalism, and it sets the terms under which most contemporary arguments about race unfold. In this chapter, I examine color-blind liberalism's central features, its primary sources in American life, the ways in which it frames contemporary debates over race, and its view of freedom.

## THE FEATURES OF COLOR-BLIND LIBERALISM

Color-blind liberalism begins with the claim that the color of an individual's skin is a morally arbitrary fact that should make no difference in the way he or she is treated. We each have a basic moral right to be judged according to our merits, character, or accomplishments as individuals, and those who judge us according to our membership in some ascriptive social group violate this right. Discrimination on the basis of race ignores the basic moral equality of persons. This means that citizens are entitled to the same set of basic civil and political rights and to the equal protection of the laws regardless of their race. They are also entitled to equality of opportunity in economic and social life; the chance to pursue an education, a job, credit, housing, and other social goods should be open to all equally. Color-blind liberalism argues that the procedures we follow to reach political and legal decisions and distribute social and economic goods must be fair—that is, they should not arbitrarily discriminate on the basis of race. When such procedures are fair, they distinguish individuals only on the basis of morally relevant differences such as merit, ability, need, desert, and so on.[1]

Color-blind liberalism's moral vision is not of an American society where race has disappeared, but one where racial differences have no effect on one's prospects in life. It is not blind to color in the sense of not seeing it at all. Rather it is blind to color in the sense of not seeing it as morally relevant. Historian John Hope Franklin puts the distinction this way: "There is nothing inherently wrong with being aware of color as long as it is seen as making distinctions in a pleasant, superficial, and unimportant manner. It is only when character is attached to color, when ability is measured by color, when privilege is tied to color, and a whole galaxy of factors in our society are tied to color—it is only when such considerations are attached to color that it becomes a deadly, dreadful, denigrating factor among us all" (1993, 72–73). Color-blind liberalism's moral vision is of an integrated society where differences between black and white Americans have as little significance as those between Irish and Polish Americans today.

This color-blind paradigm relies on a particular set of normative categories in its understanding of race. These are its individualism, its focus on rights, its emphasis on fair procedures, its dedication to equality of opportunity, and its commitment to the principle of nondiscrimination. These categories lie at the heart of a powerful strand of liberal thought and practice over the past five decades, one that has become the dominant approach to issues of race. In spite of its rise to predominance, however, color-blind liberalism is not a tightly unified ideology. It is marked by deep internal divisions between left and right interpretations of its meaning and requirements. Its adherents on the left and right disagree sharply over how widespread discrimination still is in American society, the extent to which the state should involve itself in fighting such discrimination, and the kinds of policies it should employ in doing so—including whether policies taking account of race, such as busing and affirmative action, violate the color-blind paradigm or are in fact required by it.

## THE SOURCES OF COLOR-BLIND LIBERALISM

Color-blind liberalism has roots in many areas of American life. With a firm grounding in the historical character of American political discourse, it has developed, in the last half-century, an approach to race that draws on academic political theory, the broader intellectual and social scientific communities, the civil rights movement, the courts, political elites, and public attitudes. While these various sources contribute in different ways and are often at odds over the precise nature of color-blind liberalism, they all provide the basic materials that go into its construction. They provide the color-blind paradigm with its central categories as well as the divisions upon which its internal conflicts hinge.

## American Liberalism

The language of American political life is that of liberalism. While there is evidence of a once powerful and still resonating civic republican tradition (Bailyn 1967; Wood 1969; Pocock 1975), and while ideologies of ascriptive hierarchy have also flourished (Smith 1993), it is clear that liberalism sits at the heart of the American political experience. Liberal values like individualism, freedom, equality, rights, antistatism, and the rule of law historically structure political discourse in the United States (Young 1996; Foley 1991), and this liberal tradition provides a solid historical foundation for color-blind liberalism.

American liberalism is defined by its individualism. Indeed, while liberalism is itself a political philosophy built around the individual, the American strain is even more individualistic than its European counterparts (Waligorski 1981, 1–2). As America's "first language," individualism not only defines its politics, but it also comes embedded in its deepest cultural meanings. It is part of the country's national character, expressed in its central myths, stories, and heros (Bellah et al. 1985). This individualism is at the heart of the American celebration of freedom. The United States bills itself as a land where people are free to live their own lives as they alone see fit. From the country's founding as a place to escape the political, social, and religious tyranny of the Old World to its centuries-long experience with an open frontier, Michael Foley argues, "No other society has been so strongly dependent for its sense of identity upon the quest for freedom" (1991, 14). In this sense, Americans see their society as an independent and largely self-regulating association of free and equal individuals, one that provides plenty of opportunities for people to pursue their own goals in life, but then stays out of their way while they do so (Seligman 1992, chap. 3). The American notion of freedom is a negative one, centering on the individual unrestrained by any interference with his or her actions by fellow citizens, the larger society, and especially the state. What threatens freedom are the barriers thrown up in front of individuals by others, barriers that prevent them from achieving their goals. The American ideal of freedom lies in the individual's avoiding or overcoming such barriers.

This is why the commitment to a substantial zone of privacy runs so deep in the United States. It is a sphere in which individuals should be left alone, and it is one defined and protected by the rights they carry. Rights are held as trumps against intrusive action by others or the state. They allow individuals to fend off threats to their freedom. This means, as Mary Ann Glendon (1991) points out, that American political discourse is often dominated by rights-claims and the kinds of legalistic arguments that they entail. Formal concepts like rights produce a formalistic and procedural language of politics. This kind of language gives American liberalism what Kenneth Dolbeare calls its "penchant for legalism, the belief that established legal means and regular procedures are the only proper way to resolve issues" (1984, 520). On this view, if individuals are to be free, then they must enjoy certain formal rights and procedural protections that prevent others and the government from abusing them and limiting their independence. Indeed, this focus on formal and procedural issues—on rights as trumps against interference and on mechanisms designed to insure a fair political process—has become particularly prominent within American liberalism during the last half-century (Sandel 1996 and 1984a; Lowi 1979).

Strong individual rights and procedural protections do not simply promote freedom by protecting individuals from arbitrary interference by fellow citizens and the state. They also do so by guaranteeing them equality of opportunity in social and economic life. They insure that individuals have an equal chance to pursue their fair share of public goods according to their own individual preferences, talents, and initiative. As Bellah and his colleagues write: "Our American traditions encourage us to think of justice as a matter of equal opportunities for every individual to pursue whatever he or she understands by happiness. Equal opportunities are guaranteed by fair laws and political procedures—laws and procedures applied in the same way to everyone" (1985, 25). Equality of opportunity, then, is a version of equality that retains the strong American emphasis on individualism, self-reliance, and negative freedom. It seeks to guarantee a situation in which individual action rather than external interference determines each person's success or failure. When this is not the case and opportunities are not available to all on a fair and equal basis, then the core of individual freedom is threatened.

According to the traditional liberal view of freedom, once the basic rights and procedural guarantees of citizenship are secure, the state should let social and economic life unfold in a private sphere without interference. This view came under heavy pressure in the late nineteenth and early twentieth centuries, however, as liberalism tried to come to terms with dramatic changes in American economic and social life. As local markets gave way to national ones, as more people began living in large and complex cities rather than on farms or in small towns, and as the American scene became increasingly dominated by large and powerful organizations such as corporations, factories, railroads, and trade unions, individuals experienced new and frightening kinds of inequality, dependency, and vulnerability. Individual freedom, in short, faced threats it had never faced before, as people had less control over their lives and particularly over their livelihoods. With the populist and especially the progressive movements, many liberals began to focus on the implications that growing social interdependence within large economic structures like national markets, corporations, professions, trusts, unions, and so on had for individual freedom (Lustig 1982). They began to look to the state to take an active role in protecting individuals by regulating these structures through its economic, welfare, and health and safety policies.

A powerful reformist wing of American liberalism grew out of this period, calling on the state to help secure individual freedom and equality of opportunity by combating threats to these values coming from concentrations of power and privilege in economic and social life. Finding its most powerful expression in the New Deal era and extending into the present, this strand of liberal thought and practice has created a sharp division within contemporary American liberalism. The "laissez-faire liberalism" of the right continues to stress property rights and a narrow role for the state in accordance with the classical interpretation of liberalism, while the "reform liberalism" of the left stresses the need for market regulation, health and safety requirements, and social welfare policies to protect individuals from the vulnerabilities that come with a modern capitalist economy (Young 1996, 6–7; Barker and Jones 1994, 52–53; Foley 1991, chap. 7). In this way, contemporary American liberalism still centers on its traditional values of individualism, freedom, rights, fair procedures, and equality of opportunity, but it is split over how much modern economic conditions promote or hinder these values and the role the state should take in securing them through its public policies. It is this liberal tradition that provides the background against which color-blind liberalism unfolds. The color-blind paradigm relies on its core normative categories, and it is also marked by the same kinds of internal divisions between left and right interpretations of these categories.

The color-blind paradigm, then, borrows its individualistic focus from the larger tradition of American liberalism, but there have been those within the liberal tradition who have sought to broaden it to include a theory of community and cultural groups as well, especially in the early decades of this century. Ultimately, however, these efforts were not particularly influential, and they had little impact on the development of color-blind liberalism in the postwar era. During the same period in which American liberalism began facing the challenge of growing economic complexity and demands for state intervention, it also experienced a movement among intellectuals and social reformers to pay closer attention to the social nature of persons expressed in the communities and cultural groups to which they belonged. People like John Dewey, Josiah Royce, Jane Addams, and Louis Brandeis pointed to the importance of social and intellectual diversity to American democracy, a diversity provided by the vast array of communities, associations, and expressive groups in the United States. Cultural pluralists like Horace Kallen and Randolph Bourne blasted attempts to "Americanize" ethnic immigrant groups, claiming that the country's cultural diversity was something to be celebrated, and that ethnic identity often played a critical role in how individuals pursued their own views of the good life in the United States (Quant 1970; Young 1996, chap. 10; Graber 1991, chap. 3). The early part of this century, therefore, did see challenges to the dominant individualism of the American liberal tradition, with many thinkers recognizing the importance of cultural communities and associations in American life. But this trend was overshadowed by the larger movement within American liberalism for greater economic intervention and regulation by the state. Both strands within early-twentieth-century liberalism challenged the traditional liberal view of the individual and society, but it was the arguments for economic regulation and social welfare policies by the state to help bolster individual freedom and equality of opportunity that ultimately proved more influential.

The liberalism that emerged in the years following the Second World War returned to focus as closely as ever on the individual. The attention to community and cultural groups of the progressive era gave way to the rights-based liberalism of the postwar years. An emphasis on universal citizenship rights and equal protection of the laws for all individuals became dominant in most areas of liberal thought and practice, including constitutional law, political rhetoric, civil rights, women's rights, and political theory (Young 1996, chap. 15; Sandel 1996). To the extent that postwar liberalism did look at groups, its focus was now primarily on interest groups, which it considered nothing more than the temporary, voluntary, and shifting associations of discrete individuals with similar individual interests. This was the context in which color-blind liberalism developed its understanding of race, an understanding that centered on postwar principles of rights-based individualism rather than on Progressive Era concerns with community and cultural pluralism.

Indeed, the color-blind paradigm's focus on the individual rights carrier apart from the cultural groups to which he or she belongs became an influential American export in the postwar years. According to Will Kymlicka, contemporary liberalism's hostility to minority group rights around the world springs in large part from the influence of postwar American liberalism's individualistic focus on universal human rights, a focus expressed in the desegregation and nondiscrimination legislation and judicial decisions of the civil rights movement. Kymlicka argues that the postwar American trend toward restricting issues of cultural group membership to the purely private sphere and limiting the state to guaranteeing individual rights, equal protection of the laws, and equality of opportunity for all citizens regardless of race or ethnicity has undermined the liberal dedication to minority group rights traditionally found in countries outside of the United States (1995a, chap. 4; 1989, chap. 10). In this way, the color-blind paradigm itself has come to define the heart of American liberalism in its influence on other parts of the world during the postwar era.

*Academic Political Theory*

Color-blind liberalism draws much of its theoretical strength from a particular strand of liberal political philosophy in the United States over the past several decades associated with theorists like John Rawls, Bruce Ackerman, and Ronald Dworkin.[2] They make a strong case that liberal principles of justice—the way we distribute fundamental rights and duties and allocate basic social and economic goods in a liberal society—should be blind to ascriptive differences that are "arbitrary from a moral point of view," to use Rawls's language. In order to design principles of justice that do not discriminate on the basis of such arbitrary differences, they employ a variety of hypothetical devices in which rational and self-interested individuals choose the rules that will govern the basic structure of their society prior to that society's actual existence. As Melissa Williams writes, "Rawls' original position with its veil of ignorance, Dworkin's desert island with its insurance scheme, and Ackerman's spaceship journey to a new planet all serve the purpose of ensuring that ascriptive group differences play no role in the definition of justice" (1995, 68). This view that principles of justice must be blind to social differences such as race, gender, or ethnicity has become particularly powerful within the Western liberal tradition since the second World War, and it owes much of its strength to the influence it has had in the United States (Kymlicka 1989, 210–214; Taylor 1992, 53–58).

Rawls, Dworkin, and Ackerman all formulate their theories of justice by taking individual agents out of their particular social circumstances and placing them in procedural situations designed to produce agreements that are fair toward all parties. This procedural approach is necessary given their common claim that principles of justice cannot rest on any particular conception of the good. They reject "substantive" theories of justice—those based on certain views of the good—in favor of "formal" or "procedural" theories—those based on principles of right. On their account, since individuals have different and often conflicting views of what is good in life, the rules regulating their association in society must be neutral among such views. If particular versions of the good are off-limits, then the rules by which individual agents interact must be ground in procedural principles—the rights, duties, and distributive mechanisms agents reach by common agreement for their mutual benefit. In order for such agreements to be fair toward all parties, they must be reached under conditions that are themselves fair—conditions that, at least in theory, constitute what Ackerman calls "a perfect technology of justice" (1980, 21). Rawls, who provides the most sophisticated and influential theory of this kind, writes: "The idea of the original position is to set up a fair procedure so that any principles agreed to will be just. The aim is to use the notion of pure procedural justice as a basis of theory" (1971, 136). The primary way Rawls insures that his original position is characterized by pure procedural justice is to place its participants behind a "veil of ignorance," which denies them knowledge of their particular social traits, positions, talents, and conceptions of the good. He writes: "This ensures that no one is advantaged or disadvantaged in the choice of principles by the outcome of natural chance or the contingency of social circumstances. Since all are similarly situated and no one is able to design principles to favor his particular condition, the principles of justice are the result of a fair agreement or bargain" (1971, 12). Since individuals in the original position cannot tell what their particular social circumstances will be, they will not agree to "pointless or arbitrary principles" like "basic rights should depend on the color of one's skin or the texture of one's hair" (1971, 149).

Theories of this sort are highly individualistic. Their procedural arrangements rely on rational and self-interested agents with few or no social attachments. As Michael Sandel (1982) points out, such agents come unencumbered by any deep communal commitments or specific conceptions of the good; they are constituted prior to their social contexts and prior to their particular ends. These theories see society as an association of independent individuals voluntarily coming together for their mutual advantage, and the principles of justice determine how the costs and benefits of that association are to be distributed to individual members as fairly as possible and in ways that respect their moral status as individuals. This is a view that rests on the traditional liberal commitment to the claim that each and every individual is by nature free and equal. Dworkin writes that "justice as fairness rests on the assumption of a natural right of all men and women to equality of concern and respect" (1978b, 182). On his account, the essential moral equality and dignity of each person is the deep theory behind the conceptions of social justice offered by thinkers like Rawls, Ackerman, and himself.

The actual principles of justice that emerge from these theories generally fall into two categories: a strong emphasis on individual rights and a relatively egalitarian distribution of social and economic resources. Rawls writes: "I suppose, then, that for the most part each person holds two relevant positions: that of equal citizenship and that defined by his place in the distribution of income and wealth" (1971, 96–97).[3] Rawls's first principle of justice states that each citizen should have an equal share in a scheme of basic civil and political liberties. These are traditional liberal rights to such things as speech, association, conscience, voting, holding public office, and security in one's person and one's personal property under the rule of law (1971, 60–61). Dworkin also puts a strong emphasis on these kinds of liberties, claiming that they are required by the underlying right of individuals to be treated with equal concern and respect (1978b, chap. 12; 1978a, sec. 4). Rawls's second principle of justice states that social and economic inequalities are just only so far as they benefit the least advantaged and are attached to social positions open to all under conditions of fair equality of opportunity (1971, 302). Dworkin too argues that justice demands a much more egalitarian distribution of social and economic resources than most liberal societies, including the United States, currently practice (1981; 1978a, sec. 3). Both Rawls and Dworkin reject a laissez-faire theory of equality of opportunity—one arguing that if everyone starts with an equal share of goods, then any distribution that results over time is just so long as nobody cheats or steals. This formulation still rewards or punishes morally arbitrary factors resulting from an individual's natural endowments or particular social contingencies (Rawls 1971, 106–107; Dworkin 1981, 307–309). Their version of equality of opportunity depends upon a much more egalitarian distribution of goods and positions over time, one that provides each individual with access to a share of goods large enough to pursue his or her goals in life. If persons are to have a fair and equal opportunity to act on their own preferences and live the kinds of lives they want to, then resources and offices must be as equally distributed and open to all as possible.

The strand of liberal theory represented by Rawls, Dworkin, and Ackerman retains liberalism's traditional dedication to equal civil and political rights, but it departs from the classical version that privileges private contract and property rights over economic redistribution or regulation by the state (Paul 1984, 376–377). It offers philosophical justification for the reform wing of American liberalism that supports significant state action to secure individual freedom and equality of opportunity, especially in the economic realm. In liberalism's internal theoretical conflicts, it represents the egalitarian interpretation favored by the left that opposes the right's libertarian interpretation, which finds its strongest defense in theorists like Robert Nozick (1974). While disagreeing sharply over the content and priority of various rights, over the limits of state action, and over the need for economic redistribution, these rival interpretations of liberalism do find common ground in what Michael Sandel calls an "individualistic, rights-based ethic" (1982, 66–67; 1984b, 4, 8–9). They share a commitment to the liberal ideal described by Iris Marion Young: "The state and law should express rights only in universal terms applied equally to all, and differences among persons and groups should be a purely accidental and private matter. We seek a society in which differences of race, sex, religion, and ethnicity no longer make a difference to people's rights and opportunities. People should be treated as individuals, not as members of groups" (1990, 157). So over the last several decades, liberal political philosophers in the United States have developed theories of justice that center on individualism, rights, fair procedures, equality of opportunity, and nondiscrimination, and their work has provided a powerful theoretical foundation for color-blind liberalism. Liberal political theory is not, however, without internal divisions over the meaning and requirements of its central values, and these divisions also provide the background against which color-blind liberalism's own internal conflicts unfold.

## Myrdal and American Intellectuals

As the Second World War drew to a close, Gunnar Myrdal and his colleagues published their landmark *An American Dilemma* (1944), and the way their book conceptualized the problem of race in the United States would play a pivotal role in the development of color-blind liberalism. Myrdal claimed that the dilemma of race lay in the gap that existed between the nation's professed ideals and its actual treatment of black citizens. The American creed, as an expression of both secular liberal and Christian ideals, affirmed the basic equality, dignity, and rights of each individual and promised a fair and equal opportunity to succeed in American life to all citizens. While Americans affirmed this creed in public, their blatantly unjust treatment of black citizens, a practice rooted in irrational prejudice and hatred, contradicted it in practice. Myrdal wrote:

> From the point of view of the American Creed the status accorded the Negro in America represents nothing more and nothing less than a century-long lag of public morals. In principle the Negro problem was set-

tled long ago; in practice the solution is not effectuated. The Negro in America has not yet been given the elemental civil and political rights of formal democracy, including a fair opportunity to earn his living, upon which a general accord was already won when the American Creed was first taking form. And this anachronism constitutes the contemporary "problem" both to Negroes and to whites. (1944, 24)

For Myrdal, white discrimination and prejudice created a "vicious circle" that kept black Americans in an inferior political, social, and economic position, a fact that further reinforced negative stereotypes among whites and led to more discrimination (1944, 75–78). Myrdal, however, was hopeful that the United States would eventually shake itself free of prejudice, segregation, and discrimination. It would eventually extend the promise of the American creed to all citizens regardless of color, and this would be America's greatest moral triumph, one that would once again make it an example of individual freedom and equality for the rest of the world (1944, 1021–1024).

Myrdal's book had a profound impact on the way Americans, especially white Americans, thought about race in the decades following its publication.[4] It played a critical role in inspiring and galvanizing America's white intellectual community to begin addressing the evils of racial bigotry, segregation, and discrimination. It was widely read by journalists, educators, social scientists, writers, religious leaders, and political activists. The book's argument was summarized in the popular press and in academic journals, and condensed versions became a staple in many college courses across the country (with the exception of the South). A host of government agencies, from local police departments to presidential commissions, either directly or indirectly relied on its findings in their reports, and its most famous reference came in footnote 11 of the Supreme Court's 1954 decision in *Brown v. Board of Education.*[5] Most black intellectuals were pleased with its direct attack on discrimination and segregation and with its focus on the gap between America's democratic ideals and its practice of white supremacy. They were also pleased that white America was finally listening to the kinds of arguments they had been making for years. The book focused the attention of America's mainstream intellectual and social scientific communities on the issue of race. Walter Jackson writes: "For twenty years after its publication, *An American Dilemma* remained the leading work of social science concerning Afro-Americans. Myrdal's strategy of moral exhortation and social engineering won converts among scholars in many fields, and his program of civil rights, integration, assimilation, and equal economic opportunity became a liberal orthodoxy among American intellectuals" (1990, 273). The book was followed by many others, both popular and scholarly, exploring and condemning the irrationality and injustice of racial prejudice. In the years that followed its publication, the nation saw a dramatic rise in the number of white intellectuals, social scientists, political activists, and religious leaders speaking out against bigotry and discrimination.

Beginning in the mid-1960s, many would denounce the book's view of black culture as a "pathological" response to white bigotry and find its optimistic prediction of an eventual end to racial injustice naive. In the first few decades after its publication, however, Myrdal's book played a pivotal role in preparing the ground for appeals made during the civil rights movement, and its formulation of America's racial dilemma as a conflict between the nation's ideals of individual freedom and equality and its actual treatment of black citizens is still a central feature of the color-blind paradigm.

## The Civil Rights Movement

Color-blind liberalism received its most powerful expression in the modern civil rights movement that stretched from the mid-1950s through the late-1960s. It was a movement in which black Americans demanded nothing less than their freedom through full and equal membership in American public life. On the most immediate level, this required that the state recognize and protect their basic citizenship rights. Martin Luther King Jr. opened his speech at the Montgomery bus boycott's first mass meeting with the words, "We are here in a general sense, because first and foremost—we are American citizens—and we are determined to apply our citizenship—to the fullness of its means."[6] Segregation made a mockery of citizenship by denying black citizens the most basic rights, privileges, and protections of citizenship. When the movement challenged this, it was government officials—local police, city council members, mayors, county clerks, state legislators, and governors—who provided segregation's front line of defense. City officials in Montgomery led the campaign against the bus boycott through arrests, harassment, and lawsuits; state and local officials coordinated attacks on the Freedom Riders in several states; Mississippi saw its legislature pass laws requiring the names of all new voter applicants to be printed in local papers two weeks before being accepted, and at least one member of that body personally murdered one of his own constituents who was involved in registration efforts; clerks charged with registering citizens to vote instead pistol-whipped those trying to do so; governors blocked schoolhouse doors, and school officials either ignored or designed policies to avoid desegregation orders; state and local courts refused to provide even the semblance of equal protection of the laws; and staggering numbers of civil rights workers were beaten, raped, tortured, or simply killed by police officers across the South.[7]

In their efforts to overcome this resistance by the state at one level, civil rights leaders tried to force the federal government to intervene, thereby putting pressure on the state at another level. From the Montgomery bus boycott to the Freedom Rides to Birmingham and Selma, the movement attempted to force confrontations with local government officials that would compel federal officials to step in and protect the basic rights of its citizens. At the center of the civil rights movement, then, was a long and bloody effort to shift the state from a position of either officially enforcing segregation—in the case of local and state governments in the South—or knowingly tolerating it—in the case of the federal government—to a position acknowledging and protecting full and equal rights for every individual citizen regardless of race.

While its most dramatic focus was on the challenge to state-enforced segregation in the South, the civil rights movement also linked the struggle for freedom to a broader demand for equal treatment, respect, and opportunity in American society generally. In the words of James Meredith: "I feel that every citizen should be a first-class citizen and should be allowed to develop his talents on a free, equal, and competitive basis. I think this is fair and that it infringes on the rights and privileges of no one" (1992, 49). The movement claimed that the basic moral equality of persons, regardless of arbitrary traits like race, demands that they be treated as equals. As a group of Atlanta students wrote, "Every normal human being wants to walk the earth with dignity and abhors any and all proscriptions placed upon him because of race or color."[8] Civil rights activists called on white Americans to close the gap between their professed dedication to individual freedom and equality on the one hand and their unequal, and thus unfair, treatment of African Americans on the other. In his "I Have a Dream" speech, King echoed Myrdal, saying, "I have a dream that one day this nation will rise up and live out the true meaning of its creed" (1992, 124), and in his "Letter from Birmingham Jail," he urged white Americans to practice the religious ideals they preached (1970). Going beyond an exclusive concern with the state, civil rights leaders articulated the vision of an integrated society where individuals would be treated fairly and afforded equal opportunities regardless of membership in some racially defined group.

The civil rights movement demanded an end to political, social, and economic discrimination against black Americans. It claimed black citizens deserved full and equal citizenship rights, the equal protection of the laws, fair treatment in American society, and the same social and economic opportunities as other citizens. It based its powerful moral appeal for the freedom of black citizens on the values of individualism, rights, fairness, equality of opportunity, and nondiscrimination, claiming that justice demanded that individuals "not be judged by the color of their skin but by the content of their character" (King 1992, 124). In so doing, it represented the most powerful source of color-blind liberalism in the postwar era.

## The Courts

In the last five decades color-blind liberalism has found one of its strongest allies in the courts. This is not surprising given its focus on individual rights and fair procedures, categories particularly suited to judicial interpretation and enforcement. From at least the landmark *Brown* decision to the most recent affirmative action and voting rights cases, the courts have been at the center of debates over civil rights, fair political and legal procedures, and efforts to identify and defeat racial discrimination.[9] In their attempts to convince the Supreme Court to declare de jure segregation unconstitutional, civil rights lawyers relied on the claim, articulated first by Justice Harlan in his dissent to *Plessy v. Ferguson* in 1896, that the Constitution is color-blind.[10] As Thurgood Marshall wrote in a 1947 brief: "Classifications and distinctions based on race or color have no moral or legal validity in our society. They are contrary to our constitution and laws, and this Court has struck down statutes, ordinances or official policies seeking to establish such classifications."[11] But when the Court did begin to dismantle segregation with *Brown* and the cases that followed, it declined to officially endorse this view that the Constitution prohibits any and all racial distinctions. It essentially declared that legally mandated segregation or invidious discrimination on the basis of race violates a citizen's basic right to the equal protection of the laws, but it did so without binding itself to a strict and inflexible rule of absolute color-blindness. In the postwar era, then, it has developed a strong rule of nondiscrimination by making race a suspect category subject to strict scrutiny, but not one that is prohibited altogether.

This allowed the federal judiciary to influence the actual implementation of color-blind liberalism. During and following the civil rights movement, the courts were at the center of efforts to fight school segregation, voting rights violations, and discrimination in employment, housing, and public accommodations. Refusing to endorse an absolute prohibition on racial classifications left constitutional room to consider policies such as affirmative action, minority set-asides, school busing, and election redistricting that deploy racial distinctions in order to help battle continuing discrimination and repair the lingering effects of past discrimination. In recent years a more conservative Supreme Court has continued to allow for such policies in theory, but it has moved ever closer to a strict rule of race neutrality as Justice O'Connor, the swing vote on such cases, has pressed to subject these kinds of policies to strict scrutiny and left little room for the state to prove it has a compelling interest in pursuing them.[12] In this way, the judiciary, which played such a crucial role in the rise of color-blind liberalism by declaring that all citizens are entitled to full civil rights and the equal protection of the laws without regard to race, has continued to carve out a central role for itself in the internal debates over the precise meaning and applications of the color-blind paradigm.

*Political Elites*

Color-blind liberalism owes much of its influence in the postwar era to its being embraced by the mainstream political establishment. In the early part of the century most African Americans still lived in the rural South, where they were disenfranchised and, thus, of little real interest to the two major political parties. By mid-century, however, many had migrated northward and more were following. As black voting strength grew in the North, the parties began to take notice. The late 1940s and the 1950s saw both parties testing the waters on civil rights with moderate appeals to black voters, though the Democrats were severely hampered in such efforts by the violent reaction of their southern wing.[13] The confrontation in Little Rock over school desegregation forced a reluctant Eisenhower to intervene, and in an address to the nation in September of 1957, he claimed that a country locked in a struggle with the Soviet Union in defense of freedom could not afford to deny its own citizens basic human rights simply because of their race (Eisenhower 1992). Both parties made stronger, though still tentative, appeals to civil rights in their 1960 platforms, and Kennedy's narrow margin of victory was due in large part to his success among black voters following his call to Coretta Scott King expressing concern for her husband who was in a Georgia jail cell at the time (Branch 1988, chap. 9).

With Kennedy and Johnson in the early to mid-1960s, the political establishment was finally forced to fully endorse the principles of color-blind liberalism under enormous pressure from the civil rights movement that reached its peak during this period. In his June 1963 address to the nation, Kennedy claimed that it "ought to be possible, in short, for every American to enjoy the privileges of being an American without regard to his race or his color," and that "the question is whether all Americans are to be afforded equal rights and equal opportunities." He continued, saying, "If an American, because his skin is dark, cannot eat lunch in a restaurant open to the public; if he cannot send his children to the best public school available; if he cannot vote for the public officials who represent him; if, in short, he cannot enjoy the full and free life which all of us want, then who among us would be content to have the color of his skin changed and stand in his place." Kennedy told Americans that "the time has come for this nation to fulfill its promise," urging them to support the civil rights legislation he was sending to Congress that committed the country to the "proposition that race has no place in American life or law" (1992, 117–119). With Kennedy's assassination, it was left to Johnson to push through this legislation, telling Congress: "We have talked long enough in this country about equal rights. It is time now to write the next chapter—and to write it in the book of law."[14] In March 1965 Johnson told a Joint Session of Congress and a national television audience that the country's founding principles of liberty, equality, and human dignity were at stake in the fight for civil rights. He said, "These are not just empty theories," but rather "a promise to every citizen that he shall share in the dignity of man," that "he shall share in freedom, he shall choose his leaders, educate his children, provide for his family according to his ability and his merits as a human being." Johnson said that to deny basic rights and opportunities to any citizen on the basis of race was a grave injustice, and to reverse this injustice was "to make good the promise of America" (1992, 159–162).

By the mid-1960s both political parties would officially endorse the principles of color-blind liberalism, even while disagreeing sharply over the kinds of state action they demanded. In 1964 Goldwater cast his opposition to the civil rights agenda in the language of limiting state activism generally, not in the language of white supremacy used by segregationists. The division between progressivism and racism before the mid-1960s became one between racial activism and racial conservatism following the decade's legislative accomplishments in civil rights; for party leaders, the issue was no longer whether one supported or opposed segregation or discrimination, but rather what one proposed government do about them (Carmines and Stimson 1989, chap. 8). In the wake of the civil rights revolution, political elites on both the right and left would praise the virtues of individualism, fairness, equal rights, and equality of opportunity when it came to issues of race. They could all say, in the words of Ronald Reagan, "I am opposed with every fiber of my being to discrimination," even while strongly opposing each other over the extent of discrimination in society and what exactly to do about it.[15]

## Public Attitudes

The postwar period has seen a dramatic shift in the attitudes of white Americans on race. In their study of public opinion over the last half-century, Benjamin Page and Robert Shapiro write: "The expressed attitudes of white Americans toward black Americans have undergone a great transformation over the last forty or fifty years, a change greater than on any other issue. On a wide range of policies related to public accommodations, employment, schools, neighborhoods and housing, and intermarriage, whites moved from advocating total separation and an inferior status for blacks to favoring legal equality and substantial desegregation" (1992, 68). The majority of white Americans today profess support for nondiscrimination, full and equal rights for all citizens, and equality of opportunity. They publicly claim that a person's actions, achievements, and character, rather than his or her membership in a racial group, should determine how he or she is judged. White Americans are far less supportive, however, of government action that tries to put these ideals into practice, especially if it relies on what they see as unfair racial quotas or preferences, policies they say violate the American commitment to individualism and self-reliance.[16] African Americans also express strong support for nondiscrimination, equal rights, and equality of opportunity. However, they tend to see much more discrimination still remaining in American society than do whites, and they are more likely than whites to support government policies designed to protect civil rights and bring about racial equality, policies they claim help make it possible for the American ideals of individual achievement and self-reliance to become more of a reality for black citizens as well (Sigelman and Welch 1991; Hochschild 1995). Both black and white public attitudes, then, reveal broad support for the core values of color-blind liberalism, but they also show sharp divisions over what these values imply for political practice.

## FRAMING THE DEBATE ON RACE

Over the last five decades political theorists, intellectuals and social scientists, civil rights activists, jurists, politicians, and the American public have made color-blind liberalism the dominant normative understanding of race in the United States. It is an understanding that centers on the values of individualism, rights, fair procedures, equality of opportunity, and nondiscrimination. It considers race a morally irrelevant trait that in no way should impede an individual's freedom. It is not a hegemonic ideology; there are those on the radical left and the racist right who reject it out of hand. But the country's principle political positions all endorse some version of it, and its central categories have come to frame most contemporary debates over race.

This of course does not mean the debates are not intense. As the divisions within the various sources that I reviewed in the last section reveal, those arguing from within the color-blind paradigm often disagree sharply over its meaning and requirements. Ronald Dworkin makes a distinction that is important to keep in mind here: there is a crucial difference between disagreeing on abstract "constitutive principles" and disagreeing on more specific "derivative positions" that flow from such principles (1978a, 120–121). Most Americans now agree, at least in theory, on the broad constitutive principles of the color-blind paradigm, but the specific policy positions they derive from them are often very much at odds. As Sniderman and his colleagues point out in their study of American attitudes on race, the old conflict between the liberal creed of equal rights and basic fairness on the one side and the rhetoric of bigotry on the other has been replaced by arguments between different interpretations of the same liberal creed (1993, chap. 10). Those on the right and left have come to embrace the same color-blind paradigm, but they interpret it very differently.

Those on the right advocate a narrow interpretation of the color-blind paradigm. They claim equal citizenship rights are sufficient to protect black Americans in a society where discrimination has been dramatically reduced and individual effort is now the primary determinant of success or failure. Now that segregation has fallen and African Americans are on the same legal and political footing as anybody else, they should start relying on values like hard work, discipline, creativity, self-reliance, and initiative to take advantage of the opportunities America has to offer and raise themselves up as members of other groups have done before them. State action beyond guaranteeing the formal equality of individual citizens is misguided. It tends to undermine self-reliance by fostering dependency on the state's largesse, and in a hopeless effort to mandate equality, it only restricts individual independence as state activism inevitably does. Discrimination that still exists is relatively isolated among a few disgraceful bigots, but it does not amount to much more than what members of most groups in the United States have successfully overcome without becoming wards of the state. The right, then, considers the state's work largely finished, claiming that the rest is up to individual black Americans. Indeed, it frequently offers examples of individuals who have succeeded through hard work and individual initiative—Colin Powell is the most recent—to buttress its argument for taking the state out of the race arena.

Over the past three decades, the Republican Party has embraced this narrow reading of the color-blind paradigm and found considerable success translating it into public policy. It has sung the praises of full civil and political rights and the equal protection of the laws, even as it has worked hard to reduce the role of government in fighting discrimination

that remains, in facilitating integration, in protecting
black voting strength, and in alleviating harsh economic
disproportionately afflict African Americans.[17] Starting
and Nixon in the 1960s, the Republican Party has used the argu....
reducing the state's role on matters of race to attract white voters, especially in the historically Democratic stronghold of the South. Skillfully
using issues like busing, crime, and welfare, the right has benefitted from
and helped fuel a white backlash against state activism to enforce civil
rights, promote integration, and address urban poverty. In the last
decade, the right has been particularly successful in attacking affirmative
action policies as themselves a violation of color-blind principles. In the
words of Charles Murray, one of the right's house intellectuals: "Race is
not a morally admissible reason for treating one person differently from
another. Period" (1984, 223). Equating affirmative action with
"reverse-discrimination" in this way, the right has waged an increasingly
successful campaign both through the courts and state ballot measures
like California's Proposition 209 to eliminate racial preferences designed
to open up more employment, contracting, and educational opportunities to black citizens.

Those on the left respond with a much broader interpretation of
color-blind liberalism. They claim that unjust racial discrimination and
de facto segregation are still widespread and that they both continue to
sharply limit the options African Americans face in today's society. Furthermore, economic inequality now presents the most significant obstacle to the full participation of black citizens in American life. Economic
problems like poverty and unemployment—along with social problems
like poor health, drug abuse, crime, and lack of a quality education that
are tied to economic inequality—all fall disproportionately on African
Americans, creating a burden that prevents them from enjoying real
equality of opportunity. The left argues that as long as individuals in this
country still face barriers to their freedom created by discrimination, de
facto segregation, and economic inequality because of a morally arbitrary trait like race, the state must take an active role in eliminating these
barriers so black citizens can enjoy the same opportunities to pursue
their goals in life as other Americans. The state can do this through
much stronger enforcement of existing civil rights laws prohibiting discrimination in most areas of American life, enforcement the right has
worked hard to relax. It can also do so through programs that bring
about greater economic equality between white and black Americans.
Such programs usually rely on race-neutral criteria; economic status
rather than race determines who qualifies. But by raising any individual
suffering from economic disadvantage to a level of greater equality
regardless of his or her race, they provide a major benefit to black indi-

viduals who disproportionately suffer from the problems they seek to remedy. Finally, the left argues that sometimes taking race into account, as in programs like affirmative action and busing, is the only way to overcome entrenched discrimination and de facto segregation and, thereby, achieve the ultimate goals of the color-blind paradigm. We do not yet have a color-blind society, and acting as if we do only forecloses those actions we must take in order to reach it. According to this view, sometimes taking race into account is the only way to move towards a genuinely integrated society free of racial discrimination and economic exploitation.[18]

As the Republican Party began to articulate its argument for minimal state activism on matters of race in the 1960s, the Democrats continued to push for strong civil rights enforcement and antipoverty programs, as well as measures like busing and affirmative action designed to facilitate integration. While this helped solidify the party's hold on black voters, white support continued to move toward the Republicans, exemplified by those who came to be known as "Reagan Democrats" in the 1980s. Since the mid-1970s, the Democratic Party has had little success in preventing the retreat of activist public policy on issues of race, a retreat fueled by a powerful white backlash and a revitalized right. Indeed, as Clinton showed in his two successful campaigns for the presidency in the 1990s, the Democratic Party is most successful in attracting back white voters when it adopts positions on issues like crime and welfare more like those of Republicans. It was the Clinton administration, after all, that pushed through and campaigned on the kind of "welfare-reform" plan that Ronald Reagan could only have dreamed of achieving.

The left and right, then, do offer important differences on issues of race, differences they push more or less successfully through public policy. These differences exist, however, against a deeper background of agreement about the basic categories of color-blind liberalism. For example, while the right takes a very individualistic line in its arguments against state action, the left also relies on the same kind of individualism in its arguments for state action. Both sides claim that, morally speaking, membership in a racial group should not matter to an individual's prospects in life, but they disagree on the extent that it still does and what the state should do about it. Unlike the right, the left claims that things like discrimination, segregation, and economic status are still deeply attached to race, and so individuals still face the kinds of morally arbitrary barriers to their freedom that the state has the ability and responsibility to help remove. In this way, the left and right certainly argue with each other, but they do so using the common language furnished by color-blind liberalism. They both appeal to individualism, rights, fair procedures, equality of opportunity, and the need to over-come discrimination. Their disagreement comes over what these values require in practice, especially by the state. In order to see more clearly how the arguments deployed in such conflicts over race are now framed by the categories of color-blind liberalism, I think it is useful to take a closer look at what is perhaps the most hotly contested question since the fall of de jure segregation. This is the question of whether or not remedial policies that take explicit account of race are permissible, and the two issues that dominate this question are school busing and affir-mative action.

Busing was one of the first issues in the post–civil rights era to really open up internal conflicts within the new color-blind orthodoxy that the nation had just committed itself to in the mid-1960s. Bernard Boxhill points out that the Supreme Court in its *Brown* decision left a crucial issue unresolved. This was whether (1) assigning students to different schools by race is unconstitutional or (2) segregated schools in and of themselves are unconstitutional (Boxhill 1984, 74–75). No doubt this ambiguity springs from the fact that *Brown*'s importance lies in its effect rather than in its legal reasoning, which was designed to obscure rather than illuminate the underlying constitutional issues at stake.[19] Oppo-nents of school busing embrace the first and narrower interpretation of *Brown*, while its supporters push for the second interpretation with its much wider constitutional mandate. The important thing to notice is that each side in the busing debate is able to ground its position in one of color-blind liberalism's central legal texts, and each side claims to uphold the general spirit of the color-blind paradigm itself.

Those opposed to busing simply say that the color of a child's skin is no reason to assign him or her to one school or another; individual children should be free to attend neighborhood schools regardless of their race. Parents of any race have a right to work hard, move into any neighborhood they wish, and send their kids to its schools without the state coming in and trying to achieve some artificial racial balance at the expense of a quality education. On this view, parents and kids should not be punished for residential patterns that result from the free choices made by black and white citizens or from general economic conditions unrelated to education. As long as residential or school segregation is not mandated by law, then the state should have no role in the racial composition of schools. Instead, it should concentrate on making all schools, regardless of location or racial breakdown, good ones. Assign-ing students to schools by race is precisely the kind of practice the civil rights movement fought against.

On the other side, supporters of busing respond that it is the only way to truly integrate the nation's public schools. In order to undo the effects of generations of legally mandated segregation, strong measures like busing are necessary.[20] Segregated schools, whether by law or not, are discriminatory and prevent us from achieving a society characterized by true equality of opportunity. In an article on busing, Ronald Dworkin argues that while the state must treat each individual with equal concern and respect, this doesn't mean the state must treat each individual exactly the same. Sometimes a right to equal concern and respect demands that the state take steps that are necessary to protect its citizens from the harmful effects of racial prejudice, and one of the policies it should use to fight prejudice and work for an integrated society is school busing (Dworkin 1977, 278–280).

Affirmative action has become even more controversial than busing. Opponents, including many strong supporters of the early civil rights movement, claim that affirmative action is a new form of racial discrimination that violates King's vision of a society where people are judged by the content of their character rather than by the color of their skin.[21] They are fond of quoting the early writings of leaders like Thurgood Marshall and pressing for new "civil rights" legislation that prohibits the government from discriminating on the basis of race or gender for any reason. In the words of Clint Bolick, "Only when we finally curb the power of government to discriminate on the basis of race and gender can we turn our attention to ensuring equal opportunity for all Americans" (1995, 56). Affirmative action "violates the American creed that we must be judged as individuals, not on the basis of race or sex—a group membership over which we have no choice" (Cohen 1995, A15). It is a fundamentally unfair practice that distinguishes between ascriptive groups rather than individuals, violates equal protection rights, subverts equality of opportunity, and introduces invidious racial categories just when we had committed ourselves to setting them aside. Opponents claim that affirmative action only divides Americans into hostile groups competing in a racial spoils system, rather than upholding the American vision of a society where individual citizens compete on equal terms. They also claim that affirmative action reinforces and helps perpetuate stereotypes of black inferiority among whites, as well as in the minds of African Americans themselves (Steele 1991, 87–88). Finally, they reject the argument that affirmative action is an acceptable solution to discrimination, since it practices the very thing it claims to fight. As Justice Scalia writes in his 1989 opinion in *Richmond v. Croson*: "The difficulty of overcoming the effects of past discrimination is as nothing compared with the difficulty of eradicating from our society the source of those effects, which is the tendency—fatal to a nation such as ours—to classify and judge men and women on the basis of their country of origin or the color of their skin. A solution to the first problem that aggravates the second is no solution at all."[22]

Supporters of affirmative action respond that it is sometimes the only way to keep still powerful and debilitating discriminatory practices at bay or to heal the lingering effects of past discrimination, to promote integration, and to provide for genuine equality of opportunity. In the words of Bill Clinton, "I have always believed that affirmative action is needed to remedy discrimination and to create a more inclusive society that truly provides equal opportunity."[23] On this view, affirmative action is a way to address the structural foundations of inequality and help insure equality of opportunity by bringing more African Americans into the mainstream occupational strata of American society (Takaki 1987b, 231). Rather than always treating everyone in exactly the same way, justice sometimes requires that we compensate individuals who suffer from morally arbitrary disadvantages. While not endorsing affirmative action directly, Rawls does include the "principle of redress" in his second principle of justice. He writes that "we are led to the difference principle if we wish to set up the social system so that no one gains or loses from his arbitrary place in the distribution of natural assets or his initial position in society without giving or receiving compensating advantages in return" (Rawls 1971, 102). Sometimes we must treat individuals differently if we are to treat them as equals and establish a society where arbitrary differences such as race do not matter to one's prospects in life. Dworkin is much more explicit, arguing that affirmative action does not violate individual rights, because it is not based on racial prejudice but rather on an attempt to treat individuals with equal concern and respect (1986, 381–397; 1985, 301–302; 1978b, 227–239). He claims that affirmative action's ultimate goal is to reduce the degree to which race makes a difference in American society by taking measures necessary to integrate American economic and social life (1985, 294–295). He writes: "If the strategic claims for affirmative action are cogent, they cannot be dismissed on the ground that racially explicit tests are distasteful. If such tests are distasteful, it can only be for reasons that make the underlying social realities the programs attack more distasteful still" (1985, 295).

The Supreme Court justices who supported affirmative action in the landmark *Bakke* case of 1978 rely upon just these kinds of arguments.[24] In their joint opinion, Brennan, White, Marshall, and Blackmun declare that the state may use race-conscious programs to correct for the effects of past discrimination, thereby elevating members of minority groups to positions they would have enjoyed had such discrimination not been present. They write that "a state government may adopt race-conscious programs if the purpose of such programs is to remove the disparate racial impact its actions might otherwise have and if there is reason to believe that the disparate impact is itself the product of past discrimination, whether its own or that of society at large."[25] Unlike segregation, the purpose of affirmative action programs is not to stigmatize or subordinate a particular group, but to "overcome the effects of segregation by bringing the races together."[26] Thurgood Marshall writes in his own opinion:

> It is because of a legacy of unequal treatment that we now must permit the institutions of this society to give consideration to race in making decisions about who will hold the positions of influence, affluence, and prestige in America. For far too long, the doors to these positions have been shut to Negroes. If we are ever to become a fully integrated society, one in which the color of a person's skin will not determine the opportunities available to him or her, we must be willing to take steps to open those doors. I do not believe that anyone can truly look into America's past and still find that a remedy for the effects of that past is impermissible.[27]

In their arguments, Marshall and his fellow justices claim that since race should not matter to an individual's opportunities in life, and since it clearly does given the country's history, then policies that use racial categories to negate the effects of this history actually uphold the principle that race should not matter. Such policies try to cancel out the destructive effects of discrimination, thereby restoring the state of affairs that would have existed had discrimination not been present in the first place.

When listening to arguments over affirmative action, I think it quickly becomes clear that each side is arguing with the same normative goal in mind: ensuring equality of opportunity by designing procedures that treat individuals fairly in a competitive American society. This is why a popular metaphor in affirmative action debates is the famous "level playing field." One side says that since we now have a level playing field, it is only fair that each person play by the same set of rules; while the other side answers that the field is still uneven, and so fairness demands that those facing an uphill battle have certain procedural advantages to even things out.[28] We can also see the shared normative assumptions at work in the other frequent context of the debate: the hypothetical job interview. Here, both sides agree race should not matter to a candidate's prospects. One party claims this necessarily rules out any racial preference, but the other claims the only way to compensate for the influence of discrimination on the one side is to attach a racial preference on the other; in order to control for the harmful effects of discrimination, we must factor it out of the competitive equation by weighing it equally on both sides. Both parties to the debate claim that membership in a particular racial group should be an irrelevant factor in a person's opportunities in life, but they disagree over how to achieve this goal. One says only treating it as irrelevant will make it so, while the other says only compensating for the fact that it continues to be relevant will ultimately defeat this relevance. Contemporary debates over affirmative action, then, are like most debates over issues of race in the United States. They revolve around questions of how individuals should be treated so that their race has no impact on the opportunities they face. They center on what barriers still exist that block an individual's freedom due to race and on how such barriers should be overcome. In short, they unfold against a background commitment to the values of individualism, rights, fair procedures, equality of opportunity, and nondiscrimination provided by the color-blind paradigm.

## COLOR-BLIND LIBERALISM AND FREEDOM

In a famous essay, Isaiah Berlin makes a distinction between two concepts of freedom or liberty. The first is a negative notion of freedom as noninterference by others. It relies on the defense of a sphere in which the individual is free from external obstruction or coercion at the hands of others, a sphere that hinges on a "frontier" between public and private life marked off and protected by strong individual rights (Berlin 1969, 122–130). The second concept is that of positive liberty, which relies on the idea of internal self-realization or rational self-direction. To be truly free under this notion of liberty, people must live their lives according to the demands of their true, rational, or higher selves. The question for positive liberty is not what the limits of action are or how far we are free to do something, but rather what standards we use to decide how to live our lives. On Berlin's account, positive liberty translates easily into authoritarian or totalitarian rule, because the claim is often made that people must be educated or even coerced into embracing their true selves. Irrational people must be freed from the slavery of ignorance and led into the light of reason if they are to be liberated. Sometimes they must be forced to be free, to use Rousseau's famous (or infamous) image. Positive liberty, then, is mastering oneself in accordance with truth or reason, rather than the enjoyment of noninterference and individual rights within the private sphere that negative liberty celebrates (Berlin 1969, 130–153).

Negative liberty has always been at the center of liberalism. At least since John Locke, liberals have defended the "*equal right* that every man hath *to his natural freedom*, without being subjected to the will or authority of any other man" (1982, 33, italics in the original). Modern liberalism, however, has moved away from an exclusive focus on formal rights against coercion or interference by others. As we saw earlier in this chapter, many liberals have been especially concerned with how economic inequality and exploitation threaten freedom. On their account, formal rights against interference do not necessarily guarantee that an individual is free if he or she is still left vulnerable by forces such as poverty or unemployment. Such a person may be free in a formal sense, but this means little in the very real economic context of his or her life. Some observers see this trend toward egalitarian interpretations of freedom within liberalism as a movement toward positive notions of liberty, because it pays attention to broader conditions necessary for freedom rather than just formal rights against noninterference (Waligorski 1981; Volkomer 1969). In my view, however, this trend in liberalism is not an embrace of the positive liberty that Berlin has in mind, because it does not focus on the kinds of internal self-realization or rational self-mastery that he associates with positive freedom. Instead, it simply expands the negative view of liberty to cover more sources of external interference. Now it is not only an oppressive state or unjust coercion by fellow citizens that obstruct freedom, but economic factors such as poverty and unemployment as well. Both egalitarian and libertarian interpretations of liberalism still rely primarily on a view of freedom as noninterference, they just disagree on what sorts of things interfere with an individual's liberty. In this way, they both share what Charles Taylor calls an opportunity-concept of freedom. This is an understanding of freedom as the lack of external obstacles that block an individual's opportunity to do what he or she wants to do in life (Taylor 1985b, 212–215). It is a view of freedom as being able to pursue one's own goals without interference from a host of external factors that can range from the state to other people to general economic conditions.[29] This opportunity-concept of freedom, as well as its internal disagreements over what constitutes interference with freedom, is at the heart of color-blind liberalism.

The historical language of American liberalism upon which the color-blind paradigm rests defines freedom as being left alone. It celebrates America as the land of opportunity, where political protections and open social and economic conditions make it possible for people to make their own way in life. The theories of liberal justice that the color-blind paradigm rests upon also employ an opportunity-concept of freedom. Rawls defines liberty as the freedom to do certain things without interference from a host of political, social, and especially economic constraints (Paul 1984, 386–387). Rawls writes, "Thus persons are at liberty to do something when they are free from certain constraints either to do it or not to do it and when their doing it or not doing it is protected from interference by other persons" (1971, 202). Dworkin also relies upon this view of freedom, claiming that to deny individuals strong civil and political rights as well as a just distribution of social and economic resources is to raise barriers to their liberty and prevent them from pursuing the kinds of lives they want to live, in addition to denying them the equal concern and respect that they deserve as human beings (Dworkin 1981; Guest 1991, chap. 10). This is also the view of freedom that the civil rights movement based its powerful moral appeals upon, as black Americans launched a frontal attack on the forces that denied them the opportunity to live their lives as full and free citizens of the United States. As Manning Marable writes: "The leaders of the modern Civil Rights Movement mobilized millions with one simple demand: freedom. In the context of the racially segregated society of the South in the post–World War II period, 'freedom' meant the elimination of social, political, legal and economic barriers that forced black Americans into a subordinate status" (1991a, 187). It is a measure of the movement's success that in its wake the courts, political elites, and a significant portion of the American people all embraced the notion that the freedom one enjoys should not depend upon the color of one's skin.

This opportunity-concept of freedom that the color-blind paradigm embraced in the postwar era is a thoroughly individualistic one. It tries to break the connection between membership in a racially defined group and individual opportunity, a connection that has historically contributed to the subordination of black Americans. It claims that racial group membership should not matter one way or the other to an individual's freedom. All individuals deserve an equal opportunity to live their lives as they see fit regardless of their race. This is why color-blind liberalism puts such a strong emphasis on individual rights and fair procedures; they protect persons from the external interference and unjust abuse that threatens their freedom. It is also why equality of opportunity is so important. If all individuals deserve the opportunity to live their own lives as they see fit with as few external obstacles as possible, then anything that raises higher barriers to some on the basis of a morally arbitrary fact like membership in a racial group is unjust and must be dismantled. Chief among such barriers is discrimination. For color-blind liberalism, racial discrimination threatens freedom because it restricts opportunities in life, raising obstacles that block an individual's ability to pursue his or her goals and constraining his or her choices.

It is important to notice that both the right and left interpretations of color-blind liberalism share this individualistic, opportunity-concept of freedom. Their disagreements come over how many and what kinds of external barriers tied to race still exist in American life, and over what if anything the state should do to dismantle them. While the right sees relatively few barriers and would restrict the state to protecting a narrow set of basic rights, the left extends the color-blind view of race and freedom in two important ways. First, it argues that black individuals still face external barriers to freedom due to their race and that the state must make strong efforts to attack these barriers. Second, it identifies economic inequality and exploitation as one of the most important of these barriers. The left, in short, offers a broader and more activist view of race and freedom, one going beyond traditional negative rights to include state intervention in American society, and especially the American economy, to promote the liberal value of individual freedom, a value long denied on an equal basis to some of its citizens because of their membership in an ascriptive racial group.

Color-blind liberalism's understanding of race and freedom is critical to my argument in the rest of this book, because reevaluating and expanding it is a promising way for liberalism to move beyond the limits of the color-blind paradigm. In the chapters to follow, I argue that while the left's interpretation of color-blind liberalism is richer than that of the right, it is nonetheless insufficient. This is because color-blind liberalism itself, in both its right and left interpretations, suffers from the severe shortcomings I identify in the next chapter. The key to overcoming these shortcomings, however, is to reconsider the value of freedom within liberalism, and, by doing so in chapter 4, I show just how incomplete color-blind liberalism's view of race and freedom turns out to be. First, this view, even in its broader interpretation by the left, still overlooks significant external factors critical to the freedom of black Americans. Second, by relying exclusively on an opportunity-concept, it also ignores the importance of the internal realm to the meaningful exercise of freedom. Both of these flaws are rooted in color-blind liberalism's excessive individualism, which is shared by both its left and right interpretations and which leaves unexamined the importance of culture and membership in cultural groups, especially to the exercise of freedom within the institutions, practices, and meanings of civil society. A view of freedom, however, that does take account of these factors provides a way for American liberalism to develop a richer and more compelling understanding of race. This is the understanding I develop in chapter 5 and apply to public policy in chapter 6.

# CHAPTER 3

# *The Limits of Color-Blind Liberalism*

Color-blind liberalism has had a profound and positive impact on American life and law. Its achievements, however, also reveal its limits. While color-blind liberalism is certainly superior to the public philosophy of de jure segregation that it replaced, it nonetheless suffers from severe shortcomings. In this chapter, I describe color-blind liberalism's accomplishments and the reaction of the left in the wake of these accomplishments. I then examine the critical shortcomings that prevent the color-blind paradigm from providing a full and compelling understanding of race in American life.

## THE STRENGTHS OF COLOR-BLIND LIBERALISM

It is clear that color-blind liberalism has been a potent tool in the fight for racial justice in the last five decades. With the civil rights movement, it provided a powerful context in which African Americans and those who allied themselves with the cause of black civil rights challenged the blatant disregard for black freedom and equality throughout the United States. The courts and Congress have used its categories to strike down the formal edifice of segregation and to battle the pervasive practice of racial discrimination. Its message has convinced unprecedented numbers of white Americans that their black fellow citizens deserve the same rights, protections, and opportunities as anybody else. Color-blind liberalism has underpinned successful efforts to destroy legally mandated apartheid in the South, to extend long-awaited civil and political rights to black citizens, and to reduce the most blatant forms of discrimination in American life. It has drained the rhetoric of white supremacy of its public legitimacy and dismantled its formal machinery, and it has helped to open doors of opportunity once firmly shut in social and economic life to many African Americans. By the mid-1960s, its role in the defeat of Jim Crow was, in the words of Gary Orfield, "one of the greatest triumphs of American liberalism" (1988, 313).

Color-blind liberalism has been particularly powerful at the level of the state. Using its arguments, civil rights activists and their allies managed to shift the state from a position enforcing, or at least endorsing, segregation and white supremacy to a position upholding what Roy Brooks calls "formal equal opportunity" (1990, 25). On Brooks's account, formal equal opportunity is now the state's fundamental public policy on race. It holds that black and white Americans share an equal legal status as citizens and are therefore entitled to full and equal civil rights and to equal legal treatment. Formal equal opportunity's two "operational tenets" are racial omission—the position that racial differences should not matter in the distribution of rights, duties, and social resources such as education, housing, or employment—and racial integration—the position that racial separation in all areas of American life must be discouraged and dismantled (Brooks 1990, 25–30). By pursuing this policy of formal equal opportunity, the state has officially embraced the principles of the color-blind paradigm and attempted to put them into practice.

The positive influence color-blind liberalism has had fits very well with its central categories. Its focus on individual rights and fair procedures is well-suited to action by the state, since such concepts translate easily into law. Judicial decisions such as *Brown* in 1954, legislative milestones such as the Civil Rights Act of 1964 and the Voting Rights Act of 1965, and the passage and enforcement of a host of other antidiscrimination and civil rights measures by the state in the last several decades all write color-blind liberalism's central categories into the law of the land. The formal legal and political institutions of the state have proven themselves highly receptive to the language of the color-blind paradigm. It has provided the state with the kinds of conceptual tools it has needed to attack de jure segregation, to identify and prosecute blatant racial discrimination, and to enforce basic civil rights and the equal protection of the laws regardless of race.

## COLOR-BLIND LIBERALISM AND THE LEFT

Following the stunning triumphs of the civil rights movement in Congress during the mid-1960s, the movement began to fragment over the question of what to do next. Only a few days after the movement's zenith at the signing of the Voting Rights Act in 1965, riots broke out in Watts, and the United States entered a new era in its struggle with the dilemma of race. The liberal consensus, including significant levels of white support across the country, that existed on the need to dismantle legally-mandated segregation in the South and to guarantee basic civil and political rights to black citizens, splintered as activists turned their attention to issues of de facto segregation, poverty, unemployment, crime, police brutality, poor education, and despair throughout black

America, especially in the urban ghettos of the North (Sitkoff 1993, chap. 7; Orfield 1988). The right, with the support of growing numbers of white Americans, claimed that the country had done enough by striking down de jure segregation and formally endorsing equal civil and political rights for all. On its account, the United States had put its civil rights house in order, and the rest was up to black individuals themselves; any special help they received from the state was unnecessary and unfair. Most of those on the left, however, recognized that more was needed. The country had taken a huge step with the judicial and legislative victories of the 1950s and 1960s, but it was only a first step toward building a racially just society in practice. The left argued that formal equality and an end to de jure segregation at the level of the state would not automatically guarantee genuine equality and integration in American society, so an unjust racial status quo would remain unless deeper economic and social issues were addressed.

A significant number of those on the left during the civil rights era never put much faith in liberal solutions to begin with (Haines 1988). Many in the radical and black nationalist traditions had always advocated revolutionary change or some form of black separatism rather than liberal reforms within the existing economic and social system. While many within these traditions supported the civil rights movement, they did so as a way to challenge what they considered the structural injustice of a racist/capitalist system or the American cultural addiction to white supremacy. As the civil rights movement began to fragment in the 1960s following its achievements within the broad formula provided by color-blind liberalism, some activists, frustrated with the limited scope of color-blind reforms, returned to or embraced for the first time these radical or nationalist paradigms. In doing so they rejected the liberal formula of integration, racial equality, and color-blind justice as hopeless, naive, imperialistic, or an expression of false consciousness.[1]

While these radical and black nationalist traditions have been an important presence on the American left over the last several decades, they have received little public support from either white or black Americans, most of whom have still endorsed some version of the color-blind paradigm. Indeed, most of those on the mainstream left remained committed to the broad paradigm of color-blind liberalism in the wake of the civil rights movement (Orfield 1988, 332–334). Realizing that the right's interpretation was inadequate, they developed and pushed for their own broader interpretation, hoping that extending the paradigm's understanding of race would provide a way to overcome the right's narrow interpretation that claimed enough had already been done. So on the heels of the landmark civil rights legislation of the 1960s, the left began urging the nation to take the next step and address the deeper sources of economic and social inequality existing between white and black Americans. In his speech at Howard University in 1965, President Johnson used his famous metaphor of a runner hobbled by chains for many years who is then expected to run a race on equal terms against a well-conditioned opponent. He claimed that if black individuals were to compete in American society on equal terms, then they had to have the economic and educational resources to do so rather than just formal civil and political rights (Jackson 1990, 297). This theme was echoed with even more urgency by government commissions formed to study urban riots sweeping the nation during the mid to late 1960s. They reported that it would take more than formal rights to secure racial peace and justice; it would also take jobs, education, and genuine social integration.

This question of "whether the winning of formal political rights will now enable blacks to progress economically" has been at the center of the left's efforts to address issues of race in the post–civil rights period (Piven and Cloward 1977, 256). Roy Brooks articulates the concern of those on the left nicely: "African Americans have certainly received a legalistic, formalistic type of equality. But that is a poor proxy for the real thing—an equal chance to improve or protect one's chances for worldly success and personal happiness" (1990, 32). Stanford Lyman echoes the same theme, saying, "In America, the toppling of the outer bastion of the white republic's institutionalized racism—legislatively established segregation, 'Jim Crow' laws, and juridically enforced race discrimination—has made its second line of defense—the walls built against job opportunities and occupational advancement—both more visible and less vulnerable to assault" (1991, 234). In order to attack this "second line of defense," the left has advocated stronger state intervention. The National Urban League, for example, has called for a domestic "Marshall Plan" to fight the poverty, unemployment, and inferior education that disproportionately afflict black Americans (Jacob 1994). The left has pushed for federal policies favoring full employment and a higher minimum wage, and it has supported more extensive programs targeting job training, income maintenance, primary and secondary education, drug treatment, health care, and child care, all programs it claims will help reduce the effects of economic inequality tied to race and open up opportunities still denied black citizens. Finally, the left has advocated stronger enforcement of antidiscrimination laws and programs like affirmative action and busing designed to counter the continuing effects of discrimination and to integrate the nation's primary employment and educational institutions (Carnoy 1994; Larson 1988; Solomon 1988). As we saw in the last chapter, these efforts have been part of the left's attempt to attack barriers to individual freedom that are still disproportionately tied to a person's race, an attempt that centers primarily on issues of state activism and economic inequality.

Compared to the achievements of the civil rights movement of the 1950s and early 1960s, the left has met with considerable frustration in its attempts to extend color-blind liberalism, to "take the next step" toward social and economic equality and genuine integration, in the years since. At best these efforts have seen far less success than the color-blind paradigm's early victories at the level of the state. While the post–civil rights era has seen the rise of a significant black middle class and African Americans are visible in positions of power and prestige throughout American social and economic life, as approximately 12 percent of the U.S. population, black Americans by the early to mid-1990s still carried a grossly disproportionate share of economic and social burdens, many of which have become worse rather than better in recent years. This fact has led observers such as Manning Marable and Leith Mullings to claim that "despite the concrete victories in the legal and political sphere for blacks and the growth of a professional and managerial elite, the actual material conditions for the majority of black people have grown clearly worse in the last fifteen years" (1994, 67–68).

Over the past several decades, black family income has remained about 50% to 60% that of white families, and the poverty rate for black Americans, currently around 30%, has remained three to four times that of whites. This puts 42% of black families in the poorest 20% of all American families. Even when controlling for differences in family structure and educational levels, a wide gap between black and white income remains. These disparities are particularly pronounced for children: 45% of black children live in poverty compared to 16% of white children. Since the civil rights movement, African Americans have also made little progress in overcoming the country's employment disparities. Black unemployment still consistently runs about twice that of whites, meaning it stays at recession levels during economic upswings and rises to depression levels when the country goes through a recession. In the early 1990s, official black unemployment stood at 12.5% compared to 6% for whites, and the National Urban League, accounting for those no longer looking for work, estimates actual unemployment rates to be even higher, at around 13% for the country as a whole and 23% for black Americans. This unemployment crisis is particularly evident among black urban youth. Closer to the top of the economic ladder, disparities in the professions also remain high: between 1970 and 1990 African Americans had only risen from 1.3% to 3.2% of lawyers, from 2.2% to 3% of doctors, and from 3.5% to 4.5% of professors. Of *Business Week*'s 1992 list of heads of America's thousand largest firms, only one was black. These economic problems are not limited to urban areas.

Rural African Americans have always been among the country's poorest, and they continue to absorb the heaviest shocks brought about by nationwide economic dislocations. Almost one third of black farmers, for example, lost their farms during the 1982 to 1987 farm crisis, making the decline in the number of black farmers in recent years ten times that experienced by white farmers.[2]

While the continuing disparities between white and black Americans in such areas as income and employment are dramatic, the gap between white and black wealth is even wider. In a recent study, Melvin Oliver and Thomas Shapiro (1995) point out that annual lists of the highest paid Americans, those with the highest income, routinely include black entertainers and sports figures, but the much longer lists of the wealthiest Americans, those who pay such high salaries to people on the first kind of list, rarely if ever include any African Americans. On their account, this fact illustrates just how deep racial inequality remains in the United States. While income represents the flow of money to an individual at a particular time in his or her life, wealth represents a person's accumulated assets or net worth. As such, wealth is a much more secure and substantial economic foundation, one that also can be transferred and enlarged from generation to generation. As a much better measure than income of the real economic power that an individual wields in the United States, the differences in wealth between white and black Americans are striking. Oliver and Shapiro report that on average white Americans possess almost twelve times as much median net worth as black Americans ($43,800 versus $3,700), and when equity in a house and car are excluded to look simply at the average nest egg families have in financial assets such as stocks, bonds, mutual funds, and so on, white families are worth about $7,000 on average, while the average for black families stands at zero (1995, 85–86). These kinds of wide disparities continue to exist for white and black Americans at the same educational, occupational, and even income levels. There is on average a $43,000 difference in net worth between black and white Americans at the same socioeconomic levels. College-educated whites, for example, control four times as much wealth as college-educated blacks, and while the black middle class in general manages to earn seventy cents for every dollar earned by the white middle class, it only possesses fifteen cents for every dollar of wealth held by the white middle class (1995, 7–8). In short, historical patterns of segregation and discrimination, especially in the twentieth-century housing market that has fueled an unprecedented wealth accumulation by middle-class whites, have left a legacy of massive economic inequality between white and black Americans stretching across generations. This is why Oliver and Shapiro point out that celebrating the rise of the black middle class may be premature, since it is one built on income rather than wealth, making it much more vulnerable, insecure, and less able to pass along its economic status to its children.

In addition to continuing, and in some cases widening, economic disparities, black Americans also continue to suffer disproportionately from a host of social problems, and this is particularly true of black urban youth. African Americans enjoy less access to quality health care, experience more health problems, have a shorter life expectancy, and have higher rates of infant mortality. They are more often the victims of crime, especially violent crime, and their attackers are usually black themselves. By the early 1990s, black men, only 6% of the population, made up almost half of the United States prison population, a rate of incarceration seven times that of the U.S. as a whole and higher than that of South Africa at the height of its apartheid regime. In some central cities, approximately half of all black males ages eighteen to thirty-five are in prison, on parole or probation, out on bail, or being sought by the police for arrest. During the 1980s, the homicide rate for black males in their late teens and twenties, now their leading cause of death, soared to almost nine times the rate for their white male cohorts. While black Americans do provide about half of the prison population, they account for less than 10% of those in college. White Americans have more than twice the rate of college graduation, and this gap widened among young people during the 1980s. At the primary and secondary levels, black students are disproportionately concentrated in underfunded and understaffed schools with higher dropout rates and lower academic achievement. The decline of the American family also continues to disproportionately burden African Americans, with higher rates of divorce, teenage pregnancy, and out-of-wedlock births. In 1991, the percent of female-headed households stood at 46% for black Americans compared to 14% for whites, and among those twenty to twenty-nine years of age, the rates were even higher at 60% and 18% respectively. Finally, in spite of laws prohibiting housing discrimination, residential segregation has actually risen across the nation since 1960.[3]

The left, then, has seen little success in trying to extend the color-blind paradigm and attack the economic and social inequality tied to race that still exists in American life. Instead, it is the right's narrower interpretation that has proven far more successful. The state's role in trying to bring about greater economic and social equality between white and black Americans through its public policy programs has remained relatively limited. Those trying to fight discrimination through the courts face the difficult standards of proof established by the Supreme Court in cases such as *Washington v. Davis* in 1976, *McCleskey v. Kemp* in 1987, and *St. Mary's Honor Center v. Hicks* in

1993.[4] Busing as a tool to integrate the country's schools has remained fairly narrow in scope, especially given the Supreme Court's 1974 decision in *Milliken v. Bradley* not to require busing across district lines that separate urban from suburban school systems.[5] Finally, the right has enjoyed considerable success in using the language of color-blind justice to indict affirmative action programs, which have always been rather narrow in scope and seem to be gradually losing ground with each new political campaign, state referendum, and court decision.[6]

All of this has put the left on the defensive and in a very difficult position when it comes to issues of race. It has never accepted the right's narrow interpretation of color-blind liberalism, but it has also grown frustrated with the apparent weakness of its own broader interpretation. This weakness has produced a mounting dissatisfaction with color-blind liberalism itself, yet the left still lacks any real alternative. More radical paradigms attract some, but the mainstream left is compelled to stay within the broad language of liberalism if it is to preserve any political relevance it still has. The left, in short, has fallen on hard times. It simply has not been able to recapture the moral clarity and force of argument it enjoyed during the civil rights era. It still relies on a color-blind paradigm that has not proven particularly successful since the mid-1960s, but it cannot seem to fix upon anything better without setting liberalism aside altogether, something it also cannot afford to do. As a result, the left presently suffers from a pervasive sense of frustration when it comes to questions of race. There is a sense that the "old grounds for hope for racial justice have fled" (Roediger 1992, 114–115). In the words of Derrick Bell:

> How are we to assess the unstable status of a struggle that all but the most perversely pessimistic predicted would end in triumph many years ago? Even the most deeply involved in this struggle are at a loss for a rational explanation of how the promise of racial equality escaped a fulfillment that thirty years ago appeared assured. . . . The discrepancy between the nation's deeply held beliefs and its daily behavior add a continuing confusion to racial inequalities that undermine effective action. Thus, we take refuge in the improbable and seek relief in increasingly empty repetitions of tarnished ideals. (1987, 5)

Essentially, the left stands in the same position it stood in thirty years ago: the state is formally committed to the tenets of color-blind liberalism, but deep and significant problems tied to race nonetheless remain, and the question is still where to go from here.

Much of the left's failure to achieve the goals of its broader and more activist interpretation of color-blind liberalism clearly lies with the decline of its political fortunes over the last several decades. The right simply has had the political power to eliminate or sharply limit the scope of state programs the left has advocated to help bring about racial equality and integration (Carnoy 1994; Marable 1991a, chaps. 7–8). I think, however, that there is more to this failure than a simple lack of implementation. The seeds of the left's failure to realize its broader interpretation of color-blind liberalism and its growing frustration with the entire paradigm lie in the limits of color-blind liberalism itself. This underlying weakness is often overlooked because, when compared to the right's alternative, the left's interpretation of color-blind liberalism is clearly stronger. The right's strict interpretation provides a cramped, incomplete, and often callously distorted understanding of race in the United States, one that overlooks critical economic and social barriers that still block the opportunities black individuals must have in order to live full and free lives. So compared to that of the right, the left's reading of the color-blind paradigm is much more compelling, and this is why much of it remains in the alternative liberal understanding of race that I develop in chapters 5 and 6. Nonetheless, the left's interpretation suffers from many of the same underlying problems as that of the right. This is because color-blind liberalism itself suffers from critical shortcomings that prevent it, in both its left and right versions, from providing an acceptable understanding of race in American life.

## THE LIMITS OF COLOR-BLIND LIBERALISM

Color-blind liberalism's strength is also the source of it weakness. Its central categories are very effective in focusing our attention on some issues, but in so doing they also obscure other considerations that turn out to be critical. Its understanding of race is not entirely flawed, but it is partial and incomplete; its problem is not what it pays attention to but what it overlooks. Color-blind liberalism has been very effective in addressing issues of race at the level of the state and its formal political and legal institutions. There is much more to American public life, however, than the formal realm of the state. There is also the informal, but still very much public, realm of civil society, and color-blind liberalism is simply unable to adequately come to terms with race at this level. It overlooks and obscures a host of factors at work in civil society that are critical to a full and compelling understanding of race in the United States.

Over the last two centuries, the idea of civil society has developed along two main lines within political thought. The first is the Marxist tradition that stresses the contradictions and conflicts embedded in civil society and how they find political resolution in the state. The second is the liberal tradition that offers a view of civil society as a self-regulating realm of rights-carrying individuals, a realm that should be as free as possible from state interference and one that is often described in economic terms, as an independent and nonpolitical sphere of production, consumption, and trade (Seligman 1992, 10–11; Taylor 1995, 215–216). The second view, of course, has been the dominant one in the United States, and it is firmly entrenched within color-blind liberalism. This liberal view of civil society has come in for considerable criticism over the years, with many thinkers pointing to its difficulty in accounting for sources of power outside the formal realm of the state. As Michael Walzer points out, the liberal project is traditionally one of carving out a private sphere for individual freedom, one defined and protected by rights against interference by arbitrary state power. What it often fails to notice, however, are the less formal sources of power that threaten freedom from within this sphere itself (Walzer 1984). Marx himself is disdainful of a liberalism that promises freedom through formal rights that in practice only wall off and protect a civil society where individuals are oppressed by informal economic, social, and religious practices. On his account, rights against interference by state power still leave individuals vulnerable to much deeper and much more oppressive sources of power within civil society: "Thus man was not liberated from religion; he received religious liberty. He was not liberated from property; he received the liberty to own property. He was not liberated from the egoism of business; he received the liberty to engage in business" (Marx 1963, 29). For many critics, early and modern, the flip side of liberalism's intense suspicion of state power has been an overly benign view of power in civil society.

Such critics have been particularly concerned with American liberalism's view of civil society. John Keane points out that one of America's earliest thinkers, Thomas Paine, relied on a sharp distinction between what he considered a naturally peaceful and harmonious civil society and threats to it coming from despotic state power. According to Paine, if only state power could be controlled and minimized by natural rights and the consent of the governed, then individuals would be free to flourish in a largely benign and self-regulating civil society (Keane 1988b, 44–50). On Gordon Wood's account, the generation that gave the country its constitution also gave it a cramped view of politics, one that focuses almost exclusively on formal political power and mechanisms designed to limit it. This view obscures the very real sources of informal power in civil society that frame the background against which political forces operate (Wood 1969, 562). Finally, thinkers like Mary Ann Glendon and Robert Bellah argue that the American language of politics has a great deal of difficulty identifying and making sense of deeper sources of power in civil society. In its focus on formal rights and, to a lesser extent, issues of economic distribution, this language overlooks the underlying cultural and social texture of American life (Glendon 1991, 109–117; Bellah et al. 1985, 204–208). By focusing almost exclusively on the "individual-state-market grid," American political discourse misses the importance of cultural and communal forces to both an individual's identity and to his or her prospects in life (Glendon 1991, 143).

The problems liberalism has in taking proper account of forces at work in civil society lie behind its current communitarian and politics-of-difference critiques. Communitarians argue that liberal theories of justice are too individualistic, rights-based, and procedural. They rely on an "unencumbered" or "atomistic" self, a view of the person as an independent bundle of rights existing prior to his or her social attachments or particular conceptions of the good. Communitarians claim that a liberalism of this sort overlooks the extent to which human beings are constituted by their places in particular communities and cultural traditions and by the views of the good that flow from these attachments.[7] A related but distinct line of criticism comes from those who think contemporary liberalism has either neglected or is simply unable to take proper account of social differences. The uniform rights, difference-neutral procedures, and public-private dichotomy instituted by liberalism all obscure and thereby contribute to deeply-rooted social practices and cultural meanings that oppress certain groups based on differences like race, gender, ethnicity, sexual preference, age, or disability.[8] Liberalism's critics claim that those things it tends to overlook in civil society—things like culture, informal social practices, community, and group membership and identity—all turn out to be very important to the way individuals live their lives. My contention is that, in its understanding of race, color-blind liberalism overlooks the same sorts of things.

Eliminating racial discrimination is perhaps the chief concern of the color-blind paradigm. But while the formal rights and procedural guarantees of equal protection that it relies upon so heavily are powerful tools for attacking discrimination written into law, as was the case under segregation, such tools have far more difficulty reaching the kinds of informal discrimination practiced in civil society, discrimination that is still pervasive. For example, studies show that black and white applicants matched on all other traits (education, experience, references, and so on) are treated very differently in employment markets. White applicants are about three times as likely to advance further in the interview process and receive a job offer. Not only are black applicants less likely to receive a job offer, but they also get less favorable treatment along the way. They experience longer waits and shorter interviews, receive less information about the opening, and are asked tougher questions about the accuracy of their credentials (Turner, Fix, and Struyk 1991; Fix and Struyk 1992, chap. 1). Similar studies of housing markets show a discrimination rate of between 50% and 60% in both renting and buying. Black housing applicants are steered toward different neighborhoods, shown fewer units, quoted higher prices, and provided with fewer financing options. When looking for apartments to rent, they are often simply told that no units are available when in fact there are (Smith 1995, 64–65; Fix and Struyk 1992, chap. 1). African Americans trying to get a home or business loan also face considerable discrimination. Black applicants with the same qualifications as white ones are far less likely to get a loan, and when they do, it is more often for less money and at a higher rate of interest. Poor white applicants actually have a better chance of getting a home or business loan than middle- to upper-income black applicants. Part of this is due to the outright redlining of black neighborhoods by financial institutions, but the evidence also shows that even black applicants in predominately white neighborhoods face such sharp discriminatory treatment (Oliver and Shapiro 1995; Smith 1995, 65–66; Bates 1993, chap. 5). Finally, more than forty years after *Brown* struck down de jure segregation, the country's schools remain largely segregated in practice, and even integrated schools show high levels of discriminatory treatment. In such schools black students are more likely to be selected for special education programs, including those for the mentally retarded; they are more often placed in lower ability groupings and in vocational rather than college curriculum tracks; and they are more often disciplined and with harsher penalties (Meier, Stewart, and England 1989a and 1989b; Schofield 1986). African Americans, in short, still face routine and pervasive discriminatory treatment throughout civil society in spite of holding explicit rights against such treatment (Feagin and Sikes 1994; Feagin 1991).

The left urges stricter enforcement of nondiscrimination rights and procedural protections in response to this evidence of continuing discrimination in American life, and undoubtedly stricter enforcement would have some positive effect. Formal rights and procedures, however, can only go so far when it comes to the informal sources of discrimination embedded in routine social practices throughout civil society. Subtle forms of discrimination with a smile, which are supported by race-neutral justifications that appear entirely reasonable on the surface, are exceedingly difficult for formal laws to identify and prosecute. Stricter enforcement would help, but it would only scratch the surface, because discrimination in civil society is much more informal, widespread, diffused, and elusive. It takes place in the countless number of routine social encounters that occur throughout the country each and every day, and to which the state is simply unable to be a party. As such, it is remarkably resistant to attack by state-guaranteed nondiscrimination rights. Rights to an equal opportunity in employment, housing, credit lending, and education have opened doors once firmly shut in these areas to black Americans, but they often have little impact on what happens to people once they actually walk through these doors in countless specific instances across the country every day.

For example, the law prohibits employers from screening out applicants by race, but they still have enormous discretion over how they conduct interviews, who they call back for second interviews, and to whom they ultimately offer the job. In a large pool of applicants, they can cite a host of factors other than race to justify any decisions they make. Indeed, many employers, particularly in the vast small business sector dominated by white Americans, draw their workers from informal social networks of family and friends, networks that rarely include African Americans (Bates 1993, 9–10). Even programs that mandate the hiring of more black applicants in larger enterprises are often defeated by informal social practices on the job. In their study of the New York construction industry, for instance, Roger Waldinger and Thomas Bailey find that formal guarantees of equal employment opportunity and programs requiring more African American hiring are easily frustrated by the industry's informal networks of recruiting and on-the-job training. Black applicants may get hired, but they are often frozen out of the web of social relations that determine success or failure on the job (Waldinger and Bailey 1991). Similarly, real estate agents must show houses to all applicants, but they have tremendous flexibility over the neighborhoods they focus on, the units they show, and the prices and financing options they discuss. Credit lenders also have similar kinds of discretion in making decisions about who they lend money to and the terms of the loans. Finally, while schools must accept children of all races and state mandated busing can even guarantee an integrated school, individual teachers and administrators have a great deal of discretion over how they treat different students in the school when it comes to practices such as ability grouping and discipline. Formal rights and procedural guarantees, then, have only limited effectiveness in fighting discrimination given the scope of informal discretion that individuals in all these areas of civil society necessarily wield. These rights and procedural guarantees can eliminate discrimination at the state level and even reduce some of the most blatant forms of discrimination in civil society itself. But they are simply unable to eliminate those deeper, informal, and far more subtle kinds of discrimination that still exist.[9]

Color-blind liberalism's problems with discrimination, however, go even deeper, because it tries to isolate and eliminate an informal social practice built into the very structure of American life itself. It relies on an overly simplistic view of discrimination as consciously choosing to favor an individual of one race over one of another race out of mere prejudice. But discrimination also lies much deeper; it is a routine, unconscious, and inescapable practice that structures our everyday social relations. In its most basic sense, discrimination is recognizing and attaching meaning to difference. Someone with a discriminating taste in wine, for example, is an expert at detecting differences in wine and making qualitative judgements based on those differences. It turns out Americans are very discriminating when it comes to race. We note race as a matter of course. When a television anchor tells us that the police are seeking a black male or a white female, we know what they mean. When a coworker mentions the "black woman" in accounting or the "white guy" in the mailroom, we know who they are talking about. These kinds of distinctions make sense to us. Each time we come into contact with another person we discriminate, because we notice that person's race, just as we notice that person's gender. This is why those people we have difficulty placing into a racial category grab our attention, in the same way those who's gender we can't establish grab our attention. In such instances our routine and unconscious discrimination hits a snag. This isn't to say that simply noticing a person's race is paramount to refusing to let your daughter date him because of it. Rather, it's just to say that continually taking note of racial categories insures that race will continue to matter in the way we interact with people, even while color-blind liberalism tells us it shouldn't. The color-blind paradigm's overly simplistic view of discrimination obscures the fact that the very existence of race in American society depends upon our regularly discriminating between black and white. Indeed, without such discrimination the concept of race would be meaningless in American life.

But of course race is far from meaningless. Racial distinctions are built into the underlying structure of American social relations because race is one of the primary categories Americans use to determine how they associate with one other. It is one of those preexisting categories that individuals use as cognitive shortcuts to tell them about the people with whom they come into contact. A racialized social structure in the United States carries built-in cultural notions of who members of racial groups are and how they should behave (Omi and Winant 1994, 59–60). All this depends upon pervasive meanings attached to black and white bodies, meanings that turn out to continually and systematically devalue African Americans. As Iris Young writes, "The experience of racial oppression entails in part existing as a group defined as having ugly bodies, and being feared, avoided, or hated on that account" (1990, 123). The standards of physical beauty expressed in American

culture—those tied to skin, hair, lips, noses, and hips—powerfully com-
municate white superiority, and they have had profoundly destructive
effects on the self-images of generations of African Americans (Russell,
Wilson, and Hall 1993; West 1993, chap. 7). Similarly, cultural meanings in the United States also devalue black intelligence, character, and
ability, and studies show that these meanings still powerfully influence
attitudes toward African Americans. Views of African Americans as
lazy, prone to violence, and less intelligent are still widespread among
white Americans and are even shared by a significant portion of black
citizens themselves (Smith 1995, chap. 3). African Americans still bear
the mark of slavery and all the images of moral and mental inferiority
attached to it. In this way, racism goes well beyond the prejudice of a
few misguided individuals in need of moral suasion. Instead, it is bound
up with American culture and the web of meanings, norms, and assumptions it communicates to its members, both white and black.

Color-blind liberalism, however, pays little if any attention to culture and the way its meanings structure American social relations. It is
something too slippery for individual rights and fair procedures to grasp.
Color-blind liberalism tells us to judge people as individuals rather than
as members of ascriptive groups, but its categories have little to say
about the underlying cultural meanings that shape our reactions to and
judgements of various individuals in social life. This is a significant oversight, since culture is an essential ingredient in the institutions of civil
society, one that has a profound impact on the way people live their
lives. To quote Young again: "Culture is ubiquitous, but nevertheless
deserves distinct consideration in discussions of social justice. The symbolic meanings that people attach to other kinds of people and to
actions, gestures, or institutions often significantly affect the social
standing of persons and their opportunities" (1990, 23). The cultural
meanings attached to race matter very much in the shape and operation
of American civil society, and they matter in ways that the color-blind
paradigm leaves largely unexamined.

Color-blind liberalism, especially in its left interpretation, does try
to go beyond the level of the state and address issues of race in civil society. Its attempts to do so, however, focus almost exclusively on questions of economic distribution and equality of opportunity. This focus
retains the paradigm's strong individualism and proceduralism, since it
essentially asks what procedures we should follow when trying to allocate economic resources and social positions to discrete individuals as
fairly as possible—that is, so that race matters as little as possible in the
ultimate distribution of such resources and positions. Hence the left's
emphasis on programs to attack poverty and unemployment and its support for affirmative action. This focus on questions of distribution, how-

ever, overlooks factors that are neither material nor divisible and therefore not subject to allocation among discrete individuals. Young is particularly helpful here in pointing out the shortcomings of such an approach. On her account, a distributive paradigm of justice looks at discrete goods and positions held by specific individuals rather than at nonmaterial sources of power embedded in culturally defined social relations; it restricts political debate to issues of distribution, obscuring underlying institutional structures and contexts (Young 1990, chaps. 1 and 3). This is why affirmative action, which revolves around questions of how positions are awarded to specific individuals, leaves an institution's background patterns of decision-making as well as its cultural norms and informal social practices largely unexamined (Young 1990, chap. 7). Power, in Young's view, is not just a discrete commodity to be distributed to individual agents; rather, it is a relational concept that exists in interactions between persons and between groups (1990, 31–32). Taking schools as an example of a specific social institution, she writes:

> Providing educational opportunity certainly entails allocating specific material resources—money, buildings, books, computers, and so on—and there are reasons to think that the more resources, the wider the opportunities offered to children in an educational system. But education is primarily a process taking place in a complex context of social relations. In the cultural context of the United States, male children and female children, working class children and middle-class children, Black children and white children often do not have equally enabling educational opportunities even when an equivalent amount of resources has been devoted to their education. (Young 1990, 26)

This is the case because there is more at stake within the institutions of civil society than the allocation of resources and positions, especially when it comes to race. As Cornel West points out, those on the liberal-left who focus exclusively on political and economic factors fail to grasp questions of culture, meaning, and identity that underpin the dynamics of race in the United States (1993, 20).

Color-blind liberalism's distributive focus on divisible factors such as economic resources and social positions ignores the fact that white skin has a cultural currency in American life that is indivisible and cannot be distributed equally. Noel Ignatiev writes that "the white race consists of those who partake of the privileges of white skin in this society. Its most wretched members share a status higher, in certain respects, than that of the most exalted persons excluded from it" (1995, 1). Andrew Hacker is even more explicit: "All white Americans realize that their skin comprises an inestimable asset. It opens doors and facilitates freedom of movement. It serves as a shield from insult and harassment.

Indeed, having been born white can be taken as a sign: your preferment is both ordained and deserved. Its value persists not because a white appearance automatically brings success and status, since there are no such guarantees. What it does ensure is that you will not be regarded as *black*" (1992, 60, italics in original). As the reflections of African Americans like Lawrence Graham (1995) who have seemingly "made it" in the white world illustrate, black Americans can reach the highest levels of educational, occupational, and financial achievement and still not overcome the routine disrespect, humiliation, discrimination, and questioning of social status and worth that black Americans continually face in the United States. Graham, for example, writes: "No other group is perceived as servants more than blacks. If we are spotted in a store, hotel, restaurant, or at a wedding by a distracted white person, our black skin—regardless of our attire or demeanor—suggests that we are there to serve them" (1995, 90–91). The institutions of American civil society exist within a cultural context of meanings, norms, and informal social practices that confer power on white members as a matter of course, and an exclusive focus on distributing discrete resources and positions within such institutions to particular individuals ignores these deeper sources of power.

These kinds of problems with color-blind liberalism's approach to the institutions of civil society become more evident when we consider the principle of equality of opportunity. Equality of opportunity claims that social positions should be distributed fairly. They should be open to all, and individuals should not find themselves disproportionately excluded by race, even if we have to institute affirmative action programs to make sure they are not. But, as John Schaar (1967) points out, equality of opportunity in no way addresses the underlying structure of a social institution such as a corporation or university; it merely offers individuals an equal chance to occupy certain places within it. It does not provide each person an equal opportunity to develop his or her abilities to the fullest, because society values some kinds of abilities more than others. Equality of opportunity offers each individual a chance to succeed only to the extent that he or she possesses those traits the particular institution in question values most highly. This obscures inequalities of power embedded in the "social-cultural structure" of an institution by creating the impression that merit alone determines success or failure (Schaar 1967, 239). So the norms, standards, styles, and practices of white-dominated institutions remain intact, even while equality of opportunity promises to award offices fairly and to treat members of such institutions the same regardless of race.

This is why many black Americans working in predominately white institutions experience feelings of isolation, overwork, vulnerability, and powerlessness; and why a white institution can establish an affirmative action program to bring in more African Americans without threatening the underlying patterns of white hegemony that still structure the way the institution actually operates (Bell 1987, chap. 6; Graham 1995, 249–252). It is also why we can open predominately white schools to black students and treat each student the same without regard to race, and still see the school's underlying practices and norms—things like its curriculum; its standards of appropriate behavior, speech, or dress; its expectations about the way students should respond in the classroom; and its styles of teaching—remain that of a predominately middle-class, white school, one in which white students are at home and black students are still outsiders.[10] Equality of opportunity integrates some African Americans into white institutions, but it does little to change the informal sources of power, rooted in an institution's culturally structured norms and practices, that still privilege white members. It may shuffle social positions, but it does not address underlying social relations.

Equality of opportunity relies on a dedication to neutral and universal standards of merit that simply do not exist. Instead, a certain group's culturally-defined norms and practices become the standards against which each individual is judged equally without regard to race. As Young writes:

> Where group differences in capacities, values, and behavioral or cognitive styles exist, equal treatment in the allocation of reward according to rules of merit competition will reinforce and perpetuate disadvantage. Equal treatment requires everyone to be measured according to the same norms, but in fact there are no "neutral" norms of behavior and performance. Where some groups are privileged and others oppressed, the formulation of law, policy, and the rules of private institutions tend to be biased in favor of the privileged groups, because their particular experience implicitly sets the norm. (1989, 269)

In this way, a liberal dedication to individualism, neutrality, and universal standards of justice can obscure the underlying use of standards that actually embody the norms and interests of a particular dominant group—those of white Americans in our case.

This elevation of norms and practices that embody the experiences of white Americans to the position of neutral and universal standards used to judge everyone does more than simply put African Americans at a great disadvantage in the mainstream institutions of civil society. It also poses a threat to black identity and cultural integrity itself. It makes acting "white" the price of integration, and it makes white Americans the judges of when and where black Americans have met this standard

(Hacker 1992, 22–23; Graham 1995, chap. 6). African Americans are expected to behave, dress, walk, and especially speak in ways that the white institution does not consider overly "black." They are discouraged from wearing their blackness on their sleeve; it is divisive, distracting, and means you have a chip on your shoulder and are difficult to work with. If African Americans want to cultivate their own cultural group identity, norms, and practices, then they are expected to do so in private, rather than in the public institutions of civil society. So while the identity and cultural integrity of white Americans is recognized and expressed in the institutions of civil society as a matter of course, that of black Americans is marginalized and suppressed.

In its fight against certain kinds of racism, then, color-blind liberalism leaves other kinds intact. By claiming we should judge people according to their merits as individuals rather than their race, it has done much to defeat forms of racism that rely on explicit appeals to the essential superiority of all whites to all blacks. But the color-blind paradigm does not account for how the culturally defined norms and practices of the dominant white majority can become the standards by which we judge individuals across the spectrum. So while the color-blind paradigm is able to overcome older forms of overt, conscious racism, it is still compatible with the kinds of racism that dwell "in everyday habits and cultural meanings of which people are for the most part unaware" (Young 1990, 124). While our social reality is actually structured by practices and meanings that still devalue and disadvantage African Americans, the color-blind paradigm makes it possible for us to rest assured that the shortcomings we see in our fellow citizens who "just happen to be black" are due either to individual failings (the right) or to a poor socioeconomic background (the left) rather than to a morally arbitrary trait like the color of their skin. This enables a large number of white Americans to be what Samuel Gaertner and John Dovidio call "aversive racists," people who consider themselves supportive of racial equality and opposed to any sort of bigotry, yet who still harbor deep negative reactions toward black Americans that they need to explain away in order to protect their egalitarian self-images. In order to do so, they claim that race plays no role in their negative evaluations of particular black Americans, pointing instead to individual or environmental deficiencies (Gaertner and Dovidio 1986). As Patricia Williams points out, proponents of this view always have examples of individual blacks who have made something of themselves on hand to support their position (1991, 13). Under this kind of reasoning, my admiration for Colin Powell proves two things: first, I am not a racist, and second, more blacks can make something of themselves as well, if only they apply themselves (the right) or are given a fair and equal opportunity to compete on a level playing field (the left). What this view ignores, of course, are the underlying standards and norms that shape the way we perceive and judge individuals, as well as the culturally structured sources of power that provide the context for our actual social relations.

Much of color-blind liberalism's failure to develop an adequate understanding of race when it comes to civil society flows from its individualism. In its individualistic focus on rights, procedures, economic distribution, and equality of opportunity, it overlooks the importance of cultural groups in civil society. Cultural groups mediate how persons, both black and white, experience the broad cultural context upon which the existence and operation of race in the United States hinges. As we have just seen, membership in particular cultural groups, namely those comprising white and black Americans, plays a critical role in influencing how individuals stand within a host of practices, relations, and meanings at work in American life. It positions them within the particular institutions and social networks that shape the options they face in life. Cultural group membership, in short, locates people within the institutions, practices, and meanings of American civil society where their lives unfold. Beyond influencing their external standing, however, this kind of membership is often central to their internal identity as well. Developed, maintained, and expressed in the institutions of civil society—institutions such as churches, voluntary associations, schools, museums, the media, and so on—membership in cultural groups provides many people with a sense of purpose, history, security, and self-worth; it gives them an understanding of who they are and of what they can become; and it ties them to others within a set of common practices and experiences. It not only shapes the kind of options they face, but how they understand these options as well.

As Cornell West argues, group membership and identity, as well as the institutions that foster it, are of particular importance to African Americans as a traditionally marginalized and subordinated people. Historically, the institutions of black civil society have provided a material, spiritual, and psychological line of defense against white discrimination, brutality, and cultural devaluation (West 1993, 22–24). Color-blind liberalism, however, has little room for such things. It takes each person as a citizen with a uniform set of basic rights and procedural guarantees rather than as a member of some cultural group. This is a problem for African Americans concerned with developing and protecting their own cultural identity in a society where it is often under assault. Stuart Alan Clarke identifies "a dilemma that exists in the gap between the formal guarantees made to individuals by a liberal democratic society and the social and ideological conditions that allow particular groups to sustain, concretize, and transmit group values." Clarke claims that this "dilemma has particular salience when issues of personal identity are understood to be inextricably tied to the life and values of the group, that is, when one is a black American" (1989, 12). While cultural group membership and identity, maintained and expressed in civil society, are particularly significant aspects of race in the United States, they are aspects color-blind liberalism largely ignores, except to say that they should not matter. This is an oversight that will become increasingly important in my argument over the next several chapters.

I am not suggesting that color-blind liberalism's strengths be ignored. But we must also pay close attention to its limits. It is an understanding of race that overlooks the influence of culture and membership in cultural groups within the web of institutions, practices, and meanings that constitute American civil society. While the left's efforts to extend color-blind liberalism into civil society by focusing on issues of economic distribution and equality of opportunity are certainly superior to the right's interpretation that defends the status quo, they are nonetheless inadequate. Color-blind liberalism, in short, has taken us as far as it can; if we are to develop a more comprehensive and compelling understanding of race in the United States, then we must move beyond its limits. I do not think, however, that this project requires us to set aside liberalism altogether, or even the color-blind paradigm itself. Liberalism has the capacity to overcome its problems with race. It has the resources to develop an alternative understanding of race that retains the color-blind paradigm's strengths while overcoming its weaknesses, and in order to see how liberalism can do this, I must return to the concept of freedom in liberal political thought.

# CHAPTER 4

# *Liberal Autonomy*

A strong commitment to individual freedom is at the heart of liberalism. There is, however, considerable debate over what exactly freedom is, what it requires in practice, and why it is valuable. In this chapter, I endorse the view that in order to answer these kinds of questions and reach an understanding of liberalism's dedication to freedom, we must look at the ideal of the autonomous person that constitutes its moral foundation. Liberalism's commitment to freedom flows from its deeper commitment to autonomy as a critical ingredient in human well-being. I argue that liberalism should explicitly embrace a notion of freedom as autonomy, one that includes elements of both negative and positive liberty, and that is aware of both the external and internal conditions that living an autonomous life requires. Drawing on the work of John Stuart Mill, Joseph Raz, and Charles Taylor, I explore the nature and requirements of autonomy and then show how autonomy provides the basis for a liberal approach to multiculturalism, one that focuses on the very things that color-blind liberalism overlooks.

## FREEDOM AND AUTONOMY

In chapter 2, I described how color-blind liberalism relies on what Charles Taylor calls an opportunity-concept of freedom. This is an understanding of freedom as the absence of external obstacles that block an individual's opportunities to act freely. It is the notion of freedom as noninterference usually associated with theories of negative liberty. In his essay entitled "What's Wrong with Negative Liberty," Taylor argues that this kind of opportunity-concept is, by itself, an impoverished account of freedom, one that is "incapable of defending liberalism in the form we in fact value it" (1985b, 215). On Taylor's account, the idea of freedom celebrated by liberalism also includes an "exercise-concept," one which recognizes that freedom includes elements of internal self-realization and self-direction. This view claims that we need more than external opportunities to be truly free; we also need the internal capacities necessary to take advantage of such opportunities. Without a certain level of self-awareness, self-control, and the ability to make moral judgements, we are not able to exercise our freedom in any real way. According to Taylor, the meaningful exercise of freedom requires that we reflect upon and discriminate among our own motivations, since this is the only way we are able to achieve any level of authentic self-direction in life (1985b, 215–217). We cannot make choices about the kind of life we most want to lead and the kind of person we most want to be without this kind of internal reflection and judgement.

In making this kind of argument, Taylor draws on notions of self-realization and self-direction usually associated with positive liberty. He does not, however, fully embrace the theory as Berlin describes it. According to Taylor, the path from negative to positive liberty has two steps: "The first moves us from a notion of freedom as doing what one wants to a notion which discriminates motivations and equates freedom with doing what we really want, or obeying our real will, or truly directing our lives. The second step introduces some doctrine purporting to show that we cannot do what we really want, or follow our real will, outside of a society of a certain canonical form, incorporating true self-government" (1985b, 217). Taylor clearly endorses the first step, but he does not take the second step, the one in which Berlin sees lurking such illiberal and totalitarian dangers. Taylor's essay does not provide a systematic or complete theory of freedom. Rather, it points out the limits of a simple opportunity-concept, showing that an examination of liberalism's dedication to freedom must account not only for external constraints but also for the kinds of internal capacities necessary for the meaningful exercise of freedom. Taylor shows how liberalism is able to add some elements of positive liberty to its commitment to negative liberty without also endorsing the decidedly illiberal notion that people must be lead, by force if necessary, to embrace some version of their true selves promulgated by a centralized authority. In short, Taylor shows how an exercise-concept of freedom is able to tie the liberal celebration of negative liberty to the concept of individual autonomy.

The word autonomy means self-rule. It describes persons who are authors of their own lives, who develop and pursue projects that are authentically their own. Autonomy hinges on a distinction philosophers make between first-order and second-order desires (Frankfurt 1988, 11–25; Dworkin 1988, 15). Our first-order desires are what we want at a particular time, and negative freedom generally refers to our ability to act on these without external restraints. Second-order desires, however, are desires about first-order desires themselves. They are how we control our own desires by preferring that they be of a particular kind, and this is how we exercise autonomy. By desiring to desire or not to desire something, we exercise control over our own motivations and preferences. Gerald Dworkin writes: "It is characteristic of persons that they are able to reflect on their decisions, motives, desires, and habits. In doing so they can form preferences concerning these. Thus a person may not simply desire to smoke but also desire that he not have that desire. He may not only be motivated by jealousy or anger. He can also desire that his motivations be different (or the same)" (1989, 59). Autonomy, then, refers to the ability of human beings to reflect on and evaluate their desires and motivations, allowing them to discard some and embrace others according to judgments about their worth. In this way, autonomy rests on the ability of persons to control and shape their own desires rather than becoming slaves to them. It is how they exercise internal self-control and self-direction.

Autonomy also means that the standards one uses to reflect on and make judgments about one's desires and motivations must be genuinely one's own. If a person blindly relies on another's standards, then he or she is not truly self-directing and not acting autonomously. In the words of Joel Feinberg: "To the degree to which a person is autonomous he is not merely the mouthpiece of other persons or forces. Rather his tastes, opinions, ideals, goals, values and preferences are all authentically his" (1989, 32). Autonomy is tied to the identification a person has with his or her own goals and values. As Gerald Dworkin writes, "It is only when a person identifies with the influences that motivate him, assimilates them to himself, views himself as the kind of person who wishes to be moved in particular ways, that these influences are to be identified as 'his'" (1989, 60). Autonomy means that our projects and standards are not simply ours, but that they are our own in the sense that they are derived independently without manipulation, deception, or coercion. In short, people are autonomous when they live their lives from the inside according to their own plans of life, plans continually constructed from a set of values, goals, and standards that are authentically their own.

As this account of autonomy shows, it is a concept closely related to freedom but one that generally focuses on very different sorts of issues. The liberal concern with freedom usually centers on removing external barriers to choice, while theories of autonomy usually center on the inner cognitive processes agents use when making choices. Conceived in these ways, however, both concepts by themselves are inadequate for liberalism. An opportunity-concept of freedom is too narrow to provide a complete account of what it means to be free. It ignores how individuals make internal choices about the kinds of lives they want to lead, and how the inner capacity for self-direction is what makes freedom valuable in the first place. Most theories of autonomy, however, are too cognitive to provide a complete account of what it means to live an autonomous life. They ignore the web of external circumstances that shape how people direct their own lives and the extent to which they are ultimately able to do so. They also tend to overlook the external sources people rely upon to provide the moral standards they use to exercise autonomy by reflecting on and making decisions about their own desires and motivations.

In my view, liberalism is at its strongest when it fuses the two concepts together into a broader theory of freedom as autonomy. This requires seeing them both as part of the same liberal commitment to the value of people living autonomous lives. It requires liberalism to incorporate its negative understanding of freedom into an expanded view of autonomy. This view of autonomy understands it to refer to both the external circumstances as well as the internal capacities necessary for people to direct the course of their own lives. Such an understanding of autonomy provides a solid moral grounding for liberalism by putting a commitment to the ideal of the autonomous person at its core, an ideal that sees autonomy and both its internal and external requirements as a constituent part of individual well-being, as a necessary ingredient in genuine human flourishing.

## THE NATURE OF AUTONOMY

I should be clear from the start that negative liberty is still essential in a liberal commitment to autonomy. In order for people to live autonomous lives, to rule themselves from the inside, they still must be free of arbitrary and coercive interference from the state and from their fellow citizens. To be autonomous, individuals must not be arbitrarily subject to the will of others. This is why liberalism's traditional dedication to individual rights, limited government, and the rule of law is critical to the ideal of autonomy.[1] These kinds of considerations mark off a space in which individuals have the opportunity to construct lives for themselves, providing a political context in which the exercise of autonomy becomes possible.

Autonomy, however, requires much more. Even John Locke, one of negative liberty's greatest champions, recognizes that the meaningful exercise of freedom requires more than simply the absence of external interference. In *An Essay Concerning Human Understanding*, Locke claims that the human mind has the power to initiate or stop human action and that an agent only acts freely when thought is present (1975, 237–240). He writes that "so far as this Power reaches, of acting, or not acting, by the determination of his own Thought preferring either, so far is a Man free" (1975, 244). The human mind is able to "suspend the execution of and satisfaction of any of its desires," and "before the will be determined to action," the agent can "examine, view, and judge" the good or evil of an action. "This," writes Locke, "seems to me the source of all liberty" (1975, 263). In this way, Locke recognizes a strong cognitive dimension of freedom alongside his better known defense of negative liberty. He also relies upon the existence of certain moral standards carried within his culture—provided by a classical education for the rich and simple Christian ethics for the rest—to guide the internal judgements people use to control their desires, thus making autonomy possible. Indeed, many early liberals who are strong supporters of negative rights nonetheless recognize that autonomy also requires certain institutions in civil society to provide people with the moral standards and virtues of character they need to exercise meaningful control over their own lives (Terchek 1986). Liberalism, then, has long recognized a notion of autonomy that goes well beyond individual rights to consider issues of internal capacities and the importance of shared cultural meanings provided by common institutions in civil society. Negative liberty is only one of many ingredients that make an autonomous life possible and valuable. In order to take a closer look at what else autonomy means for liberalism, we should consider the work of three political theorists: John Stuart Mill, a liberal icon; Joseph Raz, a communitarian-minded liberal; and Charles Taylor, a liberal-minded communitarian.

*John Stuart Mill*

Mill's *On Liberty* is one of liberalism's best-known defenses of individual freedom. The essay, however, develops a view of the autonomous person that goes well beyond mere negative liberty. The epigraph, taken from Wilhelm von Humbolt, clearly indicates that Mill is concerned not just with protecting individuals from external interference, but also with "the importance of human development in its richest diversity" (1989a, 3). Mill begins the essay by claiming there is much more at stake in the quest for freedom than maintaining "political liberties or rights" and "constitutional checks" (1989a, 6). The first chapter introduces his argument that forces such as custom, public opinion, and social conformity all threaten to impose a new kind of tyranny, one "enslaving the soul itself" (1989a, 8). This kind of tyranny leaves persons formally free but deprives them of the ability or desire to think for themselves. It leads them to turn over control of their lives to others and become like sheep rather than human beings. In this sense, freedom is not just a matter of formal laws and political arrangements; it also hinges on the kind of culture and civil society people find themselves in. This is why the second chapter's defense of liberty of thought and discussion becomes so important. It is Mill's argument for the kind of culture in which people are able, indeed in which they are challenged, to think for themselves rather than blindly following a dogma that is not authentically their own. Without this kind of cultural environment, human development is cramped and stunted. It is only amid intellectual freedom and diversity that humans are able to flourish mentally and adopt their own points of view on things. Mill opposes censorship not only because it violates individual rights, but also because it leads to a cultural environment where people do not think for themselves, to one in which autonomy is not possible.

Mill claims that human beings are like plants rather than machines. Given the proper conditions, they grow and flourish along their own lines rather than conforming to some mechanical blueprint of life. Just as a tree requires not only room to grow and flourish but also the kinds of conditions that make such growth possible, people need an environment conducive to autonomy if they are to develop to their fullest potential (1989a, chap. 3). This is why he argues for the importance of a civil society characterized by "diversity," by "different opinions," by "different experiments in living," by "varieties of character," and by "different modes of life" (1989a, 57). This kind of environment promotes human well-being by promoting individuality, or the ability to grow and flourish as a self-defining person. His is not an argument for an individualism defined as independence or isolation from one's social context, but rather for a social context that encourages the development of individuality, of genuine self-definition. A civil society characterized by diversity of character, opinion, and modes of life is necessary if people are to find genuine happiness and fulfillment in the development of "the mental, moral, and aesthetic stature of which their nature is capable" (1989a, 68).

This is a vision of individual autonomy as a crucial part of human development and well-being. For Mill, a well-developed person is autonomous, living life in his or her own way. He writes, "He who chooses a plan for himself, employs all his faculties" (1989a, 59). Mill grounds this account of autonomy in his concept of character: "A person whose desires and impulses are his own—are the expression of his own nature, as it has been developed and modified by his own culture—is said to have a character. One whose desires and impulses are not his own, has no character, no more than a steam-engine has a character" (1989a, 60–61). The danger Mill warns against in On Liberty is the kind of civil society that crushes this kind of character development, a cultural environment in which "the mind itself is bowed to the yoke" (1989a, 61). His is a warning against a society with plenty of negative liberty but no autonomy.

The moral commitment to the autonomous individual that is central to On Liberty is further supported in Mill's other writings. A System of

*Logic*, for example, includes a chapter on "Ethology," or the science of character. Here Mill argues that people's mental states, types of character, feelings, habits, and ultimately their actions are all shaped by the cultural and social circumstances of their lives. He claims that taking a group of people and changing their circumstances by altering the institutions in which they live out their lives, will ultimately change the kind of people they are (1896, 566). Mill expresses confidence that a science of ethology will some day be able to predict, at least in a rough way, a person's character, the kind of person he or she is, by examining the cultural and social context in which he or she lives. The important thing to notice here is Mill's belief that an individual's character is tied to his or her cultural and social environment, and since character is a crucial factor in the extent to which an individual leads an autonomous life, this is a claim that ties one's prospects for autonomy to such an environment. This means that Mill's concern for people living their own lives from the inside, for their being autonomous, leads him to focus on the kinds of cultural conditions and social institutions they require to do so.

In his "Inaugural Address Delivered to the University of St. Andrews," Mill tells his audience that the purpose of an education is not simply to pass along skills to be used in life but also, and more importantly, to help create the kind of culture in which persons can flourish. More important than dispensing facts, as useful as they might be, is the broad training of the intellect that gives people the ability to think for themselves (1984a, 234). This is why "the dogmatic inculcation from authority, of what the teacher deems true," especially in religious and moral instruction, is not the proper role of education. Rather education should develop and elevate a general culture in which people are able to form their own points of view on things as thoughtful beings (1984a, 248–250). Mill is arguing that individual autonomy rests, at least in part, on the cultural context provided by one's education.

It is in *The Subjection of Women*, however, that Mill makes what is perhaps his most powerful case for the relationship between autonomy and one's cultural and social circumstances. Mill opens the essay by decrying the "legal subordination" of women, but within just a few pages it becomes obvious that he also has in mind the deeper "social subordination of women" (1989b, 137). He argues for the formal equality of men and women, but at the same time he develops a powerful indictment of the ways in which informal but pervasive practices and norms cripple the autonomy of women in his society. Mill argues that women are socialized in such a way as to "enslave their minds," that they are educated to accept subservient social roles and submissive characters. This denies women the opportunity to develop their own faculties and formulate their own plans of life (1989b, 132–136). Because of the "extraordinary susceptibility of human nature to external influences," women's development becomes cramped and stunted in such a repressive environment. Mill writes: "What is now called the nature of women is an eminently artificial thing—the result of forced repression in some directions, unnatural stimulation in others. It may be asserted without scruple, that no other class of dependents have had their character so entirely distorted from its natural proportions by their relation with their masters" (1989b, 138). Drawing again on the metaphor of plants, Mill argues that in this kind of soil the character of women is forced to grow in particular and narrow ways rather than being able to flourish freely (1989b, 139). In this way, external circumstances not only shape the kinds of opportunities women face, but the development of their internal character as well. Mill argues that in order for women to achieve autonomy—in order for them to have the opportunity to develop their own faculties and talents, to plan and pursue their own projects, to flourish as human beings should—then the social and cultural environment in which they find themselves must change (1989b, 212–215).

Finally, in a brief essay called "The Negro Question," Mill makes a similar argument in response to Carlyle's claim that those with black skin are born to be ruled by Europeans who are clearly more intelligent. Mill responds to Carlyle, who had pointed to the behavior of former slaves in Britain's colonies to support his argument for their natural inferiority, by claiming that any attention to human affairs shows that laws governing the formation of character disprove Carlyle's "vulgar error of imputing every difference which he finds among human beings to an original difference of nature" (1984b, 93). Like trees, people develop along different paths according to the environment around them, only to an even greater degree than trees. Mill writes, "Human beings are subject to an infinitely greater variety of accidents and external influences than trees, and have infinitely more operation in impairing the growth of one another; since those who begin by being strongest have almost always hitherto used their strength to keep others weak" (1984b, 93). It is no wonder, on Mill's account, that former slaves have trouble adjusting in the wake of their being formally liberated, because their character has been forged in a centuries-long process of oppression and subordination. Where Africans have had the opportunity to develop under different cultural and social circumstances, ones that are actually supportive of human flourishing, they have achieved a way of life to rival that of any European people, as the case of ancient Egypt shows (1984b, 93).

Mill clearly links the capacity of persons to live autonomous lives to their well-being. Flourishing individuals develop their particular faculties and talents to their fullest potential, think for themselves, adopt their own points of view on things, and pursue their own authentic plans of life. Mill realizes, however, that this requires much more than rights against outside interference. It also requires that individuals develop the kind of internal character they need to construct their own lives, and this internal development is tied to their external environment. The kinds of internal standards and values that allow a person to exercise autonomy only flourish in a culture that encourages freedom of thought and expression and nonconformity, and in a civil society characterized by diverse ways of life and many avenues of achievement in which people, both men and women, are able to develop their own talents and tastes to the fullest. Drawing on the metaphor of growth, Mill argues that in order for an autonomous life to take root and flourish, it requires the appropriate kind of cultural and social soil. Where this soil is absent, autonomy is threatened, and Mill points to the examples of women and former slaves as evidence. More generally, Mill warns the readers of his day that their England is looking less and less like the kind of cultural and social environment that supports autonomy. He points to the forces of conformity, self-censorship, consumerism, and narrow self-interest as grave threats to individual autonomy, even while the people of England remain as formally free as ever. On Mill's account, then, the cultural and social circumstances surrounding individuals can either encourage or discourage the development of their capacity for autonomy, and so liberals should pay close attention to and work for the kind that develops and sustains rather than threatens autonomy.

## Joseph Raz

In recent years, the theorist making the strongest argument for the importance of autonomy to liberalism is Joseph Raz. According to Raz, the liberal concern for freedom is based on its deeper commitment to the ideal of personal autonomy. He writes, "Freedom is valuable because it is, and to the extent that it is, a concomitant of the ideal of autonomous persons creating their own lives" (1986, 265). According to Raz, the liberal commitment to individual freedom "is moored in a wider conception of the good person and the good society" provided by the ideal of autonomy (1992, 187). Developed in his *The Morality of Freedom* and other writings, Raz's is a reading of liberalism that sees autonomy and the conditions that make it possible as a necessary ingredient in human well-being, and thus as the basis for liberal morality.

Raz ties a person's well-being to his or her goals in life, which he defines as those things a person cares about—things like relationships, careers, activities, projects, aims, and so on. These are things that people care about because they believe them to be valuable or worthy, and that they willingly embrace and make their own because of this belief. Raz claims that a person's well-being hinges on the successful realization of these kinds of goals (1986, chap. 12). Goals and their successful pursuit, however, are only possible within a context of shared institutions, practices, and meanings. He writes, "A person's well-being depends to a large extent on success in socially defined and determined pursuits and activities" (1986, 309). For example, if one's goal is to engage in a successful, loving married life, it is only possible to do so within the social institution of marriage and all that it involves. The same is true of career goals: "One cannot pursue a legal career except in a society governed by law, one cannot practice medicine except in a society in which such a practice is recognized" (1986, 310). Pursuing the example of a medical career, Raz writes, "A doctor participates in a complex social form, involving general recognition of a medical practice, its social organization, its status in society, its conventions about which matters are addressed to doctors and which not . . . , and its conventions about the suitable relations between doctors and their patients" (1986, 310–311). For Raz, our well-being as persons hinges on our goals, which are only possible within a web of certain institutions and practices in civil society that are made meaningful by the shared conventions provided by a common culture.

According to Raz, personal autonomy is an "essential ingredient" in this view of human well-being, since it is a view that finds its realization in the ideal of individuals living autonomous lives. Raz defines autonomy this way: "The ruling idea behind the ideal of personal autonomy is that people should make their own lives" (1986, 369). This is not a claim that in order to be autonomous, persons have to carefully design and then follow a detailed blueprint of life, but rather that autonomous persons are who they are because of the choices they make throughout their lives (1992, 185–186). This kind of person's well-being hinges on the successful pursuit of his or her "self-chosen goals and relationships" (1986, 370). This is why autonomy is so valuable and why it forms the basis for liberal morality. It is an essential part of human well-being because "the flourishing life is the self-created life" (1992, 186). Indeed, for Raz, "Autonomy is a constituent element of the good life" (1986, 408). This is a version of liberal autonomy that cannot find expression through individual rights alone. They cannot define autonomy, because they only create and protect certain opportunities to be autonomous. What people make of such opportunities "is left undetermined by the sheer existence of the rights" (1986, 204–205). As a crucial element of human well-being, autonomy is tied to "wide-ranging aspects of social practices and institutions," and so it entails much more than simply rights against interference or coercion. Autonomy hinges on collective goods that rights alone cannot account for (1986, 207). Indeed, autonomy is not valuable because it flows from rights; rather, rights themselves are valuable because they play a role in building the kind of environment that supports autonomy. This kind of environment requires rights, but it also requires much more.

In order to construct an autonomous life, a person needs options to choose from. Raz writes that "to be autonomous, a person must not only be given a choice but he must also be given an adequate range of choices" (1986, 373). It is not simply the number of options that matters here, but the variety as well. I may be free to choose which of twelve seminars to enter, but if these are my only options, then I am not autonomous. Autonomy hinges on a social context characterized by what Raz labels "value pluralism," or the view that "many different activities and incompatible forms of life are valuable" (1994, 72). This means that there are a variety of mutually exclusive, yet still valuable, ways of life open to a person in civil society; I can choose the life of the priesthood or that of fatherhood. According to Raz, without an adequate range of varied and morally acceptable options to choose from, people cannot construct autonomous lives for themselves. This means that their autonomy, and hence their well-being, is grounded in the cultural and social circumstances that surround them. He writes: "One is autonomous only if one lives in an environment rich with possibilities. Concern with autonomy is concern with the environment" (1992, 187).

For Raz, the range of options individuals face certainly depends upon the distribution of private goods such as money, but it also hinges on nondistributive collective goods—the shared social institutions, practices, and meanings that structure the kinds of options available in a particular civil society. Occupations, relationships, leisure activities, personal pursuits: all of these things only exist as meaningful options within a particular culture with particular social forms (1986, 247; 1992, 187–188). What all this means is that living an autonomous life is only possible within a certain kind of environment, one that supports autonomy. It is here that he pulls together his argument about the link between autonomy, human well-being, and one's cultural and social context: "The autonomous life depends not on the availability of one option of freedom of choice. It depends on the general character of one's environment and culture. For those who live in an autonomy-supporting environment there is no choice but to be autonomous: there is no other way to prosper in such a society" (1986, 391). For persons living in this kind of environment, "their well-being depends on their ability to find their place in their environment which includes having what is basically an autonomous life" (1986, 391). In this way, autonomy, as a critical ingredient in human well-being, is bound up with the very character of one's culture and civil society. So if liberals are concerned about protecting individual freedom, they must concern themselves with the kind of general cultural and social environment that supports the living of an autonomous life. Raz writes: "An autonomy-sustaining common culture is a presupposition of the freedom of one and all" (1992, 188). For Raz, autonomy is inescapably a culturally and socially embedded good.

Since autonomy is bound up with the cultural context and institutions, practices, and meanings of civil society that surround an individual, much of what makes an autonomous life possible, according to Raz, flows from his or her membership in particular cultural groups. He writes, "Concern for individual freedom requires recognition that an important aspect of that ideal is the freedom of people to belong to distinctive groups, with their own beliefs and practices, and the ability of such groups to prosper" (1990, 3). On his account, one's "individual freedom and prosperity depend on full and unimpeded membership in a respected and flourishing cultural group" (1994, 69). Autonomy hinges on this kind of group membership because it depends upon an adequate range of options, options that in turn depend upon the "shared meanings and common practices" provided by groups to be at all meaningful. Options only exist within complex social interactions, and people rely on their particular cultural groups to make sense of these interactions. He writes: "Only through being socialized in a culture can one tap the options that give life a meaning. By and large, one's cultural membership determines the horizon of one's opportunities, of what one may become, or (if one is older) what one might have been" (1994, 71). Raz argues that the "commonality of interlocking practices making up the range of options open to anyone socialized into them is what cultures are," and so it is little wonder "that membership in cultural groups is of vital importance to individuals" (1994, 71). For Raz, the cultural, as well as material, resources of one's group are of vital importance to one's autonomy and well-being, because they provide a context for one's projects and relationships, one's goals in life, the range of options one faces, and what these options ultimately mean (1994, 71–72).

Raz makes a powerful argument for an autonomy-based liberalism. It is a liberalism that recognizes the value of autonomy as a constituent element of human well-being, as a necessary part of the good life for persons. His is a liberalism that recognizes how autonomy goes well beyond what is provided by negative liberty. For Raz, autonomy also depends upon one's place within the culturally structured web of institutions, practices, and meanings that make up civil society. Individual autonomy is not individualistic in nature. Rather, it is culturally and socially embedded, and one of the most important ways this becomes evident is the extent to which individuals rely on their membership in particular cultural groups to provide the internal and external resources they need to construct autonomous lives for themselves. According to Raz, one's cultural and social circumstances make a critical difference, one way or the other, to one's prospects for an autonomous life. They can either support autonomy or undermine it. This means that liberals who care about individual autonomy must concern themselves with issues of culture, membership in cultural groups, and the character of civil society.

*Charles Taylor*

In his philosophical work on the nature of human agency, Charles Taylor provides one of the richest explorations in recent years of the nature, importance, and requirements of autonomy. For Taylor, the capacity for autonomy is at the very center of what it means to be a person. It defines the internal process of human agency itself. His view of autonomy, however, is also inseparable from morality and community. This gives autonomy, an internal capacity of persons, an external grounding in particular cultural and social contexts.

In his "The Concept of a Person," Taylor argues that we usually think of persons as having a certain moral status or as being bearers of particular rights, and that such agents require certain capacities that make these views of them possible. These capacities include having a sense of self, a notion of past and future, the ability to hold values, and the ability to make choices—in short, the ability to adopt a plan for one's own life. Taylor writes, "A person must be a being with his own point of view on things" (1985a, 97). He then goes on to introduce what he sees as a decisive feature of human beings: "What is crucial about human agents is that things matter to them" (1985a, 98). Furthermore, things matter to them in moral ways; they recognize and acknowledge certain standards that make them moral agents. For Taylor, the ability to construct one's own plan of life according to one's own moral judgements about what really matters is at the heart of human agency.

Taylor explores how and why things matter to agents in his treatment of what he calls "strong evaluation," and this concept is what provides them with the capacity for autonomy. In "Self-Interpreting Animals," Taylor argues that people experience emotions that they understand only in a "subject-referring" sense (1985a, 55). These subject-referring emotions hinge on qualitative judgements about what is worthy or good in life. Taylor writes: "Our emotions make it possible for us to have a sense of what the good life is for a subject; and this sense involves in turn our making qualitative discriminations between our desires and goals, whereby we see some as higher and others as lower, some as good and others as discreditable, still others as evil, some as truly vital and others as trivial, and so on" (1985a, 65). This exercise of control over desires through qualitative judgments about them is what Taylor labels strong evaluation. It is the capacity to rank motivations according to judgments of their value rather than according to our desires themselves. Taylor writes, "It means we are not taking our de facto desires as the ultimate in justification, but are going beyond that to their worth" (1985a, 66).

Taylor discusses strong evaluation in greater detail in his essays "Responsibility for Self" and "What Is Human Agency?". He begins by contrasting weak and strong evaluation. Weak evaluation is judging desires on the basis of convenience, or how best to attain them, while strong evaluation is judging desires as belonging "to qualitatively different modes of life" (1976, 282). Under weak evaluation, something is judged "good" if it is desired, but, under strong evaluation, something is judged "good" by standards independent of desire itself. The weak evaluator is nothing more than a simple weigher of alternative desires who delays the gratification of one only if it conflicts with another. The strong evaluator, on the other hand, rises above calculating maximum satisfaction of desires to an evaluation that employs a "vocabulary of worth" (1976, 287). This is a "language of contrastive characterization" that allows people to articulate the qualitative superiority of one alternative over another (1985a, 24). Taylor employs words like good/bad, noble/base, virtue/vice, and higher/lower as examples of this capacity to contrast alternatives in terms of qualitative worth. The strong evaluator does not reject desires on the basis of their contingent conflict with other desires but, rather, on the basis of their incompatibility with the mode of life he or she wants to lead or kind of person he or she wants to be (1985a, 19). In this way, strong evaluation allows agents to reflect on and control their desires according to judgments about what constitutes a good life. In other words, it allows them to exercise autonomy. The process of strong evaluation provides human beings with the capacity for autonomy by giving them the ability to reflect on and construct their own lives in coherent and meaningful ways according to moral standards they deem most worthy. According to Taylor, the "capacity for what I have called strong evaluation is an essential feature of a person" (1985a, 43). It allows persons to exist "as beings for whom things can have significance," the central characteristic of human agency (1985c, 260–261). On Taylor's account, the capacity to employ strong evaluation—the capacity for autonomy—is an essential ingredient of human agency.

In *Sources of the Self*, Taylor discusses where the standards that guide strong evaluation come from, and we find that in his view morality is inseparable from agency, and thus from autonomy. Taylor argues that human beings have "moral and spiritual intuitions" that inform their reactions to issues like justice, human dignity, and respect for the lives and well-being of others. He goes on to say that these issues "all involve what I have called elsewhere 'strong evaluation,' that is, they involve discriminations of right or wrong, better or worse, higher or lower, which are not rendered valid by our own desires, inclinations, or choices, but rather stand independent of these and offer standards by which they can be judged" (1989a, 4). Moral intuitions, which are "deep, powerful, and universal," provide the basis for strong evaluation. These moral intuitions are subject to dramatic shaping by different cultures in different ways, but the fact that the intuitions are universal insures that every culture will have some kind of moral language. He concludes that, from these deep moral intuitions and the moral reactions they cause in us, we can discover a "given ontology of the human" (1989a, 5). According to Taylor, the ontology of human agents is fundamentally a moral one.[2]

Different cultures shape their members' moral ontology through what Taylor calls "inescapable frameworks." These incorporate a "crucial set of qualitative distinctions" that provides people with the sense that certain modes of life or ways of acting are "incomparably higher" than others. In this way, such frameworks guide strong evaluation (1989a, 19–20). Taylor claims that "doing without frameworks is utterly impossible," that living within the moral horizons they provide is "constitutive of human agency" itself, and that human identity is necessarily "oriented in moral space" marked off by these frameworks (1989a, 27–28). Since, in these ways, human agency is rooted in moral space, Taylor concludes that people "cannot do without some orientation to the good," an orientation provided by their culturally-grounded moral frameworks (1989a, 33, 42–44). He writes, "Selfhood and the good, or in another way selfhood and morality, turn out to be inextricably intertwined themes" (1989a, 3). In Taylor's view, then, morality is not just an important feature of human agency; it actually constitutes the stuff of human agency by shaping identity through connections to the good, whatever that might be from person to person and culture to culture. We are moral creatures in the most basic sense, and this makes our moral judgments—our strong evaluations—central to our identity. Moral materials are prior to and, in fact, form the basis for strong evaluation, and, as we saw above, the capacity for strong evaluation is central to an agent's having autonomy. Thus, autonomy and morality are inseparable in Taylor's treatment of agency.

This link between moral standards and strong evaluation uncovers the critical importance of cultural communities to the exercise of autonomy. According to Taylor, such communities provide their members with the moral language they need to become strong evaluators. He pays particularly close attention to the necessity of language to human agency through the process of strong evaluation, and this ties autonomy to the cultural communities that provide language. Taylor asks, "How can there be a sense of some goals or desires as higher and others as lower without a symbolic medium in which this can be articulated?" He answers, "Without language we could not have a sense of this distinction between what is really important and what we just from time to time desire" (1985a, 73–74). This emphasis on the role of language flows from Taylor's claim that human life is "fundamentally *dialogical*" in nature. He says, "We become full human agents, capable of understanding ourselves, and hence of defining an identity, through our acquisition of rich human languages of expression" (1991, 33, italics in original). Humans only understand themselves in a cultural dialogue with those around them, with those who share their membership in particular cultural groups in civil society. Their agency is therefore rooted in their existence as interlocutors in particular cultural communities (1985c, 276).

In *Sources of the Self*, Taylor further explores the link between language, culture, and human agency. Particular cultures mold an individual's innate but highly variable moral intuitions into specific moral frameworks. They can transform the same moral materials into frameworks as different as the honor ethic of a warrior society or the ethic of reason over desire found in Roman Stoicism (1989a, 5, 20–21). These moral frameworks are rooted in specific cultural characteristics, the most influential of which is language. Taylor writes, "To study persons is to study beings who only exist in, or are partly constituted by, a certain language." He continues: "A language only exists and is maintained within a language community. And this indicates another crucial feature of a self. One is a self only among other selves. A self can never be described without reference to those who surround it" (1989a, 34–35). In this way, Taylor locates agency in cultural and social as well as in moral space. He writes, "We first learn our languages of moral and spiritual discernment by being brought into an ongoing conversation by those who bring us up. . . . The full definition of someone's identity thus usually involves not only his stand on moral and spiritual matters but also some reference to a defining community" (1989a, 35–36). He faults those who think individuals can break away from "webs of interlocution" as if they were "training wheels" for true atomistic independence in adulthood. Taylor replies that it is impossible to "leap out of the human condition," that people can certainly be original and independent but that they still understand themselves only through a "relation to the language and vision of others" (1989a, 36–37). Even rebels remain embedded in their culture, because their rebellion only makes sense in terms of that culture. On Taylor's account, a person's ability to engage in strong evaluation, to exercise autonomy, hinges in the deepest way on his or her participation in a particular cultural community that provides the moral materials he or she needs to do so, even if such a person ultimately uses those materials to decide to reject that community.

Taylor's view that autonomy, and thus human agency itself, is inseparable from morality and community is the basis for his claim that a coherent formulation of liberalism cannot be rooted in what he calls "atomism." In his introduction to *Philosophy and the Human Sciences*, Taylor identifies atomism as an "understanding of the individual as metaphysically independent of society," and he criticizes this position, saying, "But what it hides from view is the way in which an individual is constituted by the language and culture which can only be maintained and renewed in the communities he is part of." Given this misunderstanding of human agency, Taylor claims we need to "purge our key normative notions—freedom, justice, rights—of their atomist distortions" (1985b, 8). In an essay entitled (not surprisingly) "Atomism," Taylor sets out to do just this. He argues that the liberal commitment to concepts like rights and individual freedom cannot rest on anything resembling atomism but, rather, rely on communitarian foundations. Taylor claims that if we truly value freedom and its protection through individual rights, then we must also work to develop and sustain the internal capacities that make these values possible and meaningful. These are, of course, the capacities central to the exercise of autonomy. Taylor writes, "What is truly important is that one be able to exercise autonomy in the basic issues of life, in one's most important commitments." The internal capacity for autonomy, however, is culturally and socially constituted, and "the free individual or autonomous moral agent can only achieve and maintain his identity in a certain type of culture" (1985b, 204–205). This is why liberals who value freedom and rights have an obligation to help develop and sustain the kind of cultural community that supports autonomous capacities, and this obligation includes a responsibility to work for and participate in the kinds of social institutions and practices that support such a community (1985b, 208). In this way, Taylor uses the concept of individual autonomy to show how liberalism cannot consider the freedom of individual human agents apart from the particular cultural and social circumstances in which those agents come embedded.

Taylor's is a powerful and nuanced account of autonomy. He shows how the capacity for autonomy is built into the very notion of what it means to be a human being. Autonomy, or the ability to engage in strong evaluation, makes possible the moral depth and complex inner life that characterizes human agents. Taylor also shows, however, that autonomy is not an internal capacity that exists independently of external factors. Autonomy rests on qualitative judgments made possible by the moral standards individuals carry, standards that they develop within certain cultural and social settings. Our sense of who we are, of who we can become, of the kind of life worth living, and so on flows from our participation in a particular cultural dialogue with those around us. Liberals who are committed to autonomy, therefore, must concern themselves with how it comes embedded in particular cultural contexts and is supported by particular institutions, practices, and meanings in civil society.

## LIBERALISM, AUTONOMY, AND MULTICULTURALISM

I am claiming that a close look at the work of Mill, Raz, and Taylor helps uncover the implications of autonomy for liberalism. They show how the ideal of autonomy is able to provide a solid moral grounding for liberalism. They also show how liberalism must employ a broad view of autonomy, one that includes both external and internal factors, and one that looks to the importance of culture, membership in cultural groups, and civil society, rather than just individual rights and procedural protections alone.

At its best, liberalism is committed to the ideal of men and women living their own lives from the inside. This is a liberalism that recognizes the importance of developing and pursuing one's own projects, of living by one's own authentic plan of life, as a necessary part of one's well-being. Autonomy is a constituent element of the good life for human beings. It is a necessary ingredient in genuine human flourishing. This ideal, however, goes far beyond freedom as noninterference; it requires much more than the right to be left alone. Negative liberty is a necessary but not a sufficient condition of a full liberal commitment to autonomy. If liberalism is to provide a compelling account of individual autonomy, then it needs to acknowledge its cultural and social nature.[3] Alasdair MacIntyre makes the point that in order to be compelling, a political and moral philosophy must offer a vision of its social embodiment (1984, 23). Liberalism is no different. If liberalism's moral strength flows from its commitment to individual autonomy, then it must pay attention to the kind of culture and civil society in which living an autonomous life becomes possible. It must recognize that both the internal and external requirements of autonomy come embedded in the kinds of cultural and social circumstances that surround persons.

Externally, autonomy depends upon the existence of an adequate range of options from which to choose. If we are to decide what paths are best for us at different points in our lives, then we need a variety of distinct paths to choose from at these points. What Mill and Raz bring out so well is how the kinds of options people face hinge on their cultural and social contexts. Some people who have the same menu of rights and formal procedural protections as their fellow citizens can find themselves far more vulnerable than others when it comes to their participation in civil society. They can find their development as persons cramped by the narrow and impoverished range of choices they actually face. I think it is important to notice here that while economic circumstances certainly have a large impact on the kinds of choices we face, there is also more involved. The range of options individuals face hinges on more than just their income and what it can buy. The kinds of power that come embedded within informal practices and meanings also shape the range of options available to people. The positions a person occupies within the web of institutions, practices, and meanings of civil society are critical to the kinds of options he or she faces in life. Since these things influence a person's range of options, they also influence the kind of life he or she imagines living and, in turn, the kind of person he or she becomes. The range of options open to us not only shapes the pursuit of our goals but their very formation, shaping in turn the kind of person we turn out to be, the kind of inner character we develop. This is why a secure environment rich in valuable alternatives supports the development and exercise of autonomy, while an environment characterized by vulnerability and few if any meaningful choices does not. As both Raz and Taylor point out, much of this turns on our membership in particular cultural groups. Group membership plays an important part in locating us within institutions, practices, and meanings of civil society and hence determining our range of options. It provides access to the resources we need both to have options and to make sense of them. Our membership in particular groups orients us in that cultural and social space where individual autonomy becomes possible.

In addition to the external range of options persons face within their particular cultural and social environments, autonomy also hinges on internal elements. It depends upon an individual's ability to evaluate his or her own desires and motivations, to engage in Taylor's strong evaluation. Exercising the capacity for autonomy requires people to make moral judgments about the kind of life they want to lead and the kind of person they want to be. It requires persons to act on their moral nature according to standards that are authentically their own. Developing authentic moral standards, however, does not mean inventing them out of thin air. Individuals draw such standards from their social relationships, their communities, their participation within a cultural dialogue. As both Taylor and Mill point out, the moral character upon which autonomy hinges is forged within particular cultural and social settings. In order to exercise the inner capacity for autonomy, people must take part in the moral language or languages that surround them. As with external options, these internal considerations and the external conditions that make them possible depend in large part on membership in cultural groups. These groups provide access to the moral languages people draw upon to become autonomous by either embracing, rejecting, or modifying the standards they offer. They provide the cultural norms that make the lives people choose for themselves meaningful. In short, the cultural groups that make up civil society constitute a critical part of the cultural and social context in which individuals define themselves as persons, a process of self-definition that is at the heart of autonomy.

I am not offering an account of liberal autonomy that considers it a static adherence to established cultural norms. The fact that autonomy hinges on particular cultural and social environments does not mean that to act autonomously people must live their lives in the same way people traditionally have in such environments. Cultural norms and the institutions, practices, and meanings of civil society are not static but fluid. They are open to challenge and revision. Marriage, for example, has remained a central institution in American life, but notions of gender roles within it, of the acceptability of ending it through divorce, and even of its requiring partners of different sexes have all undergone and continue to undergo important transformations. What is important is not that institutions, practices, and meanings remain the same, but that they comprise a shifting and contested context in which our lives, as we choose to live them, take on meaning (Kymlicka 1989, 166–168). As Taylor points out, even rebels need a cultural and social context to define themselves both within and against; otherwise their rebellion is meaningless.

Mine is also not an account of autonomy that defines it as losing oneself within groups. Cultural group membership is a critical part of autonomy, but not when individuals let groups live their lives for them or when groups hold on to their members through manipulation or coercion. Groups are important because they locate their members within the web of institutions, practices, and meanings of civil society, and this shapes the kinds of options their members face in life. They provide the cultural and social resources their members use to construct their own lives. In so doing, they influence both the internal and external requirements of autonomy. Cultural groups, then, are an integral part of an autonomy-supporting environment. But they can also be part of an autonomy-inhibiting environment, especially when members are not free to distinguish themselves from the group or to leave it entirely.

It is important to notice, then, that all of these factors—cultural norms, social institutions and practices, membership in cultural groups, and so on—in no way guarantee autonomy in and of themselves. Rather, for an autonomous life to become possible, they must be of a certain kind. Just as an individual right may either contribute to or obstruct autonomy—the right to freely practice one's religion versus the right to own slaves as property, for example—these factors can either support or hinder the development of an autonomous life. They can make autonomy possible or they can crush it. What is critical to recognize, however, is that they matter very much to autonomy one way or the other.

The importance of cultural groups to autonomy provides liberalism with a promising way to address the general issue of multiculturalism. Indeed, many political theorists in recent years have used autonomy to push liberalism to be more accommodating toward cultural pluralism in a variety of ways. Raz, for example, argues that autonomy provides the basis for a more generous liberal response to the issue of multiculturalism than that offered by a purely individualistic, procedural, and rights-based approach. According to Raz, since cultural group membership is so important to autonomy, "multiculturalism requires a political society to recognize the equal standing of all the stable and viable cultural communities existing in that society" (1994, 69). He writes, "Because individual freedom and well-being depend on unimpeded membership in a respected and prosperous cultural group, there is little wonder that multiculturalism emerges as a central element in any decent liberal political program for societies inhabited by a number of viable cultural groups" (1994, 72). According to Raz, the liberal commitment to multiculturalism needs to go well beyond a narrow and individualistic emphasis on individual nondiscrimination rights to a public recognition of the importance of cultural group membership to the autonomy and well-being of persons.

Taylor makes a similar claim. In "The Politics of Recognition," he lays out two ways in which liberalism can respond to the problem of multiculturalism. The first is dedicated to individual rights, equal treatment under the law, and fair procedures that are neutral on any substantive questions of the good. According to Taylor, this approach, which is the dominant one in the United States, is "inhospitable" to multiculturalism. Its overriding emphasis on the uniform application of rights and procedures and its individualistic suspicion of collective goals both trump the claims made by distinct cultural groups, claims rooted in their particular views of the good life, their particular material and social interests, and indeed in their very survival as vulnerable minority communities (1992, 53–58, 60–61). In contrast, Taylor outlines a second liberal approach to multiculturalism, one that acknowledges the importance of membership in cultural communities to human beings as autonomous agents and recognizes the survival and flourishing of such communities as a matter of public concern. This alternative approach, while remaining dedicated to fundamental rights, does consider "the broad range of immunities and presumptions of uniform treatment" open to compromise based on claims by distinct cultural groups. It is able to do so because it is nonprocedural and grounded in substantive judgments about the good life for persons, ones which include the importance of membership in a secure cultural community (1992, 58–61).

Finally, Will Kymlicka (1995a and 1989) relies heavily on autonomy in his influential arguments about liberalism and multiculturalism. On his account, postwar liberalism pays little if any attention to the importance of cultural group membership because it usually assumes a homogenous culture that all citizens share and draw upon in common. This oversight, however, becomes a problem in racially or ethnically plural societies where minority cultures are often threatened by the majority's dominant cultural norms and require special measures in order to protect their cultural integrity. In his attempt to correct this oversight, Kymlicka claims that cultural group membership is a significant part of individual well-being, because it forms the context in which people choose how to live their lives (1995a, chap. 5; 1989, chap. 8). He argues that membership in a particular culture is necessary to the exercise of autonomous choice, because it provides both the options from which individuals choose and the values that make such options meaningful. Kymlikca claims, in short, that "the liberal value of freedom of choice has certain cultural preconditions, and hence that issues of cultural membership must be incorporated into liberal principles" (1995a, 76). Kymlicka goes on to argue that this requires that liberalism make room for special group rights and a distinct legal status for certain minority cultures.[4]

Autonomy, then, is a powerful way to shift liberalism away from an exclusively individualistic, universal rights-based, and procedural approach to one that recognizes the public importance of cultural group membership to individuals living in countries containing more than one distinct cultural group. In some cases, however, this use of autonomy to reformulate liberalism's approach to multiculturalism is not without its problems. As William Galston (1995) points out, the very cultural values that autonomy relies upon—open and unrestrained individual choice from among a wide array of diverse options—is not something all cultural groups share. Indeed, it is something sharply at odds with the cultural practices and traditions of some. On his account, autonomy can actually make liberalism less hospitable to some forms of multicultural-ism, since "the decision to throw state power behind the promotion of individual autonomy can weaken or undermine individuals and groups that do not and cannot organize their affairs in accordance with that principle without undermining the deepest sources of their identity" (521). This goes to the problem of how much liberalism should accom-modate illiberal groups, and it is one of the most difficult in the general debate over liberalism and multiculturalism. It is a problem, however, that fortunately does not apply to the case of white and black Americans in the United States. This is so because the cultural identity of African Americans, while distinct in many ways, is as liberal, or at least no less liberal, than that of white Americans. The problem of illiberal cultural groups becomes pressing when looking at groups—usually small, insu-lar, and religiously based—within Western liberal democracies that strongly reject the broad liberal values of the mainstream society. This simply is not the case for most African Americans, who remain as com-mitted to the broad liberal values of autonomy, free choice, tolerance, equality, rights, and so on as white Americans.[5] While white and black Americans are distinct cultural groups with much dividing them, they are nonetheless groups that both share in and contribute to a broader cultural and social context in the United States, a context that is broadly speaking a modern liberal democratic one. So at least in the case of black and white Americans in the United States, autonomy still provides a promising way to address the issue of cultural pluralism within liberal-ism without threatening the fundamental cultural integrity of either group. Indeed, as I argue in the next chapter, autonomy provides a way for American liberalism to accommodate the cultural integrity of black Americans as much as it has traditionally done for white Americans.

Given the broad view of autonomy that liberalism is capable of employing, what then can we say about color-blind liberalism and its view of race and freedom? First, color-blind liberalism's central cate-gories do in fact focus on issues critical to autonomy. Strong individual rights and procedural protections are an important part of any liberal commitment to autonomy, because it does depend upon our being free from arbitrary interference by the state and our fellow citizens. A sphere marked off by formal rights, therefore, is essential to an individual's opportunity to freely live his or her own life. Furthermore, the left's interpreting the color-blind paradigm to require greater economic equal-ity between white and black Americans is also very important. Auton-omy depends in large measure on the range of options provided by our economic status. Economic power opens many doors that remain closed without it, so attention to distributive issues remains an important part of any liberal commitment to autonomy. All this means that the left's view of race and freedom within its interpretation of the color-blind paradigm is still valuable. The state's taking an active role to protect the basic civil rights of black Americans, to battle continuing discrimination that presents a barrier to black opportunity, and to work to reduce the economic inequality that disproportionately narrows the options facing black citizens is still critically important to a liberal understanding of race informed by autonomy.

I think it is clear, however, that color-blind liberalism also fails to account for many other factors that are necessary for autonomy. First, autonomy is in large part an internal dimension of human agency that color-blind liberalism's opportunity-concept of freedom misses. Autonomy hinges not simply on the absence of barriers to choice, but also on the actual exercise of choice in meaningful ways, and this is something the color-blind paradigm and its concern with external barriers to freedom does not account for. It fails to grasp the close link between internal and external factors and their importance to autonomy. Second, even color-blind liberalism's opportunity-concept of freedom misses critical external factors upon which autonomy hinges. Indeed, autonomy's external requirements include just the sorts of things I showed color-blind liberalism overlooks in chapter 3. Autonomy depends upon the broad cultural context and the character of the institutions, practices, and meanings of civil society that surround people, the very things the color-blind paradigm has so much trouble accounting for. Finally, both of these shortcomings are tied to color-blind liberalism's failure to account for how membership in particular cultural groups influences an individual's prospects for an autonomous life. Cultural group membership is critical to both the internal and external requirements of autonomy, and so the color-blind paradigm's failing to properly account for this is a serious shortcoming. Color-blind liberalism, in short, relies upon a narrow and incomplete view of freedom in its understanding of race. The broader theory of autonomy I have outlined in this chapter, however, is able to provide American liberalism with the resources it needs to overcome the shortcomings of the color-blind paradigm. Autonomy is able to provide the basis for an expanded liberal understanding of race in the United States.

# CHAPTER 5

# Expanding the Liberal Understanding of Race

Black and white Americans still experience the ideal of autonomy very differently. First, African Americans continue to face greater cultural, social, economic, and political barriers to autonomy in the United States. This is not to say that white Americans are guaranteed a full and flourishing autonomous life, or that black Americans are incapable of such a life. Instead, it is to say that African Americans still face greater obstacles to such a life, some of which color-blind liberalism addresses and some of which it overlooks. Second, black and white Americans frequently draw both the internal and external elements necessary for autonomy from different places. Their membership in distinct cultural groups and the spaces such groups occupy in American civil society plays a critical role in providing the kinds of resources that individuals in each group need to both construct and overcome threats to an autonomous life. In a profoundly important way, then, the autonomy of African American men and women hinges not on making their membership in a racially defined group irrelevant as color-blind liberalism argues, but rather on that very group membership itself and its relevance in their lives. Autonomy, in short, demands that those concerned with its promotion see the continuing struggle for black freedom in the United States in a much broader cultural and social context than that considered by color-blind liberalism. In this way, autonomy provides liberalism with a powerful way to push its understanding of race beyond the limits of the color-blind paradigm, even while retaining its strengths.[1] In this chapter, I describe the features of such an expanded understanding of race, outlining the kinds of factors it must consider to be more complete and compelling than color-blind liberalism alone.

## COMPLEXITY

In his *Spheres of Justice*, Michael Walzer argues that no single distributive principle—such as free exchange, need, merit, birth, desert, and so on—applies to every kind of social good in every sphere of social life.

Rather, different principles are called for in different spheres. Walzer argues that "principles of justice are themselves pluralistic in form," and this means that different normative categories are appropriate in different settings (1983, 6). Trying to apply a single formula to every setting produces a rigid and narrow approach to social justice that overlooks much of importance, because looking at every setting through the same normative lens distorts one's view of what is particular and unique about each. Walzer offers an account of social justice that is complex— the view that different principles and categories are appropriate in different spheres of public life—rather than simple—the view that a single formula applies across all these various spheres. John Keane also picks up this line of argument, claiming that we must understand our central normative goals as complex concepts (1988a, 11–15). On his account, their realization often demands different kinds of considerations in different spheres of public life, and one of the most important differences comes when we apply them either to the state or to civil society.

In my view, complexity is an idea especially appropriate to individual autonomy. As I demonstrated in the last chapter, autonomy is a normative goal that necessitates a variety of considerations. It becomes possible only in an environment characterized by a host of different cultural, social, economic, and political factors. What it requires at the level of the state, for example, is not the same as what it requires in civil society. Autonomy, therefore, is a complex ideal, requiring different sorts of normative principles to understand its meaning in different areas of public life. A focus on only some of its features—such as formal rights or economic opportunity—while overlooking others—such as informal social practices or cultural group membership—yields an overly simplistic and incomplete view of autonomy. A comprehensive view of autonomy, on the other hand, is complex. It recognizes that autonomy has different kinds of features in different spheres of public life, and so the normative categories that we use to think about autonomy in these various spheres will also be different. A liberal understanding of race that is informed by autonomy must therefore be a complex one. It must recognize that we need to think about race and autonomy in different ways in different spheres of public life. No single normative formula can grasp something as multidimensional as race. It is something that cuts across so many different areas in American life that we should fully expect to find different normative considerations appropriate depending upon the particular area in question. Just as we would not use the same set of tools to repair a watch as we would to landscape a yard, we should not expect the same set of normative categories to be appropriate when considering America's experience with race in all of its dimensions.

A normative understanding of race that is informed by liberal autonomy and characterized by complexity should not set aside color-blind liberalism. It should not try to replace it with an entirely different normative formula. Rather, it must incorporate the categories of color-blind liberalism into a broader approach. It must use the ideal of autonomy to retain the color-blind paradigm even while moving beyond it, focusing on the very things it overlooks. This is an understanding that recognizes that color-blind liberalism's categories are appropriate in some spheres but not in others. Sometimes color-blind considerations are called for, but sometimes, especially when it comes to civil society, explicitly group-conscious considerations are necessary. Here group-conscious and color-blind considerations do not simply refer to noticing or not noticing an individual's race. Rather, they mean taking the position that a person's race is or is not morally relevant in a particular setting. Relying on color-blind considerations means embracing the view that individuals should be treated as such—which is to say, without regard to their membership in certain racially defined groups. This is the view that an individual's race should make no difference to his or her prospects in a particular area of life. Relying on group-conscious considerations, on the other hand, means recognizing that an individual's prospects in some areas are inescapably tied to his or her membership in a racially defined cultural group. Taking a group-conscious view means acknowledging the role that institutions, practices, and meanings tied to race play in the structure of American life, and thus to autonomy. In short, color-blind considerations focus on the individual apart from his or her membership in a racially defined cultural group, while group-conscious considerations focus on the individual as a part of that group. I am arguing that a liberal understanding of race must depend upon both of these views, because each is appropriate in different spheres of American life.

## THE CONTINUING IMPORTANCE
## OF COLOR-BLIND LIBERALISM

As I argued in chapter 3, color-blind liberalism does have many strengths, and so its categories are still critically important to a liberal understanding of race. They continue to have a vital role to play both at the level of the state and in civil society.

### Citizenship

Citizenship is one sphere in which color-blind principles are still appropriate. It is an area critical to autonomy in which an individual's race should not be morally relevant. The basic rights of liberal citizenship are vital to autonomy, because individuals need protection against arbitrary interference by the state and fellow citizens in order to construct autonomous lives for themselves. They need the measure of security and independence that the rights and protections of liberal citizenship provide. In order to become a real possibility, then, autonomy requires the negative freedom provided by liberalism's traditional commitment to individual rights: the rights to worship, speak, assemble, and travel freely; the rights to live and work where we choose; the right to privacy in our own affairs and those of our family; the procedural rights we have when accused of a crime; the right to vote for and hold elected office; the right to own and transfer property; and the right to equal treatment under the law. These formal rights and protections help create a space in which autonomy becomes possible, in which people are able to direct their own lives without undue interference. They are the fruits of liberal citizenship, and they should belong to each individual on an equal basis.

One of the most direct and effective ways in which the United States has historically subverted the freedom of its black citizens is the simple denial of citizenship rights. From the era of slavery, in which the Supreme Court declared in the infamous 1857 case of *Scott v. Sandford* that black Americans were not citizens under the Constitution and therefore enjoyed none of its rights and privileges, through the invention and implementation of the Jim Crow system, under which they became citizens in name only, the basic rights and protections of United States citizenship have rarely applied to African Americans.[2] In the almost four centuries that black Americans have been part of this country's history, they have only really begun to enjoy the basic rights and protections of citizenship in any meaningful way in the last few decades. Over the vast majority of their years in the United States, then, African Americans have been left open to any and all forms of direct interference with their freedom—enslavement, disenfranchisement, lynching, rape, theft, beatings, and so on. They have generally been subject to violent, humiliating, and exploitative treatment according to the whim of any white American so inclined with little or no protection by the state. Under conditions such as these, living an autonomous life becomes impossible, or at least exceedingly difficult.

This is why the success of black Americans during the postwar era in defeating de jure segregation and winning recognition of their full civil and political rights from the state are essential steps in striking down barriers that historically burden their ability to live autonomous lives. The ability of black Americans to enjoy the rights and protections of citizenship on the same basis as any other citizen without regard to race is necessary to the creation of a space in which individual autonomy becomes possible. Given the historical pattern in the United States of denying such rights and protections to black citizens, and of even taking them away after they have already been granted as was the case following Reconstruction, a strong commitment to their protection must remain at the center of a liberal understanding of race. This is why color-blind liberalism's powerful emphasis on the individual rights, procedural protections, and equal protection of the laws that flow from citizenship is still critical. A liberal understanding of race must remain committed to the position that the fundamental rights and protections of citizenship are necessary for liberal autonomy and should be the same for each individual regardless of his or her membership in a racially defined cultural group.

This view of citizenship is at odds with the leading alternative to color-blind liberalism within liberal thought and practice in recent years, an alternative that claims group-differentiated citizenship is the best way to solve liberalism's problems with multiculturalism. Proponents of this view of citizenship argue that liberalism sometimes must make room for formal group rights designed to protect cultural minorities.[3] These might include specific rights or immunities for group members, veto power over legislation touching on fundamental group concerns, some level of guaranteed group representation in government bodies, special regional government status, or special language rights. Under such schemes the formal civil and political rights of citizenship vary according to an individual's membership in a particular cultural group. Within contemporary liberal political thought, the work of Will Kymlicka (1995a and 1989) is perhaps the most significant along these lines. As I discussed in the last chapter, Kymlicka argues that freedom hinges in large part on the context of choice provided by one's membership in a cultural group. This means that members of certain cultural minorities are at a disadvantage in some countries if their cultural integrity is threatened by the norms and practices of the dominant group. Kymlicka claims that secure cultural membership should be considered a primary good in the Rawlsian sense, and thus a proper subject for distributive justice. On his account, justice as fairness demands that each individual be entitled to an equal share in the benefits of cultural membership, and so those who are placed at a morally arbitrary disadvantage by belonging to vulnerable minority cultures deserve special protective measures (1995a, chap. 6). Kymlicka writes, "Once we recognize cultural membership as an important good which underlies our choices, then special political rights and status for minority cultures may be required" (1989, 199). In this way, Kymlicka argues that the liberal theories of justice articulated by thinkers like Rawls and Dworkin actually justify "special status for minority cultures in a culturally plural state" (1989, 162). On his account, granting cultural minorities special rights and a distinct legal status is in many cases not only consistent with liberal justice, but in fact required by it.

Kymlicka's case for minority group rights hinges on a distinction he makes between "national minorities" in a "multination state" and "ethnic groups" in a "polyethnic state" (1995a, chap. 2). National minorities are generally the result of a state incorporating a previously self-governing and regionally concentrated cultural group—often with its own language, traditions, political institutions, and so on. Such groups usually want to protect their own regional and cultural independence, self-government rights, and language within a broader political federation. Ethnic groups, on the other hand, are generally the result of individual or family immigration to a new land, and they tend to be regionally dispersed. Rather than wanting to remain separate and independent political entities, such groups generally want full membership in the larger society, though they often press for recognition and respect for their ethnic identity and for mainstream institutions to be more accommodating of cultural differences. Kymlicka's primary concern is that national minorities not be treated like ethnic groups. While ethnic groups may deserve some forms of group-differentiated citizenship—exemptions from dress codes in the military or from Sunday closing laws for religious minorities, for example—the goal is to insure full and equal participation in the dominant culture and civil society without discrimination on the basis of ethnicity (1995a, 96–97, 113–115, 127). National minorities, on the other hand, do not want to integrate into the mainstream culture and civil society, and they frequently require special self-government rights and a distinct constitutional status in order to remain separate and independent. On Kymlicka's account, such groups constitute separate nations with their own cultures and civil societies that are not part of the dominant culture and civil society with which they happen to share a political affiliation at the state level. His main argument for group-differentiated citizenship focuses primarily on these kinds of national minorities.

Kymlicka makes a powerful case for why liberalism must sometimes make room for group rights, a case that in some instances is legitimate. He correctly argues that group-differentiated citizenship may in fact be appropriate in countries that contain a number of separate, clearly defined, and relatively stable national minority groups. Indeed, such a model is the basis for consociational democracy in countries like Belgium and for special constitutional arrangements for nationality groups in countries like Canada. Group-differentiated citizenship may even be appropriate for some national minorities in the United States. Kymlicka points out that the United States rarely makes a distinction between its ethnic groups and its national minorities. In treating all groups as if they were immigrant ethnic groups in need of nondiscrimination protections to facilitate integration, it overlooks national minorities such as indigenous Americans, the descendants of Mexican citizens in the Southwest incorporated as a group into the United States, and native Hawaiians. He writes, "In the USA, there is ample recognition that the country is polyethnic, but difficulty accepting that the country is also multinational, and that national minorities have special claims of cultural rights and self-government" (1995a, 22). I think that Kymlicka is correct to argue that certain national minorities in the United States do have some claim on differentiated citizenship rights, a claim long recognized at least in U.S. treaties with various American Indian tribes. Special group rights and legal provisions that recognize the need for regional self-government, language protections, exemptions from educational requirements, and so on are therefore appropriate in the case of some national minorities in the United States, especially when it comes to indigenous Americans or traditionally isolated religious communities such as the Amish (Svensson 1979). I do not think such measures are helpful, however, when it comes to black and white Americans, a fact Kymlicka himself acknowledges.

The argument Kymlicka develops rests on his distinction between national minorities and ethnic immigrant groups, but he recognizes that some groups are "hard cases" that fall in the "grey areas" between the two types (1995a, 101). African Americans are one such group, because they lack the regional homeland, separate language, or history of independent self-government that characterize national minorities, but unlike immigrant ethnic groups, their migration was not voluntary, they endured a significant period of forced enslavement, and the United States has historically resisted rather than facilitated their integration into the dominant culture and society (1995a, 24–25). Since African Americans do not fit Kymlicka's definition of a national minority, he does not count them as a group that requires group-differentiated citizenship rights. Indeed, the thrust of his argument actually seems to endorse a strong color-blind version of citizenship rights when it comes to black Americans. At the heart of his broad argument that contemporary liberalism overlooks the need for minority-group rights is the claim that this is the case because so many groups around the world are simply not like African Americans in the United States. According to Kymlicka, it is the success of the American civil rights movement in pushing a universal rights–based, color-blind, and equal-protection version of citizenship that has been over-generalized to the rest of the world. While such an approach was perhaps appropriate for African Americans long denied civil and political rights and seeking full and equal membership in American life, it is not necessarily appropriate for many national minority groups, even those in the United States like indigenous Americans, who instead want to maintain a separate status and identity through regional self-government rights and special legal exemptions (1995a, 60; 1989, 3–4, 142–150).[4] Kymlicka argues that simply because color-blind citizenship rights have been so important to African Americans in the United States, this in no way means that they are appropriate for the kinds of national minority groups around the world that are radically different from African Americans.

Kymlicka, then, rejects group-differentiated citizenship in the case of African Americans, and he is correct to do so. While it is a powerful way to address some of liberalism's problems with multiculturalism, it is not one that is particularly useful when it comes to race in the United States, because race exists within a cultural and social context that is inhospitable to the formal arrangements that group-differentiated citizenship requires. As Michael Walzer points out, the United States blends a remarkable array of different racial, ethnic, and religious groups, which are all "dispersed and inter-mixed without ground of their own" (1992a, 15). There are distinct cultural groups in the United States, including racially defined groups, but they are far too fluid, indeterminate, and interspersed to be formally fixed by the laws of citizenship (Walzer 1992a, 69–74). Race exists in a broader American cultural and social context that contains a host of "identity-defining groups" that individuals may draw upon (Rorty 1994, 157). Ethnicity, gender, class, religion, region, occupation, sexual orientation, age, and other such groups all overlap and cross-cut race in American life. In this kind of environment individuals often have multiple attachments that overlap one another and form a whole series of identities nested within each other (Bell 1975, 153, 158–159). Various cultural groups mark off and occupy their own distinct cultural and social space, but they also draw upon, contribute to, and interact in the larger cultural and social context of American life that is common to them all. In this kind of environment, many group members come and go, drawing on their membership in one group some of the time, but then drawing on their membership in other groups with other memberships at other times. This pattern of groups within American civil society is far too fluid, overlapping, and multidimensional to be reproduced in a formal scheme of group rights at the state level. This is why the American model is historically one of a dramatically differentiated population in civil society sharing a common citizenship in the state. In my view, a liberal understanding of race must take account of this broad context in which race exists, recognizing that it is one poorly suited to formalized group rights.

Indeed, resorting to group-differentiated citizenship as a way to overcome the shortcomings of color-blind liberalism begs the question, because these shortcomings lie in the realm of civil society rather than citizenship. As the leading alternative to the color-blind paradigm within contemporary liberalism, the call for group-differentiated citizenship seeks to revise that paradigm in the very sphere where it remains the most compelling, avoiding entirely the sphere of civil society where it runs into so many of its problems. The problem with color-blind liberalism is not its view of citizenship, but its incomplete view of civil society. The way to move beyond its limits, then, is not to adjust the formal rights and procedures of citizenship, but to move beyond issues of citizenship altogether when it comes to civil society. This is something that proposals for group-differentiated citizenship fail to do. They continue to rely upon the formal categories of citizenship to address shortcomings that go far beyond such categories. The problem with Kymlicka's argument, then, is not that he rejects group-differentiated citizenship when he considers the case of race in the United States. He is correct to do so. Instead, the problem is that this rejection throws us back on color-blind liberalism alone with no other alternative. Kymlicka's diagnosis of color-blind liberalism in general is accurate, but the only solution he offers is not appropriate in the case of race in the United States, something he himself recognizes. This is why moving beyond the limits of color-blind liberalism requires a much different approach than that offered by group-differentiated citizenship.

Finally, an issue often wrongly equated in American politics with group-differentiated citizenship is minority political representation, and the work of Lani Guinier (1994) provides an excellent example of this. Guinier is often accused by her critics of supporting group rights, but her work on minority voting representation is nonetheless firmly within the paradigm of color-blind liberalism and its view of citizenship. She does not demand that the United States embrace some sort of consociational democracy with group-differentiated citizenship through such measures as guaranteed seats in the government, group veto power, separate self-government rights, or immunities from U.S. laws for black Americans. Rather, she explores ways to adjust formally race-neutral democratic procedures in order to minimize the discriminatory impact of existing voting arrangements that disproportionately reduce the influence of black voters. In this way, she is well within the color-blind liberal tradition of looking at issues of procedural fairness, equality of opportunity, nondiscrimination, and inclusion. While the color-blind paradigm puts a strong emphasis on formal individual rights like the right to vote, it does not necessarily imply any specific electoral system. The principle of one person having one vote is perfectly compatible with many different kinds of electoral arrangements. As Guinier shows, certain electoral procedures such as cumulative voting, supermajorities, and multimember districts with proportional rather than winner-take-all representation that tend to enhance the influence of individual black voters in the electoral process are in fact compatible with the color-blind view of citizenship. Indeed, given the country's history of black political marginalization, attention to the ways such procedures might help boost and protect the political influence of individual black citizens should remain part of a liberal understanding of race and citizenship.

*Civil Society*

Color-blind liberalism is at its strongest in the realm of citizenship at the level of the state, but in spite of its problems with civil society, it still has much of value to offer in this sphere as well. As I argued in chapter 4, autonomy hinges in large part on the range of options individuals face in civil society. While many things can expand or narrow one's range of options, it is clear that the historical and continuing practice of racial discrimination is one of the most significant ways black Americans find their choices in life constrained. Victims of discrimination see choices about where and how they can live, work, play, go to school, worship, open businesses, travel, and buy goods dramatically narrowed. By entirely eliminating or imposing heavy costs on the kinds of options a person faces, discrimination plays a significant role in determining the kind of life he or she is able to lead. This is why discrimination is one of the most important barriers to an autonomous life that African Americans have faced and continue to face in civil society, and why color-blind liberalism's strong commitment to reducing discrimination is still essential in a liberal approach to race. Through the language of color-blind liberalism, at least in its left interpretation, African Americans and others who support black civil rights are able to push the state to intervene more actively in civil society to enforce laws against discrimination in areas such as employment, education, housing, credit lending, and public accommodations. This language can also bring public pressure and negative publicity to bear on organizations in civil society that are guilty of systematic discrimination, forcing them to examine and change their business practices, as the campaign against Denny's restaurants and Texaco in recent years demonstrates.

One of color-blind liberalism's most potent tools in such efforts is its celebration of equality of opportunity. I argued in chapter 3 that equality of opportunity does not deliver all it promises and leaves many important issues obscured, but it does provide a powerful justification for continuing efforts to open up more social and economic opportunities to black Americans. The language of equality of opportunity is a compelling one in the United States, and so it offers an opening for those who care about autonomy to push institutions in civil society such as businesses, universities, and banks to make more positions and resources available for African Americans who are underrepresented in such institutions. Doing so can help open up a wider range of options for black men and women in the United States, creating an environment more supportive of autonomy.

The left's interpretation of the color-blind paradigm also contributes a strong emphasis on an individual's economic status, as well as on social problems such as crime, poor health, and poor education that are frequently tied to economic vulnerability. This is an emphasis that I think must remain central to a liberal understanding of race. A person's economic position does much to influence the range of options he or she faces in life, and African Americans who disproportionately suffer from poverty, unemployment, and underemployment clearly find their choices more restricted. A lower income, reduced access to credit, and little financial security usually mean a narrower range of options. They mean a person is less able to pursue his or her goals in life, that the obstacles to an autonomous life that he or she faces are greater. Similarly, social problems such as crime, poor health, and poor education can also dramatically narrow the range of options an individual faces, and so they too raise barriers to his or her autonomy. This is why those concerned with autonomy must support efforts to undo the pattern of economic inequality that exists between white and black Americans, a pattern that means black individuals are more likely to face higher barriers to an autonomous life than their white counterparts. Those concerned with continuing racial inequality in the United States, then, can use the language of color-blind liberalism to push for more state efforts to close the racial economic gap, to alleviate the social problems disproportionately afflicting black Americans, and in so doing to move toward economic and social conditions more supportive of black autonomy.

Color-blind liberalism's strengths at the level of the state spill over into civil society, because its focus on individual rights, procedural protections, equality of opportunity, and nondiscrimination provides a basis for the state to take action to protect individuals in civil society. The discrimination, reduced opportunities, economic inequality, and disproportionate social burdens black citizens bear within civil society threaten their autonomy, and so state action to alleviate these burdens can help support autonomy, or at least help reduce threats to it. This is why the left's interpretation of color-blind liberalism is still critically important. It provides African Americans and others committed to the struggle for black freedom with the language to continue to push the state to help fight barriers to black autonomy that still exist in civil society. Finally, color-blind liberalism also provides a moral language those committed to autonomy can employ to directly challenge institutions and individuals in civil society, independent of state action, by shaming them into reforming discriminatory practices and working to open up more social and economic opportunities to black Americans.

I am arguing, then, that some elements of the color-blind paradigm should remain central to a liberal understanding of race and American civil society. But they are not enough. As chapter 3 demonstrated, color-blind liberalism's focus on fighting discrimination, working for equality of opportunity, and addressing economic and social inequality in civil society are only partially effective. The color-blind paradigm overlooks a host of other factors that turn out to be decisive. Color-blind principles must therefore take their place in a broader understanding of race within American liberalism, one that uses autonomy to consider factors beyond those included in the color-blind paradigm.

## MOVING BEYOND COLOR-BLIND LIBERALISM

At the moral core of color-blind liberalism lies the vision of an integrated society, one in which race does not matter to one's prospects in life. At the other extreme lies the segregated society, one in which one's race means everything. American civil society fits neither model; it is partially integrated and partially segregated. De jure segregation has fallen, but complete integration has not come. Black and white Americans are distributed across the country, but we still tend to live in largely segregated neighborhoods with largely segregated schools. Most of the nation's universities are integrated, but classes, dormitories, and cafeterias are often not. The economy is integrated in a broad sense, with the growth of a significant black middle class in the last several decades, and with black Americans visible in business, industry, government jobs, and the major professions. African Americans are, however, still grossly underrepresented in some economic sectors, overrepresented in others, disproportionately unemployed, and making less than their white counterparts. American television programs feature black characters in a wide variety of roles, but the most popular shows among black and white Americans are very different (Farhi 1994). The popular music charts are full of both white and black artists, but we tend to go to separate clubs when we dance to the music these artists produce. American courtrooms have both black and white judges, lawyers, defendants, and jurors, but our perceptions of criminal behavior and our reactions to verdicts, O. J. Simpson's for example, are often very different. Black and white Americans often shop side by side in the same malls and sit next to each other at the same sporting events, but we still go to largely segregated churches. More and more white and black Americans come into contact with each other in civil society, but such relationships are often stiff and formal. We know each other as acquaintances, but not so much as intimate friends or lovers. We see each other at work, but not so much at weddings or funerals where our family and closest friends gather.

This state of affairs should not be surprising. Integration is far from an all or nothing choice. Many people cry that we must be either one common people or two separate ones, but this dichotomy is far too simplistic. We are both. Today, white and black Americans are culturally, socially, and economically integrated to a great extent as one people. We are, however, also culturally, socially, and economically separated to a great extent as two distinct groups. Sometimes race does not matter, but other times it does. This is why a liberal understanding of race must rely on group-conscious considerations in addition to color-blind ones when it comes to American civil society.

## Race and the Shape of American Civil Society

Race is part of an American civil society with many dimensions. It is in its broadest form a space that all Americans share, a network of institutions, practices, and meanings that we all contribute to and draw upon to some extent. There is, then, a common American civil society, just as there is a common American culture that helps define it. But this broader civil society is constituted by many smaller networks of institutions, practices, and meanings that are distinct but intertwined. These establish a vast array of smaller and distinct cultural, social, and economic spaces that are nested within and overlap each other in the broader space provided by the common American civil society. It is within these smaller spaces that men and women live their everyday lives, and so what goes on within them is critical to their autonomy. Paying attention to autonomy in American civil society, then, also means paying attention to the smaller, distinct spaces that make it up. Some of the most important of these have always been those carved out by America's various cultural groups, groups formed along both ethnic and racial lines. Throughout American history, racial and ethnic groups have marked off distinct spaces in which they develop their own cultural, social, and economic resources for members to draw upon.[5] Cultural groups, then, are one of the most important elements structuring American civil society, because they play a major role in defining those spaces that give it its ultimate shape.

It is important to keep in mind, however, that the influence of cultural groups on the shape of American civil society is not all-encompassing. Cultural group identity is rarely the only aspect of a person's self-image. In the United States, as in most modern countries in the West, such an identity is usually only one element in a person's self-concept, an element that he or she may emphasize or de-emphasize in different areas of his or her life (Heisler 1991). Group identity and participation in a group's cultural, social, and economic activities are highly variable, they are far more important to some group members than to others, their salience can become more or less powerful over time, and they compete with many other sources of identity and participation in American life. This is part of the reason group membership cannot be locked into a scheme of group rights; it is simply too fluid, partial, and multidimensional to be nailed down in any formal way. For example, a person's Jewish American identity and her participation in distinctly Jewish American cultural, social, and economic space may be less important to her than to her brother, and they may be far less important to both of them than they were to their grandfather. Furthermore, this aspect of her life can grow more important as she grows older, or less so. Finally, she can also draw on her identity and status as a woman, a New Englander, an attorney, or a conservative Republican. Individuals do draw cultural, social, and economic resources from their cultural groups, but they also draw them from sources outside of these groups. Cultural groups, then, are only one of many elements structuring American civil society and the prospects for autonomy within it. They are important in civil society, but not exclusively so.

To the extent that such groups do contribute to those distinct spaces that give American civil society its shape, however, they should be of particular interest to those concerned with autonomy. Living an autonomous life becomes possible only within the specific spaces in civil society that individuals find themselves in, including those marked off by the cultural groups to which they belong. As I argued in chapter 4, membership in cultural groups is critical to autonomy, in both its internal and external dimensions, because it locates persons within those institutions, practices, and meanings that influence their range of options and give their lives meaning. In doing so, it provides them with the kinds of internal and external resources they need to construct autonomous lives for themselves. A concern for autonomy, therefore, demands attention to cultural-group membership and the resources it provides, and this in turn demands attention to those distinct spaces in civil society in which cultural groups develop and provide these kinds of resources to their members.

Black and white Americans are two distinct cultural groups, each locating their members within American civil society and providing resources their members need to construct autonomous lives. This is not to say that they are tightly unified or that they are the only cultural groups to which their members may belong. Two black Americans or two white Americans can have little else in common. Furthermore, one may be both a white American as well as a Polish American, or a black American as well as a Haitian American.[6] It is, however, particularly difficult to be both a white and black American. Even those of mixed-race heritage who consider themselves members of both groups find it difficult to have their dual membership accepted by either one. The American pattern is that you are one, the other, or neither, but you can rarely be both, and generally if you have any discernable blackness, then black you are. My point is that the division between black and white is not set in stone, and it is not the only membership one can hold, but it is nonetheless very real and very important to how one's life unfolds.

This distinct status as a cultural group is readily apparent in the case of black Americans given their existence as a historically subordinated minority. As Gayraud Wilmore argues, "within American culture as a whole there has been and continues to be an exceedingly complex and distinctive subculture that may be designated black or Afro-American," and this is a subculture forged for group survival during a centuries long process of white oppression (1983, 220). Similarly, C. Eric Lincoln and Lawrence Mamiya claim that "black people created their own unique and distinctive forms of culture and worldviews as parallels rather than replications of the culture in which they were involuntary guests" (1990, 2). Contemporary researchers continue to identify and explore a distinctive African American belief system or worldview, as well as the rich and unique cultural tradition of black language, music, dance, stories, body styles, foods, rituals, and so on, a tradition reaching all the way back to its West African roots.[7] Black cultural identity is developed, maintained, and expressed in the institutions, practices, and meanings of black civil society. Historically, the institution most closely associated with black civil society is the black church, and indeed, in the years following emancipation it was the only significant institution under black control. As Taylor Branch writes, "It served not only as a place of worship but also as a bulletin board to a people who owned no organs of communication, a credit union to those without banks, and even a kind of people's court" (1988, 3). Over the years, however, other institutions became important and joined the church in carving out what remains a distinctly black civil society. Such institutions include black mutual aid and benevolent societies, schools and colleges, fraternities and sororities, newspapers and magazines, neighborhood and professional associations, museums and libraries, businesses and credit unions, social clubs and sports leagues, political organizations and trade unions, and bars and dance halls. These institutions occupy a space that is also defined by

black cultural products such as food, music, dance, dialect, dress, stories, poetry, literature, ceremonies, and holidays. It is space structured
by shared meanings, traditions, practices, and social networks. Black
civil society, in short, is the cultural, social, and economic space that
encompasses those institutions, practices, and meanings defined and
dominated by black Americans.

While black Americans are often recognized as a distinct cultural
group with their own cultural, social, and economic space in civil society, the fact that this is also true for white Americans is often overlooked. It is often thought that white Americans do not comprise a distinct cultural group in the way black Americans do, that they are far too
numerous and diverse to be considered a single group. The fact is both
black and white Americans are numerous and diverse, but this does not
mean they cannot both be, in a crucial sense, distinct cultural groups.
Indeed, in recent years researchers have begun to uncover and examine
a distinctly white cultural identity in the United States.[8] White Americans are not somehow racially neutral, as if black group identity hinges
on a departure from some kind of nonracial norm. Rather, race structures white lives and identities just as it does those of black Americans.
In spite of dramatic ethnic, social, regional, religious, and economic
diversity, white Americans do in fact share a common cultural identity.
Those with little else in common do share white skin, and this positions
them in American life in a way unavailable to black Americans.

While we can refer to a distinctly black civil society with its own
institutions, practices, and meanings, we can also refer to a distinctly
white civil society as that complex network of institutions, practices,
and meanings defined and dominated by white Americans. Neither one,
nor even the two of them together, totally defines the shape of American civil society as a whole, and they also experience significant
exchange across their borders. They are, however, distinct and unique.
Each exists in that cultural, social, and economic space in which group
members predominate. Members of each group are to a great extent at
home within their own institutions, practices, and meanings and
strangers within those of the other. The crucial difference, however, is
that while the distinct space defining black civil society sits at the margins of American life, that defining white civil society sits squarely at its
center. Both spaces come nested within the larger context of American
civil society as a whole, but the one dominated by white Americans is
the much larger, secure, and more powerful one, and it usually squeezes
black civil society far off to the margins. This is why the importance of
white civil society to white Americans often goes unnoticed; it overlaps
to such a great extent with American civil society generally. White
Americans are often able to think of success or failure as an entirely indi-

vidual matter, because the group resources to which they have access in mainstream civil society form a largely unnoticed background to their lives. The institutions, practices, and meanings of white civil society are often taken for granted by white Americans, because they are the same ones that remain predominant in American life generally.

This overlap between white defined and dominated institutions, practices, and meanings and those of American civil society generally is why black and white Americans often find themselves positioned so differently in American life. It is why cultural-group membership is so critical to how black and white citizens stand in mainstream civil society, and thus to how they experience autonomy. White Americans have access to cultural, social, and economic resources provided them within the mainstream institutions, practices, and meanings of civil society in a way that black Americans do not. This makes white skin a resource with a powerful currency in American life. It ensures that those who have it are treated as white, that they occupy a position of privilege and power unavailable to black citizens. It means that white Americans find themselves more welcome, more at home, in mainstream institutions and networks dominated by their fellow group members. They share a common bond of racial identity with those who hold cultural, social, economic, and political power in the United States. Perhaps most importantly, they do not bear the mark of slavery and all the cultural assumptions of inferiority it carries. Their burden of proof is easier than that facing black citizens in American life: they have to prove their incompetence, ignorance, criminality, and dishonesty rather than having to prove their competence, intelligence, law-abidingness, and integrity. All this is why, as I claimed in chapter 3, black Americans are often at a sharp disadvantage within mainstream civil society. Its institutions, practices, and meanings are generally not their own. They are unable to draw on the cultural, social, and economic resources of mainstream civil society to the extent that white Americans are able to, because such resources tend to be those defined and dominated by white Americans as a distinct cultural group.

A liberal understanding of race, then, must go beyond a focus on individuals alone to recognize how cultural groups structure American civil society. It must recognize the extent to which membership in such groups shapes how both white and black Americans stand within the web of institutions, practices, and meanings that defines American life. Such membership is critical to autonomy because it influences the kinds of internal and external resources people can draw upon in civil society, resources that they need to construct autonomous lives for themselves. While white Americans enjoy secure membership in a flourishing majority group with its own cultural, social, and economic space that dominates American civil society, this is not the case for black Americans as a historically oppressed and marginalized minority. As a distinct cultural group, African Americans are vulnerable in a way the white majority is not. Their group security, integrity, and power is not a given the way it is for white Americans. This makes the space defined by black civil society particularly important for black men and women, and of particular concern for anyone committed to the ideal of autonomy. As a vulnerable cultural minority whose members are not able to draw on the institutions, practices, and meanings of American civil society in the same way the white majority is able to, African Americans rely in critical ways on their group's own distinct space in order to develop and provide resources to group members, resources critical to their autonomy.

## The Importance of Black Civil Society

The institutions, practices, and meanings of black civil society have played a vital historical role in helping African Americans survive in the United States as a persecuted minority. They provide what Cornel West calls a "cultural armor" protecting black citizens from continual assault at the hands of white America (1993, 23). Robin Kelley (1994), for example, argues that the black working class has historically relied upon distinct cultural practices—things like songs, jokes, stories, body styles, clothing, and speech—to assert its own identity and resist subordination in white-dominated institutions. It has been able to carve out its own informal cultural space both within white-controlled institutions, such as a factory floor or behind the counter of a fast food restaurant, as well as outside of them altogether in its own neighborhoods and institutions. On Kelley's account, this alternative space has provided African Americans with a refuge from the humiliations of a white society demanding deference and submission; it has offered them a location in which to resist oppressive treatment and to assert their own identity, worth, and power. Kelly writes: "Hidden in homes, dance halls, and churches, embedded in expressive cultures, is where much of what is choked back at work or in white-dominated public space can find expression" (1994, 51). This historical function of black civil society as a defensive bulwark against white oppression found what is perhaps its most dramatic expression in the modern civil rights movement. It is paradoxical that color-blind liberalism, which overlooks the importance of civil society to such an extent, relies so heavily on the language of the civil rights movement, a movement that itself was rooted so deeply in the institutions of black civil society. The mobilization of black citizens in the 1950s and 1960s to demand their freedom sprang out of black churches and colleges, and it relied heavily upon the work of the black media, black labor unions and businesses, and black voluntary associations of all kinds. At the very time that the color-blind paradigm received its clearest and most powerful public expression, then, the importance of the distinct cultural, social, and economic space controlled by African Americans to their struggle for freedom was the most visible.

It was to the task of extending and strengthening this space that many activists turned with their appeals to black power and black nationalism in the 1960s and 1970s. Such appeals are often condemned as illiberal for their departure from the color-blind paradigm. To the extent that they focus on the importance of black civil society, however, they are important to a liberal understanding of race. Figures like Malcolm X and those advocating black power, for example, contribute a powerful commitment to building and maintaining black culture and community. Malcolm X tells his fellow black Americans that the "white man controls his own school, his own bank, his own economy, his own politics, his own everything—but he also controls yours." He continues, saying, "Just like the white man has control of his, you need to control yours" (1970, 161). In *Black Power*, Stokely Carmichael and Charles Hamilton write: "The concept of Black Power rests on a fundamental premise: *Before a group can enter the open society, it must first close ranks.* By this we mean that group solidarity is necessary before a group can operate effectively from a bargaining position of strength in a pluralistic society" (1967, 44, italics in original). Just as other cultural groups throughout American history have attended to their own concerns and provided for their own members by "building Irish Power, Italian Power, Polish Power, or Jewish Power," Carmichael and Hamilton argue that African Americans must do the same (1967, 51). On their account, this means strengthening and making more independent the economic and social institutions in black communities rather than relying so much on those dominated by white Americans. It also means black Americans must define themselves through their own cultural meanings rather than living under those imposed upon them by white Americans: "From now on we shall view ourselves as African-Americans and as black people who are in fact energetic, determined, intelligent, beautiful and peace-loving" (1967, 38).

This focus on the importance of a distinct and independent black civil society in the language of black power and black nationalism is far from incompatible with a liberal understanding of race in the United States. Indeed, it has much to contribute to such an understanding, because the strength and vitality of black civil society is so important to the autonomy of black men and women. As an alternative cultural, social, and economic space defined and controlled by African Americans, black civil society plays a critical role in providing both the internal and external resources black men and women need to construct autonomous lives for themselves.

Autonomy depends upon a cultural context in which an individual's internal choices make sense. People need inner standards to guide their choices in life, and they draw these from their interaction with others. Internal ideas about the kind of person they want to be and the kind of life they want to lead become meaningful only in a dialogue with those around them, those with whom they share certain cultural norms and meanings. In this way, the cultural resources provided individuals by group membership are critical to the exercise of autonomy. They are the moral materials people use to construct autonomous lives for themselves, and they are the kind developed, expressed, and passed on within the space of black civil society. Black Americans participate in a distinct cultural tradition that provides an ongoing dialogue about the content of a good life, about the nature of a good person, about worthy values and norms of behavior, about justice and human dignity, about the proper relationship of individual members to their families and communities, and so on. African American culture, in short, provides its members with a context in which their lives take on meaning, thus making it possible for an individual's decisions about his or her life to be meaningful as well.

For African Americans, it is particularly important that the kind of cultural resources developed and passed along to members within black civil society be ones that affirm black possibility, ones that counter the cultural messages predominant in American civil society at large by celebrating black intelligence, ability, beauty, talent, worth, and integrity. They need to assert that black men and women can in fact lead a full range of rich, satisfying, and valuable lives. They must provide a cultural context that makes group members aware of the worthy kinds of people they can become and the rich kinds of lives they can lead. To enhance autonomy, black culture must awaken the black self-awareness, self-confidence, and self-respect that is continually threatened by the meanings at work in the dominant American culture. In the words of Derrick Bell, this is the work of decolonizing black minds (1987, chap. 9). It is the imperative behind the efforts of the black power movement to fight the "internal inferiorization" of white supremacy by making black beautiful and powerful (Smith 1995, chap. 5). It is the idea behind black nationalist and Afrocentric attempts to highlight a noble tradition of black cultural accomplishment, integrity, and independence (Lincoln 1994, chap. 2; Asante 1987 and 1990). And it is central to the message of Malcolm X, which, according to Cornel West, demands an internal "psychic conversion" from black men and women, one leading them to "affirm themselves as human beings, no longer viewing their bodies, minds, and souls through white lenses, and believing themselves capable of taking control of their own destinies" (West 1993, 136).

On West's account, this kind of cultural conversion is only possible through "those institutions in civil society still vital enough to promote self-worth and self-affirmation" (1993, 30). Black churches, mosques, and schools, for example, have this capacity. They are able to serve as "those intermediate institutions that affirm the humanity of black people, accent their capacities and potentialities, and foster the character and excellence requisite for productive citizenship" (West 1993, 88). Through black religious institutions and schools, the black media, black literature and poetry, black music, black ceremonies and holidays, and black museums and libraries that record black history and achievement, black civil society is able to provide the cultural meanings, values, and standards African Americans can use to reflect on and make decisions about the course of their lives. In this way, black culture and those institutions that express it are able to provide the internal materials black men and women can use to construct autonomous lives for themselves.

Autonomy also hinges in large part on the range of external options people face in life, and these options are provided by the social institutions and networks they are a part of. As a subordinated minority in the United States, African Americans have carved out the distinct space of black civil society in order to provide the kinds of opportunities and support to group members that they often lack in American civil society at large. As such, black civil society constitutes an independent and alternative social space that black men and women can draw upon in constructing their lives. Through black-controlled institutions and networks, it furnishes group members with more choices and room to develop, expanding their range of options and providing them with social support in times of need. This gives black Americans greater control over their lives in a country where they historically have had little.

In the crucible of slavery, discrimination, and exploitation, black Americans have forged a long and powerful group self-help tradition. This is a tradition created out of historical necessity, since, in the words of Marsha Jean Darling, "if African Americans did not do for themselves, no one else did" (1994, 121). The oldest and perhaps most important element in this tradition is the black family. Black family ties tend to be more extended than those of whites, with a larger group of kin sharing more family functions. This provides an extensive network of family members across several generations to help with things like income support in times of need, household chores, care for children, and job contacts during periods of unemployment. Black families tend to be more flexible in the performance of family roles depending on who is best able to fill them at particular times, and they are often better able to absorb new members into their structure when the need arises, as when the children of kin in crisis need a new or temporary home. The black family also provides an extended mentoring network to draw upon, one that often includes members in many areas of the country and in many fields of employment.[9]

The black self-help tradition has also relied upon a host of other institutions in black civil society from before the Civil War to the present. Black Americans have worked through their own churches and mosques, benevolent societies, insurance cooperatives, schools and universities, neighborhood groups, orphanages, professional and trade associations, fraternal lodges, mentoring networks, and voluntary groups of all kinds to provide mutual support, to extend aid to those in need, and to expand the range of social options available to group members.[10] Even institutions not formally designed to promote group self-help and mutual aid can perform this function. Black bars, for example, provide an alternative space defined and dominated by black men and women in which they can interact, network, exchange news and information, and engage in expressive and leisure activities such as dancing and drinking (Oliver 1994, chap. 3). These kinds of institutions help give African Americans more room to define their own identities and goals in life, as well as providing the kinds of social interaction needed to pursue these goals in cooperation with others.

There is a close relationship between the autonomy-supporting role played by institutions in black civil society and black cultural identity. Researchers have found that black individuals with higher levels of group consciousness—or a closer identification with black Americans as a proud, worthy, strong, and accomplished cultural group—tend to participate in the voluntary associations of black civil society at higher levels.[11] In this way, an internal identification with a positive African American cultural identity, something that is itself important to the inner process of autonomy, also helps to strengthen the social institutions of black civil society that provide important external resources for autonomy. This link between strengthening the internal image black Americans have of themselves as well as the external institutions of black civil society at the same time has its roots in movements like Marcus Garvey's Universal Negro Improvement Association, which tried to boost black pride and cultural awareness while building independent black social institutions, and it continues in many organizations today such as the Nation of Islam (Lincoln 1994, chaps. 2–4). It is through the distinct institutions, practices, and meanings of black civil society, then, that African Americans are able to develop the cultural and social resources that group members draw upon for autonomy, resources that help provide both the internal and external conditions that the meaningful exercise of autonomy requires.

Some of the most important external resources black civil society can provide for black men and women are economic ones. A person's individual and family economic status is clearly important to his or her autonomy, because it influences the range of options he or she faces in life. In their study of wealth inequality between black and white Americans, Melvin Oliver and Thomas Shapiro argue that it is so disturbing because "family assets expand choices, horizons, and opportunities for children while lack of assets limit opportunities" (1995, 7). This is why I argue that the left's interpretation of color-blind liberalism and its emphasis on state action to address individual and family inequality between black and white Americans is still important to a liberal understanding of race. The issue, however, goes well beyond individual or family economic status; it is also tied to the economic resources of cultural groups. The color-blind view tries to make one's race irrelevant to one's economic status, but the two are nonetheless still bound up with each other in important ways. Jeremiah Cotton (1992) and James Jennings (1992b) both argue against seeing black economic well-being simply in terms of black individuals or families. Instead, they claim that it is inescapably linked to the economic resources of the entire group. In this way, black economic self-help should refer not only to that of individual African Americans, but also to collective efforts by black Americans united together. This is why the African American tradition of collective self-help has always had a crucial economic dimension.

As such an economically vulnerable cultural group, black Americans have always relied on extended kin and friendship networks to provide an informal safety net through pooling assets and borrowing and lending money when necessary (Lincoln and Mamiya 1990, 240–241). In this way, one of the most important informal sources of group support in black civil society is the sharing of scarce economic resources. African Americans have also developed an important array of formal economic institutions from the antebellum period to the present to develop and provide economic resources to group members. Following the Civil War, black-owned banks and insurance companies grew out of many prewar mutual aid societies and benevolent associations. The nineteenth century also saw the growth of a strong entrepreneurial tradition among black Americans with the rise of many black businesses (Butler 1991; Lincoln and Mamiya 1990, chap. 9; Darling 1994). These institutions have always played a critical role in providing economic support for African Americans facing discrimination in mainstream economic life, and they continue to do so today. Black business owners, for example, continue to have a dramatically better record of hiring black workers than their white cohorts do. In his study of the American small-business sector, Timothy Bates finds that white-owned businesses almost exclusively hire white applicants and exclude black ones, even when these businesses are located in black communities, while black-owned businesses consistently hire black workers, even when these businesses are located outside of black neighborhoods (1993, chap. 5). Bates writes that even "their geographic separation from ghetto areas has not severed the employment link between black-owned businesses and black job seekers" (1993, 12). In this way, black-owned businesses and financial institutions do not simply boost the economic status of their owners, but also that of black Americans generally through their hiring, business, and lending practices. The economic resources of black civil society—things like black firms and small businesses, banks and credit unions, professional associations and trade unions—provide an alternative economic context for black men and women to draw upon. This is a space with economic power under the control of group members. It is a space that is able to retain and build capital in black communities rather than seeing it simply pass through. To the extent that the range of options facing black men and women hinges on economic issues, then, it is not simply their individual or family status, but the economic resources of black civil society itself that is critical to autonomy.

While the cultural, social, and economic space of black civil society is so important in providing African Americans with the internal and external resources they need to construct autonomous lives for themselves, it is a space that is far from secure. As a historically marginalized and subordinated minority, black Americans often find the institutions of black civil society fragile and vulnerable within a larger and often hostile American society. This means that one of the most important resources developed within black civil society is the political power necessary for its own protection. An independent and strong black civil society hinges in large part on the political influence black Americans can wield in support of it. This ability to protect black civil society, however, is not the only reason political power is so important to the autonomy of black men and women. It is also critical to efforts by black Americans to force open more economic and social opportunities in mainstream, white-dominated civil society. Political leverage is often the only way to demand an end to discriminatory and exploitative practices in American life that raise barriers to black autonomy. Such political activism is also an important symbolic way for black Americans to demand and win public recognition of group legitimacy, thereby contributing to group pride and cultural awareness. Continually fighting for a seat at the political table allows African Americans to publicly declare their status as a legitimate cultural group in the United States. In this way, then, the autonomy of black men and women often hinges on the group's using networks and institutions in black civil society to mobilize and initiate direct confrontations with state power. Through such group mobilization and empowerment, African Americans can challenge state power and carve out a share of it for themselves, using it to publicly assert their worth and influence as a distinct cultural group, while at the same time demanding public policies that both help strengthen institutions in black civil society and help fend off threats to autonomy within the larger economic and social spheres of American life.[12]

This link between civil society and political action is nothing new among cultural groups in the United States, a country in which membership in such groups has always been a powerful basis for political mobilization. Race and ethnicity are both particularly effective markers around which to recruit people to a political cause, because, as Daniel Bell argues, cultural groups combine symbolic and expressive appeals with concrete and material ones (1975, 165–166). Such groups are able to assert both their material interests and their cultural identity through political action (Cochran 1995–96). They mobilize politically to force concessions from the state, to help define and protect their own group resources, and to win public recognition of group worth, usually through the elevation of group members to positions of political power and prominence (Litt 1970, 31; Banfield and Wilson 1966, 41–42; Wolfinger 1966, 47–49). African Americans are no different. In spite of considerable social and economic diversity among black Americans, they remain a cultural group with their own distinct political identity, interests, opinions, and behavior trends (Dawson 1994). As such, their political mobilization remains critically important to their autonomy.

In the context of liberal democratic politics, the key to this kind of political mobilization, especially for a group like black Americans with little preexisting economic or political clout, is increasing political participation among members. Here political participation does not simply refer to voting, but also to a host of other activities as well—things like attending protests or mass meetings, organizing or supporting grassroots campaigns, contacting elected officials, joining political organizations, working for political parties, signing petitions, and so on. These are the kinds of activities that are rooted in black civil society. Indeed, many of the most important institutions of black civil society, from the NAACP to A. Philip Randolph's Brotherhood of Sleeping Car Porters to the Black Panthers, have been primarily political groups, and many other institutions, such as black churches and colleges, have taken on important political roles throughout their history. One activist and writer who has done much to highlight this important link between the need for black political mobilization and the strength of black civil society is

James Jennings. Jennings (1992b) argues that collective social and economic self-help efforts in black civil society are critically important to black progress, but that this is only possible in the modern United States if a responsive government provides a supportive context for such efforts. On his account, black political empowerment is the only way to ensure a government that acts in such a way. Jennings (1992a) outlines a vision of what he calls "black empowerment activism." This sort of activism goes beyond traditional coalition and party politics within the existing power structure to mobilize the black poor and working class on a grassroots community level to exercise political influence over specific local issues of concern to the life of the community. It puts its emphasis on gaining more community control over independent black institutions such as schools, neighborhoods, businesses, and political institutions. Its goal is to achieve more group power rather than mere access to the existing power structure for a few black individuals. Jennings argues that developing this kind of political mobilization requires the cultivation of black cultural awareness, unity, and group consciousness. On his account, strengthening the institutions of black civil society and politically empowering black communities on the local level are both inseparable from the need to create a sense of group cooperation, pride, and common purpose.

Jennings is correct to highlight the important relationship between political mobilization, the institutions of civil society, and cultural-group consciousness. While levels of political participation for white as well as black Americans are largely a function of socioeconomic status, they are also positively related to levels of participation in the nonpolitical associations and institutions of civil society (London 1975). Boosting participation in civil society therefore boosts political participation. Indeed, researchers have long found that when socioeconomic status is held constant, black Americans often show higher levels of social and political participation than white Americans. As we saw above, many scholars have found evidence of a "group consciousness" or "ethnic community" explanation for this.[13] On their account, black Americans tend to experience stronger group identification and cohesion as a minority amidst an often hostile majority. This means they take a more active role in the institutions and associations of their own communities and more often see their fate linked to that of their group. This heightened group identity and increased involvement in black civil society leads to higher rates of political participation. In this way, the space occupied by black civil society and the black cultural identity cultivated within it can provide a foundation for political mobilization—mobilization that can, in turn, strengthen and protect the kinds of autonomy-supporting resources developed in that space, that can publicly assert

the worth and integrity of African Americans as a distinct cul
group, and that can demand that the state help protect black citi.
from the threats to their autonomy, such as discrimination and economic exploitation, that they still routinely face in the United States.

I am arguing, then, that a liberal understanding of race in the United
States must recognize the importance of black civil society to the autonomy of black men and women. It is an alternative and independent space
in which African Americans can develop and provide the cultural, social,
economic, and political resources that group members can draw upon in
constructing their lives, and as such, it contributes to both the internal
and external requirements of autonomy. A liberal understanding of race
can begin to better account for this importance not only by recognizing
it in a general way, but also by examining how specific institutions
within black civil society contribute to the autonomy of black men and
women in various ways. Doing so can begin to open up the liberal dialogue about race to specific factors too often overlooked. While many
institutions in black civil society are good candidates for such examination, I think it is most useful to illustrate the point by briefly considering just one of them here. The black church is an excellent example of
an institution that provides the cultural, social, economic, and political
resources that we have just seen are so critical to the autonomy of black
men and women. As such, it is just the kind of institution a liberal understanding of race must concern itself with.

## The Black Church

While there is some debate over what exactly the term "the black
church" refers to, most scholars take it to mean congregations that are
part of the major independent and historically black Christian denominations in the United States (Lincoln and Mamiya 1990, 1). While many
black Americans embrace religious traditions outside of Christianity, the
dominant religious tradition among African Americans both historically
and today is Christianity, and while there are predominately black congregations in white denominations such as the United Methodist, Episcopal, and Roman Catholic Churches, the bulk of black Christians, over
80 percent in fact, still belong to one of the seven historically black-controlled denominations.[14] This black religious tradition has been at the
center of African American life from slavery through the present. Indeed,
C. Eric Lincoln and Lawrence Mamiya claim that "the Black Church has
no challenger as the cultural womb of the black community" (1990, 8),
and they argue that it is still "one of the strongest, most stable, and most
independent institutional areas in the black community nationwide"
(1990, 261).

Theologians and sociologists have long recognized that black Christianity is not simply a copy of the religion given to slaves by their European captors, but rather a unique spiritual and cultural tradition, what Lincoln and Mamiya call a distinct "black sacred cosmos," forged by African Americans during centuries of slavery and oppression.[15] As Lincoln, one of the most influential students of black religion, writes: "The black religious experience is something more than a black patina on a white happening. It is a unique response to a historical occurrence that can never be replicated for any other people in America" (1983, vii). Looking back on the history of African Americans who came before him, Lincoln finds this religious experience critically important:

> The black pilgrimage in America was made less onerous because of their religion. Their religion was the organizing principle around which their life was structured. Their church was their school, their forum, their political arena, their social club, their art gallery, their conservatory of music. It was lyceum and gymnasium as well as *sanctum sanctorum*. Their religion was the peculiar sustaining force that gave them the strength to endure when endurance gave no promise, and the courage to be creative in the face of their own destruction. (1983, vii, italics in original)

For Lincoln, then, much of the importance of black religion and black churches lies in the contributions they make in the long and difficult quest for black liberation in America. He writes, "Black persons' religion has been a critical component of their American passage from slavery to a freedom that is still to be perfected" (1983, vii). In this way, the ideal of freedom has always been at the heart of the black religious experience: "In song, word, and deed, freedom has always been the superlative value of the black sacred cosmos" (Lincoln and Mamiya 1990, 5). So from slavery to the present, the black church in the United States has developed a powerful tradition of linking religious faith with the quest for black liberation. Furthermore, this is a tradition that sees liberation as both an internal and an external process. It understands liberation to be the struggle to overcome the inner spiritual and psychological scars of white oppression as well as the many external barriers to black freedom (Wilmore 1983; Harris 1993). Working for black autonomy in both its internal and external dimensions, then, has always been and continues to be at the center of the cultural, social, economic, and political ministry of the black church.

The black church is one of the primary institutions African Americans rely upon to develop and pass along black cultural resources. It is a space in which the black cultural tradition—one expressed in such things as songs, music, stories, styles of speaking and worship, rituals, celebrations, and religious fellowship—can flourish. This tradition helps provide group members with the meanings, standards, and values they need to make their choices in life meaningful. It furnishes a moral language individuals can use to make decisions about the kind of life they want to lead and the kind of person they want to be. In this way, it helps develop the internal resources necessary for autonomy. Historically, the black church has been one of the few spaces in which African Americans can sustain the kinds of cultural meanings and values that affirm black worth, dignity, and possibility in the face of cultural devaluation and marginalization by the larger society. This potential goes all the way back to the experience of slavery, where slaves took the religion of their masters and transformed it into their own tradition of resisting the tyranny of slavery by professing their own humanity and value and keeping the hope of liberation from bondage alive. In the words of Manning Marable, "Black prophetic Christianity gave spiritual freedom to the slaves, and a sense of humanity that transcended the slavery system" (1986, 201). This tradition within black religion has continued from slavery through to the present. According to Forrest Harris, the black church has always been and continues to be one of the primary areas in which black Americans can interpret their own experience in a positive way, asserting their own humanity, creativity, ability, and power in order to envision and work toward the accomplishments they are capable of reaching (1993, 40–48). It provides a context in which black Americans can reflect on and develop goals in life that they consider worthy and valuable, a process central to the exercise of autonomy.

Autonomy also hinges in large part on the external range of options, sources of support, and avenues of achievement provided people by the social institutions and networks surrounding them, and the black church has always been one of the most important spaces in which these kinds of social resources are available to African Americans in a variety of ways. First, in a country where mainstream avenues of achievement and positions of social status and respect have been historically closed to African Americans, black churches have always been alternative institutions in which they can occupy valuable and respected social roles. The most obvious of these of course is that of minister, a position that for many years was one of the only professions open to young black men of ambition and talent.[16] Besides the job of minister, however, black churches also rely on a wide range of lay members, both men and women, belonging to church clubs and committees of all kinds and filling positions on the church staff as ushers, deacons, choir members, youth group leaders, secretaries, financial officers, and so on (Baer and Singer 1992, chap. 3; Lincoln and Mamiya 1990, chaps. 5–6; Freedman 1993). As Lincoln and Mamiya write: "The proliferation of such internal service groups in black churches helps to spread the available quantums of status, dignity, and recognition among lay members. Black people who are largely invisible or who have only marginal identities in their workday roles in the larger society receive confirmation of their humanity and dignity through such church activities" (1990, 147). The black church, then, is an important source of alternative and valuable social roles available to individuals in black civil society, helping to expand the range of meaningful options available to them throughout their lives.

Second, the black church is one of the most important independent spaces in which black social networks and activities exist. The extended-kin networks and the resources they share that are so important to many African Americans are often bound together by common membership in a black church (Scott and Black 1991; Baer and Singer 1992, chap. 5). The church itself also constitutes an even larger network of people from various walks of life and of various ages and abilities that members can rely upon for fellowship, advice and comfort, inspiration, help in times of need, mentoring relationships, job opportunities, and so on.[17] This kind of social interaction that individuals can draw upon in constructing their lives takes place within the vast array of activities sponsored by black churches. These include things like Bible-study groups, prayer meetings, special-interest clubs such as gardening or art, lectures, concerts, plays, Sunday school classes, choir practices, book clubs, revivals, youth groups, afterschool programs, cookouts, sports leagues, trips, retreats, senior citizen programs, youth scouting troops, dances, fashion shows, potluck suppers, and bazaars. Even when not organized directly by the church itself, black churches often provide facilities for other civic and family groups in black civil society to hold meetings, classes, sporting events, lectures, receptions, banquets, and so on.[18] The black church, in short, is one of the oldest and most effective institutions working to develop a space for black social life to flourish, thereby providing the kind of social interaction so important to the autonomy of black men and women.

Third, some of the most vital social functions performed by the black church in this space have always been those aimed at helping group members in need as part of the black self-help tradition. From their very founding in the late eighteenth and early nineteenth centuries, the first independent black churches launched a host of mutual aid and social-service projects, and they enlarged these efforts in the years following the Civil War (Lincoln and Mamiya 1990, chap. 9). Black churches again expanded their efforts at social outreach and aid during the twentieth century, as many poor African Americans migrated to the urban centers of the Northeast and Midwest looking for a better life but instead finding harsh social and economic conditions (Baer and Singer 1992, chap. 2; Taylor 1994, 53–64). This tradition within black churches remains a powerful part of their ministry today. It includes such things as food banks, homeless shelters, nursing homes, welfare offices, Head Start programs, prison visitation, day care centers, health clinics, mentoring programs, drug and alcohol addiction counseling, college scholarships, low-income housing rehabilitation and rent assistance, neighborhood watch and antidrug patrols, youth counseling, academic tutoring, adult education and literacy classes, programs to fight teenage pregnancy, parenting classes, gang-intervention efforts, college prep classes, adoption services, shut-in visitation and meals, clothing banks, AIDS awareness and outreach, legal services, and shelters for abused women and children.[19] Furthermore, these kinds of programs are not limited to individual black churches, but are also often the focus of broader ecumenical efforts. A wide array of black ecumenical groups in the last several decades have launched programs to fight black violence, gang activity, housing deterioration, drug and alcohol addiction, family disintegration, health care shortages, and low academic performance (Sawyer 1994). Black churches, then, have a long and powerful tradition of organizing collective efforts to reach out and minister to black Americans in need, helping them battle and overcome a wide array of social problems and thereby gain more control over their own lives.

Finally, while the black church is itself an institution at the center of black civil society that provides African Americans with access to social positions, networks, activities, and sources of support, it also provides these kinds of resources indirectly through its history of helping to create and then support with money and members other institutions in black civil society. From the early nineteenth century, black churches and denominations have helped create and then sustain black lodges and clubs of all kinds, fraternities and sororities, mutual aid societies, and newspapers and magazines (Lincoln and Mamiya 1990, chap. 1; Mukenge 1983, 47–48). Black churches have also always worked to create and strengthen black educational institutions at all levels. Many black churches have established their own neighborhood primary and secondary schools over the years, and they have always been strong supporters of black higher education. For example, the first independent black college in the United States, Wilberforce University in Ohio, was established in 1863 by the African Methodist Episcopal Church after raising money from its membership to buy the college (Mukenge 1983, 37). Indeed, over half of all historically black colleges were founded by black religious bodies (Blackwell 1985, 27). Black churches today continue to donate money to black colleges, raise money for their own scholarship funds, and announce academic achievements from the pulpit during services (Lincoln and Mamiya 1990, 251–253). In a variety of ways, then, the black church provides many kinds of social resources African Americans can draw upon in constructing autonomous lives for themselves, and it does this both directly as an important institution itself and indirectly through its influence on other institutions in black civil society.

In addition to the general social resources important for autonomy that the black church furnishes, it also provides certain economic resources that help expand the range of options open to African Americans in a country where mainstream economic opportunities are historically rather narrow. Black churches often serve as a network in which members can find jobs, and the social programs many of them offer include employment services—things like job listings, training programs, résumé and application workshops, and counseling—and small business services—things like legal and financial advice, fiscal planning workshops, business networking, entrepreneurial classes, computer demonstrations, and technical assistance (Lincoln and Mamiya 1990, chap. 9; Freedman 1993; Taylor 1994). These kinds of services provide group members with the support they often need to improve or simply maintain their economic status and security. On an even deeper level, however, the black church is itself one of the strongest and most independent economic institutions in black civil society, one supported by African American giving to religious organizations that tops $2 billion each year (Lincoln and Mamiya 1990, 260). In their survey of black churches, Lincoln and Mamiya report that just over 90% own their own buildings, with 60% having paid off their mortgage and about 50% reporting no significant debt. Additionally, they report that 16% hold investments (usually money market certificates or high interest bank accounts), 7% operate their own businesses, and 14% own revenue-generating real estate (1990, 255–260). While black churches are by no means wealthy and often lack the financial expertise to put their resources to the most profitable use, they are fairly secure economic institutions in a community with few of them. As Lincoln and Mamiya write, "There are probably very few other institutions in the black community that can match this level of ownership and independence" (1990, 258).

Throughout their history, black churches have used this economic independence and power to help foster economic development in black communities, and there is a growing trend among many of them in recent years to try to expand this tradition.[20] The earliest black banks and insurance companies evolved out of church-sponsored benevolent and burial associations, and black churches were also instrumental in the creation of early black businesses such as funeral parlors and mortuaries. Today, black ministers not only pressure local businesses to hire more black employees, but many have started opening church-owned businesses themselves, or loaning church funds to members to do so independently. Many black churches are opening their own banks, credit unions, and economic-development foundations to help foster the growth of black-owned businesses, businesses that in turn tend to hire black workers. They are purchasing and rehabilitating both retail and residential real estate to raise local property values and to improve the local supply of jobs and housing. They are also undertaking efforts to build new homes to sell at a low cost with little interest to local residents in order to address poor housing conditions and to raise levels of home ownership and equity in black communities. Furthermore, while these kinds of projects are ongoing at local levels in black neighborhoods across the country, black ecumenical groups such as the Congress of National Black Churches are trying to coordinate and expand such efforts on a national level (Sawyer 1994). The black church, then, is one of the most important black-controlled institutions that African Americans can use to build and sustain the economic resources of their cultural group, resources that are often critical to the autonomy of group members.

While the black church is a central institution within the space of black civil society where cultural, social, and economic resources so important to autonomy are developed, it has also proven itself a powerful political resource in efforts by African Americans to define and protect this space, as well as to assert their basic rights and interests in American life generally. Baer and Singer (1992) claim that while black churches do have a history of often accommodating white domination as the price of ensuring black survival in the United States, they also frequently resist this domination when they are able to, through political action aimed at securing black freedom. As such, the black church has always been one of the most important political institutions under the control of African Americans. This means, according to Baer and Singer, that "African-American politics has always had and continues to have a decidedly religious slant, while African-American religion is deeply political" (1992, xvii). This political potential for resistance within black religion goes all the way back to the slave revolts lead by black religious figures like Gabriel Prosser in 1800, Denmark Vesey in 1822, and Nat Turner in 1831 (Wilmore 1983). During slavery black churches also played a critical role in abolitionist political agitation and in helping slaves escape to the North (Lincoln and Mamiya 1990, chaps. 2–3, 8; Taylor 1994, 12–13). Following emancipation the black church was instrumental in electing black Americans to political offices across the South, including many ministers themselves. Indeed, the first black citizen ever elected to the U.S. Congress was Rev. Hiram Revels, a member of the African Methodist Episcopal clergy elected to the Senate from Mississippi. During the late nineteenth and into the twentieth centuries, black ministers became the leading political figures among African Americans, because they were among the only black Americans with extensive leadership and organizational experience; they had large, cohesive, organized, and loyal constituencies in place with their congregations; and they occupied a position of economic and social independence within black communities, one relatively insulated from white economic reprisals. During the first half of the twentieth century, many black churches under the leadership of such politically active ministers were instrumental in the creation of political organizations such as the NAACP, the National Urban League, and the Brotherhood of Sleeping Car Porters. They also played important roles as junior partners in many local political machines across the Northeast and Midwest (Lincoln and Mamiya 1990, chap. 8).

With the coming of the civil rights movement in the 1950s and 1960s, of course, the black church continued to play a decisive political role, providing leadership, mass meeting facilities, communication and transportation networks, and thousands of dedicated activists on the front lines.[21] Even the landmark *Brown* decision took its name from a black minister, Rev. Oliver L. Brown of St. Mark's A.M.E. in Topeka, Kansas, who sued his local school board on behalf of his daughter and her fellow black students who had been forced to go to segregated public schools (Lincoln and Mamiya 1990, 211). Today, black churches and ecumenical organizations continue to play critical roles in political action by black Americans at all levels, from presidential election campaigns to grassroots mobilization and protest around specific local issues such as police brutality or tenant rights (Lincoln and Mamiya 1990, chap. 8; Taylor 1994, 191–234; Sawyer 1994). Furthermore, the importance of black consciousness to political mobilization that we saw James Jennings (1992a and 1992b) emphasize in the last section holds true for black churches as well. Lincoln and Mamiya find that higher levels of black group consciousness among black clergy is positively related to their willingness to engage in political action and protest through their churches (1990, chap. 7). Using black churches to raise awareness of black cultural unity and dignity, then, can translate into political empowerment within the space of black civil society. This kind of empowerment is vital to protecting the cultural, social, and economic resources, as well as the fundamental rights and interests, of black Americans as an often vulnerable cultural minority. In this way, then, it is vital to the autonomy that black men and women are ultimately able to exercise in their lives.

As a central institution in black civil society, the black church is one of the most important foundations available to black men and women in constructing autonomous lives for themselves. It provides a space in which African Americans can develop and sustain the kinds of cultural, social, economic, and political resources group members need to exercise autonomy in both its internal and external dimensions. This is not to say that black Americans must belong to a historically black Christian church in order to be autonomous. Many other religious groups also provide similar resources. The Nation of Islam, for example, puts a strong emphasis on things like black cultural awareness, social unity and outreach, self-help efforts, moral standards, and independent economic institutions (Lincoln 1994; McCloud 1995). Furthermore, a host of non-religious institutions in black civil society also work to furnish these kinds of cultural, social, economic, and political resources. My point is that the black church is one such institution among many, and as such it is just the kind of institution that a liberal understanding of race in the United States should account for and examine.

*Forces within Black Communities That Threaten Autonomy*

Black civil society has two closely related functions in supporting the autonomy of black men and women that I think a liberal understanding of race must recognize. The first is the one I have just described. It is the ability of black civil society to provide various kinds of resources that are enabling of black autonomy, resources often not available to African Americans as a distinct and historically marginalized cultural minority. The second, which I have also touched upon when looking at the black self-help tradition of social outreach and economic support, is the ability of black civil society to struggle against certain disabling social forces that threaten autonomy within black communities. Black civil society is not a space in which autonomy is guaranteed or necessarily made easy by the various resources the last two sections examined. Rather, it is a space in which black Americans—like other cultural groups in their distinct cultural, social, and economic space in civil society—also experience and try to overcome disabling factors that undermine autonomy in both its internal and external dimensions.

As I pointed out in chapter 3, black Americans suffer disproportionately from a host of social problems such as crime, violence, family breakdown, and low academic achievement.[22] Furthermore, many of these problems are concentrated in poverty-ridden urban ghettos—areas housing what many scholars, following Wilson (1987), have come to call the black underclass. Such areas are characterized by high levels of unemployment, school failure and dropout rates, violent crime, drug and alcohol abuse, and family disintegration, as well as by widespread social alienation, hopelessness, and despair. These are the kinds of social problems that threaten autonomy by undermining both the internal and external conditions that make it possible. High crime rates, for example, lead to the massive incarceration of young black males, completely eliminating their liberty while in prison, but also dramatically shrinking the range of options they can expect to face for the rest of their lives and draining black communities of husbands, fathers, and friends. High crime rates also create fear among local residents, leading many of them to avoid social contact, to radically adjust their daily activities, and to live out their lives with the feeling of being under siege (Oliver 1994, 2–3). Indeed, as Judith Shklar (1989) argues, living in fear can be a powerful threat to a person's prospects for the free and flourishing life that liberalism celebrates. Similarly, things like low academic achievement, dropping out of school, and drug or alcohol dependency all dramatically narrow the external range of options a person faces in life. They can also undermine an individual's internal confidence and self-image, influencing the kinds of goals he or she sets and the kinds of relationships he or she is able to form. Furthermore, a pervasive sense of hopelessness and alienation can cripple a person's internal capacity to conceive of and pursue a rich and meaningful life. It can undermine his or her ability to draw on the kinds of institutions and networks that provide resources, both internal and external, necessary for autonomy.

Similarly, family breakdown can undermine autonomy by leaving children as well as the single parents left to care for them, most often their mothers, both economically and socially vulnerable. In their research, Sara McLanahan and Gary Sandefur (1994) find that single parents run a higher risk of experiencing economic insecurity, poverty, stress, anxiety, and depression. They report that children growing up in single-parent families not only run a higher risk of living in poverty, but also of experiencing social problems like dropping out of school, receiving lower grades, not going to college, having their own children while still teenagers, not finding a job in their teens and twenties, and engaging in criminal activity. Controlling for economic status, McLanahan and Sandefur find that these social problems are not simply due to the economic consequences of living in single-parent families, but also to the lack of emotional and social support, sharing of family duties, access to social networks, supervision, and stability that two-parent households are better able to provide. Summarizing their conclusions, McLanahan and Sandefur claim that "growing up with only one biological parent frequently deprives children of important economic, parental, and community resources, and that these deprivations ultimately undermine their chances of future success" (1994, 3). In addition to providing resources that contribute to autonomy, then, black civil society is also the cultural, social, and economic space in which black Americans disproportionately experience and struggle to overcome a host of social problems that can undermine their prospects for an autonomous life.

It is these kinds of disabling forces that many people looking in on black communities from the outside make their exclusive focus, frequently and mistakenly considering them the cultural core of black civil society, something the intellectual right in particular is prone to doing. Dinesh D'Souza (1995) provides a particularly dramatic recent example of this. D'Souza argues that contemporary black culture is pathological and uncivilized. It is defined by rampant crime and its glorification, sexual irresponsibility, and the persistent refusal to embrace basic mainstream values like hard work, thrift, responsibility, and honesty. On his account, civil rights and the equal protection of the laws have not brought social and economic equality, because African Americans suffer from severe cultural deficiencies that they refuse to address, preferring instead to blame their own failures on white racism that is no longer a serious obstacle to their progress. It is a black "civilizational breakdown" rather than racism that is the real problem for African Americans today. D'Souza writes: "At every socioeconomic level, blacks are uncompetitive on those measures of achievement that are essential to modern industrial society. Many middle-class African Americans are, by their own account, distorted in their social relations by the consuming passion of black rage. And nothing strengthens racism in this country more than the behavior of the African American underclass, which flagrantly violates and scandalizes basic codes of responsibility, decency, and civility" (1995, 527). D'Souza claims that racism today is nothing more than an understandable response to the gap in civilized behavior that exists between black Americans and the rest of the country. He writes that "the best way to eradicate beliefs in black inferiority is to remove their empirical basis," and that if only "blacks can close the civilization gap, the race problem in this country is likely to become insignificant" (1995, 527). On D'Souza's account, if African Americans want to overcome mainstream beliefs about their inferiority, then they need to stop acting so inferior. In short, they need to stop acting so black, and instead embrace the cultural norms of mainstream and civilized American society. According to D'Souza and those who share his views, then, black culture and civil society are themselves a burden that African Americans must set aside if they are to overcome the disabling social problems they currently experience.

D'Souza's argument, of course, ignores the fact that most African Americans simply do not engage in the kinds of destructive or irresponsible behavior that he claims defines contemporary black culture and civil society. Furthermore, these kinds of behavior are in no way limited to African Americans. Social phenomenon like crime, drug and alcohol abuse, conspicuous consumption, the glorification of violence, sexual irresponsibility, poor school performance, and family breakdown exist in American civil society generally; they reflect broad cultural norms and practices that often characterize the common American culture that both black and white Americans draw upon. In discussing the social problems of black urban youth, for example, Tommy Lott points out that "black popular culture is understandably in many ways a recoding of various elements of mainstream culture that have been adapted to fit the circumstances of extreme-poverty urban neighborhoods" (1992, 72). Indeed, it is as easy to see the same messages glorifying violence, criminal behavior, and treating women as sexual objects in many mainstream "action" films as those found in some black popular music. The primary difference between black and white Americans in this area is not the existence of certain social problems that can undermine autonomy, but rather their extent. African Americans, and particularly those in certain poor black neighborhoods, suffer disproportionately from these kinds of problems, but they in no way have a monopoly on them.

Another important difference to keep in mind, however, is that black Americans often pay a higher price for engaging in the same kinds of behavior. What Robert Halpern says of poor people generally can also be said of African Americans across the board: "The primary difference between poor people and others is in the much greater effects of mistakes when there is so little room for error" (1995, 6). Irresponsible behavior like driving while drunk carried a higher cost at the hands of the police for Rodney King than it did for Ted Kennedy, and assaulting police officers trying to make an arrest usually carries a higher price, often a fatal one, for a young black male in the ghetto than it did for a young man named Pat Buchanan. Similarly, failing to hold a marriage together and allowing a family to break apart often brings a much higher social and economic cost for poor black Americans and their children than it did for people like Ronald Reagan and Newt Gingrich. This difference in costs frequently carries over into public policy as well. For example, crack cocaine, more often used by black Americans, brings a much harsher sentence than powder cocaine, more often used by white Americans (Smith 1995, 72–73). In a similar spirit, early in the 1996 presidential campaign both Bob Dole and Bill Clinton endorsed proposals to make certain social welfare programs that disproportionately benefit black Americans contingent on passing a drug test, while neither candidate publicly extended this logic to cover the kinds of public assistance that go mainly to white farmers, white social security recipients, or white college students receiving guaranteed loans (the single program

I suspect would take a significant hit from such a proposal).

Finally, and most importantly, D'Souza and those who share his views simply fail to acknowledge the influence that larger structural issues, such as economic arrangements and pervasive social discrimination, have on the extent of the disabling social problems experienced by black Americans. As Mack Jones (1992) points out, if by the term "black underclass" people mean a group of black Americans within the social and economic structure of American life who are unskilled, undereducated, unemployed or stuck in low-paying jobs, and living amidst poverty and the desperate social conditions it entails with little hope for any sort of upward mobility, then it is nothing new in the United States. According to Jones, such a group of black Americans has always existed in larger or lesser numbers as the inevitable result of systemic economic conditions and the social and political discrimination that supports them. In the United States, a history of economic exploitation and segregation, changes in the economy that have dramatically reduced the number of blue collar manufacturing jobs available to black urban residents, and continuing practices of discrimination and ghettoization have all combined to create high rates of poverty, unemployment, and underemployment in black communities across the country. These conditions in turn lead to higher levels of crime, drug use, family stress and breakdown, violence, academic underachievement, and alienation.[23] Broad structural factors outside of black civil society, then, help create and aggravate the kinds of social problems that can threaten autonomy within it.

I think the temptation in focusing on structural issues, however, is to go to the opposite extreme from D'Souza and his ilk, looking at these issues alone without allowing for any independent influence within black culture and civil society itself. While this avoids the error of labeling black Americans as pathological or uncivilized, it also falls into the paternalistic trap of labeling black Americans as incapable of any real wrongdoing, of taking them simply as passive victims of larger systemic forces beyond their control. This too is misguided. Black Americans are as capable as white Americans of irresponsible behavior, and black culture and civil society is as capable as that of whites of accommodating destructive forces such as violence, crime, drug and alcohol abuse, misogyny, the breakdown of families, and so on. If the position of African Americans in the broad economic and social structure of the United States dramatically improved, the extent of these kinds of social problems would undoubtedly become less severe, but they would still continue to exist at significant levels, just as they do for white Americans who enjoy advantaged structural positions. While structural forces do have a considerable impact on their extent, cultural groups of all kinds, regardless of their structural status, still experience the kinds of disabling social forces that can undermine the autonomy of group members. Furthermore, these are forces that they often experience and must come to terms with in their own distinct space in civil society. So the mistake is not examining these kinds of problems as cultural and social ones capable of transformation within black civil society. Instead, it is, first, letting people like D'Souza take them to define black culture and civil society as a whole, and, second, not also paying attention to the larger structural context outside of black civil society in which they also exist.

The kind of disabling social problems that threaten autonomy in black communities do so precisely because they are multidimensional. They are tied to both structural conditions outside of black civil society and to cultural and social factors within it, and they undermine autonomy in both its external and internal realms. It only makes sense, then, to address them in different dimensions as well. Such a multidimensional approach locates these kinds of problems and their solutions in larger structural conditions, such as economic arrangements and social discrimination, but also within black civil society itself, and more specifically in the need to revitalize its ability to respond to such problems. This means working for structural change, but it also means cultivating black cultural identity and consciousness, working for group unity and cohesion, and strengthening the distinct institutions, practices, and meanings of black civil society. Such an approach does not, in short, advocate setting aside black culture, identity, and civil society as somehow pathological as people like D'Souza suggest, but rather putting such things at its very center.

A host of scholars and activists in recent years have embraced this kind of multidimensional approach to locating and addressing the kind of social problems that threaten autonomy within black communities. On the right, for example, people like Glenn Loury (1994) and James Wilson (1994) urge scholars and activists to go beyond structural issues alone when considering the social problems of the black urban poor, and to also consider the importance of normative and cultural factors, as well as the institutions in black communities such as families and churches upon which such factors hinge. Many people on the left, however, are also well aware of the importance of such considerations. Manning Marable (1991a) and Cornel West (1993), for instance, are both democratic socialists dedicated to the structural transformation of American economic and social arrangements that disproportionately burden African Americans with the kinds of disabling social problems I am considering here. But they both also see these problems existing within the context of a black civil society often failing to properly respond to them. Marable sees a breakdown within many black families, neighborhoods, and cultural institutions "devastating to the spirit and cultural consciousness of blacks," a breakdown that is allowing forces such as violence, drugs, crime, and alienation to grow to crisis levels (1991a, 191–192). It is a breakdown Marable claims must be addressed in large part by revitalizing black institutions in civil society and by raising black cultural consciousness. West also warns against what he sees as the "gross deterioration of personal, familial, and communal relations among African-Americans" (1993, 56). On his account, the institutions of black civil society are becoming increasingly weak, leading to a growing tide of "pervasive black communal and cultural chaos" threatening black men and women (1993, 86). In order to battle this threat, West urges action to cultivate black unity and cultural awareness and to reverse the decline of black civil society by rebuilding and strengthening "shattered cultural institutions" (1993, 25).

In a similar way, Frank Kirkland (1992) claims that overcoming the tangle of problems afflicting the black urban poor requires structural economic reforms that dramatically lower black joblessness and poverty, but it also requires revitalizing the crumbling institutions of such communities in order to provide the kinds of social support, cultural rootedness, and moral standards that people need to live decent and meaningful lives. Joan Wallace-Benjamin (1994) also claims that an erosion of black civil society has compounded the influence of external structural forces to produce fragmentation, alienation, and alarming levels of disabling social problems in many black communities. She argues that this means black Americans must redouble their efforts to strengthen black institutions like the family and community-based organizations, and to raise black consciousness and cultural pride, in order to mobilize their communities to fight such problems and their devastating effects. James Jennings (1992c) adds the reminder that such mobilization must also be one aiming at effective political power, because only such power can help transform both structural conditions outside of black civil society and cultural institutions within it in ways that attack the disabling social problems afflicting so many black Americans. On Jennings's (1992b) account, many black activists recognize the need to transform black civil society to battle such problems, but in ways that strengthen distinctly black institutions, cultural traditions, and sources of group consciousness, rather than rejecting these things as people like D'Souza urge.

This kind of multidimensional approach to understanding and addressing disabling social problems affecting African Americans also informs the reaction many scholars and activists have to specific instances of such problems, particularly among black urban youth. For example, Signithia Fordham and John Ogbu (1986) argue that the dominant American culture has historically told black Americans that they are incapable of academic success, and American economic and social structures have reinforced this by historically failing to reward black academic achievement in any real way. On their account, this has produced among many contemporary black students a strong cultural norm that defines academic effort and achievement as "acting white," a cultural norm that effectively lowers black academic success and thereby narrows economic and social opportunities later in life. According to Ogbu and Fordham, overcoming this problem within black youth culture requires efforts to change external structural conditions so that black educational success pays off in greater and more obvious ways, but it also requires efforts within black culture to emphasize black intelligence and intellectual accomplishment and to stress the dignity and value of black academic achievement. In a similar way, Blanche Bernstein (1991) argues that while high levels of poor single-parent families among African Americans are partly the result of structural factors, such as high rates of black male joblessness and incarceration, this is also a cultural problem that a growing number of black leaders are attacking through the moral power of black institutions such as the church, efforts that put a particular emphasis on fighting teenage pregnancy.

Jewelle Gibbs provides another example of this multidimensional approach in her look at the social problems of young black males, writing:

> The life-style of many young black inner-city males is frequently characterized by antisocial behaviors, drug addiction, exploitative and hostile relationships with women, confrontational relationships with police and other authorities, and very high-risk activities. These attitudes and activities may well be individual and/or collective responses to structural forces and environmental constraints which combine to deny these black males access to equal opportunity and social mobility. Yet they are *socially* reinforced through the black community's tolerance and tacit acceptance. (1988a, 26, italics in original)

According to Gibbs, structural factors certainly lie behind the crisis of young black males in America's urban ghettos, but this is a crisis compounded by the decline of black civil society in these areas, a decline that has drained its ability to react effectively. Addressing this crisis, therefore, means both attacking its structural causes and revitalizing the ability of black civil society to respond to it. Similarly, William Oliver (1994 and 1989) argues that while high levels of crime, violence, and alienation among young black males are rooted in structural forces such as high unemployment and the continuing influence of white racism, they are also rooted in the failure of black culture and civil society to respond to such problems effectively. He claims that while working to transform structural conditions, black Americans must also use the institutions of black civil society to intervene more effectively in the often troubled world of young black urban males through such things as direct moral confrontation, social outreach, Afrocentric education and the use of more black male teachers and role models, mentoring programs, more community centers with alternative social activities, and programs such as rites-of-passage ceremonies that raise black pride and cultural awareness.

My point here is that a great many scholars and activists concerned with addressing the kinds of social problems that can threaten autonomy in black communities recognize that such problems are rooted both in structural conditions outside of black civil society and in cultural and social conditions within it. This is why black civil society is so important in the struggle against such disabling problems. First, it is the space in which black men and women experience and must deal with them. Second, it provides the kinds of political resources black Americans can draw upon in mobilizing to attack their larger structural causes, such as economic inequality and continuing discrimination. And third, it provides the cultural, social, and economic resources black Americans can use in working to overcome them within their own communities as part of the black self-help tradition. This is why institutions such as the black church are so important. They have the potential to focus the political power of black Americans on transforming structural conditions, but they also have the potential to address the deep cultural and social roots of such disabling problems by strengthening the ability of black Americans to respond to them through social outreach and aid, moral challenge and support, and cultural awareness and pride.[24]

A liberal understanding of race, then, must recognize that overcoming disabling social problems disproportionately threatening the autonomy of black men and women does indeed demand an emphasis on attacking systemic forces such as economic inequality and continuing discrimination, an emphasis often provided by the left's interpretation of color-blind liberalism. But it also demands locating and addressing these problems in a group-conscious way. The ability of institutions, practices, and meanings in black civil society, as the space in which black Americans experience such problems in their daily lives, to respond to them in culturally specific ways is also critically important to the autonomy of black men and women.

This brings us back to the broader purpose of this chapter. My argument is that a liberal understanding of race that is guided by the value of autonomy must retain the strengths of color-blind liberalism, but it must also move beyond the color-blind paradigm's limits. A broader understanding of race in the United States, one that is more complex and multidimensional, incorporates both color-blind and group-conscious considerations. It continues to emphasize color-blind principles in the realm of citizenship, where basic civil and political rights and the equal protection of the laws should remain the same for all individuals regardless of race. It also does so in the realm of civil society, pushing for greater social and economic equality, working to open up more opportunities for African Americans, and fighting continuing discrimination. But it also includes attention to group-conscious factors that color-blind liberalism alone overlooks. It recognizes the way that distinct cultural groups comprising white and black Americans help determine the shape of American civil society, locating their members within it and providing them with the kinds of cultural, social, economic, and political resources they need to construct autonomous lives for themselves. This means that a liberal understanding of race must recognize the importance of black civil society, and specific institutions within it such as the black church, to the autonomy of African Americans as a historically subordinated and marginalized cultural group. This is an importance that includes the ability to provide resources enabling of autonomy, as well as the ability to help members overcome disabling forces that threaten autonomy.

What all this means for a liberal understanding of race, then, is the recognition that the strength and vitality of black culture and black civil society, in addition to broader structural factors affecting African Americans, are critically important to the long and continuing struggle for freedom by black men and women in the United States. Such a recognition, in turn, demands that a liberal politics of race dedicated to being a part of this struggle must focus on both color-blind and group-conscious factors in its public policy efforts, efforts I turn to in the next chapter.

# CHAPTER 6

# *Public Policy*

In trying to come to grips with America's exceedingly difficult confrontations over race, it is tempting to look for new and ingenious policy breakthroughs that will finally sort out all the issues and show us all the right answers. In this chapter, however, I do not pretend to unveil any such breakthroughs. Even if trying to develop such novel and remarkable policies were not beyond the scope of this book, doing so would certainly be beyond my capabilities, and in fact I have a healthy skepticism of anyone's ability to discover them. Nor do I pretend to offer a detailed look at the nuts and bolts of public policies dealing with race. Entire books regularly appear on the intricacies of race and public policy, and the topic is far from exhausted. One chapter, therefore, cannot furnish a comprehensive description of the subject, and this too is not my aim. Instead, this chapter provides a sketch of the general policy directions the previous chapters point toward. I examine the most promising public policy approaches—ones offered in recent years by a diverse collection of scholars and activists—that flow out of the book's expanded liberal understanding of race. The chapter, then, is not a detailed policy blueprint, but rather a look at the kinds of public policies we should consider when thinking about race, liberalism, and freedom.

## PUBLIC POLICY, AUTONOMY, AND BLACK AMERICANS

All Americans are part of the same broad political community, one built around a commitment to liberalism and its core political values. This means that all Americans, as members of a liberal regime, have a civic responsibility to uphold and work for liberal values, one of the most significant of which is autonomy. While there are many ways in which citizens in a modern liberal regime can work for political values such as autonomy, one of the most important of these is through their state's public policies. Public policy is perhaps the primary way in which political values in large and complex modern states are transformed into political practice. Autonomy, therefore, should be a central concern in any liberal state's policy debates and decisions. Indeed, as Joseph Raz argues, one of the state's most important duties in a liberal regime is to help promote autonomy, and this does not simply mean it must refrain from violating negative liberty, but also that it must work to create and sustain the kind of cultural and social environment that supports autonomy (1986, chap. 15). Through its public policies, the state can and should contribute to an autonomy-enhancing environment, and this is possible not only through policies aimed at the formal legal and political institutions of the state itself, but also through those that have a significant impact within civil society.

From the beginning of this book, I have argued that one of the longest-standing challenges to the liberal value of autonomy in the United States is the historical struggle by African Americans to overcome subordination and secure the promise of freedom, and this is a challenge that remains as important as ever. Given their group membership, African Americans have always experienced autonomy and its many requirements very differently—in the kinds of barriers to autonomy that they face in American life generally, as well as in the cultural, social, and economic space from which they often draw the various resources it requires and in which they often struggle to overcome threats to its meaningful exercise. This is a distinct and unique experience with autonomy that continues today. This means that, as a liberal regime, the United States must make supporting the autonomy of its black citizens one of its most important policy goals. Through its policies, it must contribute to and help to sustain the kinds of distinct conditions that the autonomy of black men and women depends upon. As a unique group in the United States, the autonomy of African Americans should be a unique policy concern, one with its own distinct dynamics and requirements that flow from the country's historical legacy as well as from contemporary necessity.

This is why African American confrontations with state power are so critical to their autonomy. If public policy plays such a vital role in the creation and protection of an autonomy-enhancing environment for black citizens, then their ability to influence public policy becomes critically important. As I argued in the last chapter, the autonomy of black men and women hinges in large part on their ability to mobilize and wield political power, demanding policies from the state that enhance rather than threaten their autonomy. To take a single example, I argue below in the section on education policy that hiring more black teachers and administrators in predominately black schools is an important way to reduce discriminatory treatment within schools, to provide an educational environment more sensitive to black cultural norms, to allow black children to interact with black adults in positions of authority and responsibility, and to boost black educational attainment—all things, I argue, that contribute to an autonomy-enhancing environment for black students. It is important to keep in mind, however, that changing hiring policies in local school districts to bring in more black teachers and administrators is a political process, one usually requiring black residents of those districts to put enough political pressure on school boards to institute such policies. As Meier, Steward, and England (1989a) point out, those districts where African Americans are able to elect more black representatives to school boards have much better records of hiring black teachers and administrators to staff their schools. So, as this example of hiring policies in education illustrates, black political mobilization, especially at local levels where higher numbers make such mobilization more effective, is critically important in forcing the state to uphold its commitment to protecting and enhancing black autonomy through its public policies.

A responsibility to work for these kinds of policies, however, does not simply rest with black Americans. It is one also shared by white Americans for two important reasons. First, as majority members of a liberal political regime in the United States, white Americans bear the greatest share of the common responsibility of all citizens to work for an environment that supports and sustains autonomy, including that of members of a cultural minority like African Americans. Second, and in a more direct way, white Americans as a distinct cultural group owe much of their current group status to the historical legacy of undermining or obliterating the autonomy of their black fellow citizens, a legacy still in need of redress. This second source of responsibility is the more controversial of the two. Many white Americans claim that they never owned slaves, do not discriminate against anybody, and in many cases descended from ethnic groups that experienced hardship and discrimination themselves. They claim that they should not be held responsible for the past sins of others. As I have argued, however, white Americans today, by virtue of their group membership, find themselves positioned very differently in the web of institutions, practices, and meanings that structures American civil society. They continue to have access to cultural, social, economic, and political resources in mainstream American life in a way that black Americans do not. They continue to benefit from membership in a secure and powerful majority group in the United States, something that is simply not true of African Americans as members of a far more vulnerable and far less powerful minority group that is historically subject to widespread subordination, marginalization, and exploitation.

Indeed, today's unequal levels of income, wealth, and social capital (education, job skills, access to fellow group members in positions of power and prestige, and so on) that white Americans tend to enjoy compared to black citizens are clearly the result of a cumulative process of discrimination and exploitation stretching back many generations. For example, black Americans have always been a cheap and expendable supply of labor upon which white economic development, security, and social status is often built. This of course was true during the centuries of slavery and Jim Crow, but it also continues in the comparatively brief post-segregation period. Black workers still experience levels of unemployment consistently twice that of whites and are often the last hired and the first fired, conditions that guarantee that economic shocks and dislocations will hit black Americans much earlier, much harder, and much longer, effectively cushioning the blow for the white majority. Furthermore, while many European immigrant groups did face harsh social and economic conditions themselves, they were able to surmount these over several generations in large part by winning recognition as white Americans, something that helped guarantee them a place above the very lowest social and economic positions reserved for black Americans. They were able to buy into and benefit from a system of racial exploitation and discrimination to improve their status, and they have passed this status down to their descendants living in the United States today.[1]

Finally, today's huge white middle class owes its economic and social position in large part to the phenomenal expansion of the suburban housing market since the mid-twentieth century, one made possible by government policies and one that has allowed it, across several generations, to accumulate significant levels of wealth and the things it can buy (good public schools, college and professional degrees, safe neighborhoods, and so on). This is a process, however, that most black Americans were effectively shut out of through formal government policies, pervasive discrimination, and extreme poverty (Oliver and Shapiro 1995; Halpern 1995, 2–3). As these examples show, then, the social and economic positions most white Americans presently occupy did not materialize out of thin air. Rather, they are deeply rooted in their group membership and in that group's historical mistreatment of black Americans. All this means that white Americans today still have a duty to help contribute to the autonomy of their black fellow citizens, and this duty is based not only on their general status as citizens in a liberal regime, but more specifically on their continuing to benefit from longstanding barriers to black autonomy as well. White Americans, therefore, have a responsibility to join their black fellow citizens in pressuring the state for the kinds of public policies that contribute to an autonomy-enhancing environment for black men and women in the United States.

A public policy agenda of this kind—that is, one guided by the liberal value of autonomy—is necessarily complex and multidimensional.

As I argued in chapter 4, autonomy is itself a complex and multidimensional value, and its meaningful realization hinges on a whole range of considerations. It certainly requires the protection against outside interference provided by strong negative rights, but it also requires a secure environment rich in valuable options. We need a wide range of options in order to make meaningful decisions about the course our lives will take. This means our autonomy depends upon a certain level of economic security and material opportunity. We need to be free of the intense uncertainty and vulnerability brought on by severe economic hardship and need. Furthermore, while this level of economic security is necessary for autonomy, it is not sufficient. Our range of options, and thus our autonomy, goes beyond economic conditions to hinge as well on our more general participation within the complex web of institutions, practices, and meanings that constitutes civil society. It is this participation that is provided, in large part, by our membership in secure and flourishing cultural groups. Finally, in addition to shaping our external range of options, cultural group membership of this kind also helps provide the inner resources we need to actually exercise autonomy, to make the kinds of choices that allow us to live our lives from the inside.

It is this account of autonomy that demands that we recognize the importance of a host of factors to the continuing struggle of black men and women to secure the promise of an autonomous life in the United States. These factors include strong citizenship and nondiscrimination rights, greater social and economic equality, and more social and economic opportunities in mainstream American life. They also include a renewed focus on the ability of black civil society, and institutions within it such as the black church, to provide the kinds of cultural, social, economic, and political resources that group members need to construct autonomous lives for themselves. Identifying the kinds of factors upon which the autonomy of black Americans hinges in this way means that we can also identify ways in which public policy can contribute to these factors. We can, in other words, identify various ways in which public policy can help support the autonomy of black men and women in different areas of American life. Public policy can strengthen citizenship and nondiscrimination rights. It can help alleviate economic vulnerability and insecurity and promote social and economic equality. It can help expand social and economic opportunities for black men and women. Public policy can also help strengthen institutions within black civil society itself, supporting their ability to deliver the resources so critical to the autonomy of group members. It can help revitalize institutions like black churches, schools, and businesses in ways that ultimately contribute to the ability of African Americans to carve out autonomous lives for themselves.

Autonomy, in short, is able to provide the basis for a public policy approach to race that is multidimensional while at the same time unified and coherent. Since the factors upon which the autonomy of African Americans in the United States hinges are complex, a policy approach designed to contribute to that autonomy must also be complex. It demands different kinds of policies guided by different kinds of considerations in various spheres of American life. But such an approach is also unified by its common focus on autonomy. Autonomy is the normative goal that draws the different stands together and joins them as interrelated parts of a single policy framework. In this way, autonomy offers a way for liberals, particularly those on the left, to integrate their often fragmented and unrelated policy proposals together into a broader and more unified approach. Autonomy is the normative foundation liberals can use to develop a more coherent, interrelated, and ultimately compelling agenda for public policy when it comes to issues of race in the United States.

Within this kind of autonomy-based approach, the contributions public policy can make to African American autonomy are of two broad kinds, corresponding to both the color-blind and group-conscious elements that should inform a liberal understanding of race. First, guided by color-blind principles, public policy can help lower the barriers to autonomy that black individuals still face in American life on account of their race, barriers such as discrimination, social and economic inequality, and reduced opportunities in mainstream civil society. Second, guided by group-conscious considerations, public policy can help strengthen black civil society and its ability to deliver autonomy-enhancing resources, as well as to struggle against forces threatening autonomy within black communities. A critical part of this second role for public policy, however, is to channel public resources into black civil society while not threatening its independence and distinct character as black cultural, social, and economic space. Even with more public support, black civil society must remain a network of institutions, practices, and meanings defined and dominated by black Americans in order to play the vital role that it does in supporting black autonomy.

I am claiming, then, that an expanded liberal understanding of race has important policy applications. Using autonomy as a guide, it can uncover the different kinds of policies, some guided by color-blind considerations and others guided by group-conscious considerations, that are most appropriate in different areas of American life, offering a broader, more multidimensional, and ultimately more compelling view of the critical interaction between race and public policy in the United States.

## THE STATE, CIVIL SOCIETY, AND PUBLIC POLICY

In the United States, as in most industrial and postindustrial countries in the West, the state and civil society are distinct, but they also intersect in important ways. It is at this intersection, as well as in the state's own institutions, that public policy can contribute to the autonomy of black men and women. Furthermore, it can do this in a variety of areas and in a variety of ways.

### Civil Rights

Civil rights policy is one area in which color-blind considerations, particularly the left's interpretation emphasizing strong state action to fight continuing discrimination, are critical. Since the basic rights and protections of citizenship are so essential to making autonomy possible, and since they should belong to each individual without regard to race, the state's guarding the equal rights and protections of citizenship for black citizens must be one of its primary policy concerns. The state has a duty to aggressively enforce the historically fragile rights of African Americans, and this requires active and sustained prosecution of those who violate their political rights—such as the right to vote, to run for and hold public office, and to sit on juries—and basic civil liberties—such as the right to counsel, to protection against unreasonable searches and seizures, and to freedom of assembly. It also requires strong enforcement of laws designed to fight discrimination in civil society. There are laws on the books against discrimination in housing, employment, credit lending, public accommodations, and so on, but giving them teeth is often another matter. As I argued in chapter 3, the state can have only a limited impact on discrimination in civil society, but it nonetheless can work to effectively reduce its frequency, and its leadership can set the tone for a broader fight against discrimination in American life generally. This, however, depends upon aggressive enforcement of civil rights laws by government officials and on standards of proof in the courts that allow prosecutors to battle discrimination more effectively.

As scholars such as Robert McAlpine, Billy Tidwell, and Monica Jackson (1988) and David Rose (1994) point out, the executive branch of the federal government has a great deal of flexibility in deciding how it enforces civil rights laws. Officials in agencies such as the Justice Department, the Department of Labor, and the Equal Employment Opportunity Commission, taking their cues from the White House, have considerable discretion over how broadly they interpret antidiscrimination legislation and how aggressively they prosecute violators. While the late 1960s and the 1970s saw fairly aggressive enforcement by the federal government of laws against discrimination, especially those prohibiting employment discrimination like Title VII of the Civil Rights Act of 1964, the Reagan administration in the 1980s started a trend toward interpreting such laws very narrowly and reducing federal efforts to prosecute all but the most flagrant violators. Led by the Reagan administration's Justice Department, the executive branch began pushing for much narrower interpretations of legislation like Title VII, ones favored by employers accused of discrimination rather than those established by the courts and federal agencies in the 1970s. Beginning in the 1980s, the federal government brought far fewer discrimination cases, and the Justice Department and the Equal Employment Opportunity Commission argued the ones they did bring as if regulations and guidelines designed to prove and prosecute discrimination that were on the books in their own agencies did not even exist (Rose 1994). The executive branch of the federal government, in short, has considerable power, one way or the other, over how effective civil rights laws ultimately prove to be. This is why it can make an important contribution to the fight against barriers to black autonomy still raised by discrimination. Doing so, however, means reversing the trend toward narrow interpretations and inconsistent or lax execution of antidiscrimination laws over the last two decades. It demands, in short, that the aggressive and consistent enforcement of civil rights measures must once again become a central part of the federal government's public policy agenda.

While the executive branch has considerable power over how effective antidiscrimination laws will be, the federal courts also play a critical role by deciding what standards of proof they will require in such cases. For example, in decisions like *Griggs v. Duke Power Co.* in 1971 and *McDonnell Douglass v. Green* in 1973, the Supreme Court made it clear that under Title VII of the Civil Rights Act of 1964 many hiring practices that on their face were race neutral but that had a significant discriminatory impact were prohibited.[2] This made it easier to prove employment discrimination without having to prove actual discriminatory intent, something an employer who simply keeps his or her mouth shut can often avoid. With *Washington v. Davis* in 1976, however, the Court signaled a change in direction by deciding that in cases in which Title VII does not apply and discrimination complaints are brought instead directly under the Fifth or Fourteenth Amendments, proof of actual discriminatory purpose or intent rather than simply a discriminatory or disproportionate impact is required.[3] The Court has applied this more recent and narrower standard in employment cases like *Pullman-Standard v. Swint* in 1982, *Firefighters v. Stotts* in 1984, *Wygant v. Jackson Board of Education* in 1986, and *St. Mary's Honor Center v. Hicks* in 1993, as well as in the death penalty case of *McCleskey v.*

*Kemp* in 1987, in which the Court stated that evidence of massive racial disparities in applications of the death penalty is not enough to make it unconstitutional without proof of discriminatory intent in each individual case.[4] The federal courts, then, can make proving and thus prosecuting discrimination more or less difficult, and in recent years the trend has been toward making it more so.

To the extent that effectively fighting discrimination should be a central policy goal of the state, however, this is a trend that should be reversed. As legal theorists like Charles Lawrence (1987) argue, discrimination is such a subtle, informal, culturally embedded, and often unconscious force that strict intent requirements necessarily miss much of its scope, and so constitutional standards that allow judges to account for the broader cultural and social context of laws that have a disparate racial impact are much more appropriate. Broader standards of proof, such as those favored by Lawrence or those established in *Griggs*, give the state the room it needs to fight more effectively those forms of discrimination that it is able to identify and prosecute. Furthermore, working for such standards does not simply mean doing so through the courts themselves, but also through Congress, which has the power to direct the courts to interpret certain statutes in certain ways, as it did in 1992 when it negated the narrow standards of proof applied by the Supreme Court to Title VII discrimination cases in its 1989 *Wards Cove v. Antonio* decision as well as several other cases (Davis and Graham 1995, chap. 5).[5] Working through both the judicial and legislative branches, then, it is possible to push for standards of proof that give actors like employers, credit lenders, and real estate agents less room to discriminate against black citizens in civil society and that help the state more effectively prosecute those violators it is able to identify.

Finally, one of the most controversial ways the state has tried to fight discrimination against African Americans over the last several decades is through affirmative action policies, both in its own institutions and contracting procedures as well as in policies that encourage nonstate institutions in civil society to recruit and include more black citizens. As I pointed out in chapter 2, most arguments for affirmative action today rely on the categories of the color-blind paradigm. Such programs attempt to counter the effects of previous and continuing discrimination and to open up more opportunities in American life to black Americans in order to help create a more inclusive society where one's race ultimately makes less difference to one's prospects. As such, affirmative action is still an important policy tool furnished by color-blind liberalism, one that has in fact helped many black Americans overcome barriers to their autonomy posed by discrimination and reduced opportunities in mainstream civil society, and one that can continue to do so.

The left's interpretation of color-blind liberalism, which makes a distinction between invidious and benign discrimination and thereby permits race-conscious measures that are designed to overcome the continuing legacy of racism in American life, still has a valuable role to play in a liberal policy agenda. It is important to keep in mind, however, that affirmative action's impact is less dramatic than many of its strongest supporters suggest. While it is clearly a benefit to some black individuals, it often fails to help those in most need—those with too little education, job skills, or experience to qualify for the positions it helps provide. While it facilitates the upward mobility of certain black Americans, it does little to change the broader cultural, social, and economic context in which race exists in the United States, and so its ameliorative potential remains fairly narrow. Affirmative action, in short, is a policy tool with a relatively limited impact, except for those black individuals it directly benefits. It is a tool, however, that should remain an important part of the state's civil rights policies given the role it does play in expanding the range of options facing many black individuals. This is why the continuing assault on affirmative action measures by elected leaders (both Republican and Democrat), by ballot measures such as California's Proposition 209, and by the Supreme Court in recent cases such as *Richmond v. Croson* in 1989 and *Adarand v. Pena* in 1995 should be resisted as something that weakens a civil rights policy that aims to support the autonomy of black men and women.[6]

## The Safety Net and Economic Policy

In addition to civil rights policies, many of the social and economic policies favored by the left's interpretation of color-blind liberalism are also important elements of a public-policy approach to enhancing black autonomy. Since African Americans still suffer disproportionately from economic hardship and the many social problems it aggravates, and since these kinds of forces raise barriers to an autonomous life, public policies designed to address them can make an important contribution to the autonomy of black men and women. Indeed, such policies are part and parcel of the modern welfare state, and they are generally race-neutral, relying instead on means-tested or universal criteria. These kinds of policies are designed to ease the uncertainty, insure against the insecurity, and cushion the fluctuations of a market economy, all of which threaten to undermine the secure range of options upon which the meaningful exercise of autonomy hinges. But while all modern industrial and postindustrial countries have some sort of safety net provided by these kinds of policies, the one constructed by the United States in the last century is particularly weak—by which I mean it is far less developed, comprehensive, or integrated than that of most other comparable states.[7] Furthermore, rather than expanding the kinds of policies that make up this safety net, the trend in the United States is presently toward cutting them even further, especially those that benefit the most economically and socially vulnerable. This lack of a fully developed and comprehensive safety net of course falls the hardest on a group like African Americans who are more often in need of it.

This is why it is important to work for more extensive, stronger, and better-funded safety net policies in the United States. For the most vulnerable, this requires means-tested programs like low-income housing assistance, food stamps, school lunches, Head Start, and income supplements. Such programs of course do not in and of themselves guarantee an autonomous life, but they do help make individuals less vulnerable, enlarging their range of options, or at least preventing their choices from shrinking any further. They help prevent one's life from being characterized by a ceaseless insecurity that threatens to obliterate autonomy. Simply having a place to live through a low income housing voucher, for example, does not necessarily provide a person with an extensive range of options, but it does guarantee a greater range than if one is homeless. In addition to means-tested programs, however, it is also important to work for the creation of universal programs that help provide services such as health insurance or child care. While benefiting all Americans, these programs are particularly helpful to those who, like a disproportionate number of African Americans, currently lack access to such vital services because of their income, employment status, or neighborhood residence. These kinds of universal programs also carry the built-in advantage of attracting more political backing, even while providing the greatest benefit to the most vulnerable who usually lack effective political power themselves (Wilson 1987). In this way, working to expand and strengthen safety-net policies, both the means-tested and universal varieties, is an important minimum requirement in efforts to create a social and economic environment more supportive of black autonomy given the status of black Americans as members of a group more frequently suffering from the problems these policies work to alleviate. Such policies, in short, help to provide a floor above which autonomy becomes more realistic for many black men and women.

In my view, the most important part of such policy efforts are those that address the persistent problem of black employment. Unemployment and underemployment continue to stay at alarmingly high levels for African Americans, especially in the central cities, and the prospects for improvement without state intervention are bleak. Compounding the forces of discrimination and a lack of quality education facing many black workers is the decades-long decline of blue collar manufacturing in urban areas, the decline in family farming in rural areas, and the increasing presence of immigrant workers competing for service-sector jobs. Of these, it is perhaps the loss of large-scale manufacturing jobs that has had the most severe impact on black employment prospects and earnings in recent years (Wilson 1987). As Timothy Bates points out, median black income in the Midwest, a region in which this decline has been most dramatic, fell from 73% to 52% of median white income between 1970 and 1987, a drop from $23,671 to $16,755 in constant dollars (1993, 8). Furthermore, the fragile job base of African Americans is likely to erode even further in the coming years. Black employment is still disproportionately concentrated in sectors such as manufacturing, agriculture, and the public sector that are likely to see a continuing decline, while it is dramatically underrepresented in emerging growth sectors like high technology (Marable 1991b; Watson, Austin, and Reed 1988). These increasing levels of black unemployment, especially among urban youth, not only lead to far fewer economic options in life but to the higher levels of crime, violence, drug abuse, hopelessness, and alienation that threaten autonomy as well (Marable 1991b; K. Jennings 1992; Oliver 1994). These levels of unemployment also put significant stress on the black family. First, they dramatically reduce the pool of black men, with good, stable jobs and no problems with the law, who make attractive husbands and fathers, and, second, they force many black women onto public assistance to support their families since jobs that pay a livable wage and provide benefits such as health and day care for their children are so scarce (Wilson 1987; Staples 1991; K. Jennings 1992).

Since this employment crisis in black America continues to pose a significant threat to black autonomy, it is something that public policy must address, and it can do so in large part through race-neutral economic policies that do two things: reduce unemployment and offer more support to the working poor, a group often overlooked in American social policy. We can see this need to address employment issues, for example, in contemporary welfare debates. Missing in the rhetoric of "putting welfare recipients to work," especially coming from the right, is the fact that the kinds of jobs that could adequately replace existing programs are simply not available for those who need them. If they were, then the debate would be largely moot, since most of today's recipients would be in those jobs rather than on public assistance. Moving people "from welfare to work" is a worthy goal, something most recipients themselves applaud since living on public assistance is a difficult existence, but it is not one we can achieve by simply telling them to go find a job. Rather, what is needed is more jobs for low-skilled, often poorly educated workers that pay a living wage; requirements that such jobs come with benefits like health insurance and child care; better and cheaper public transportation so employees can get to jobs; better job-training so people will be qualified to work; more adequate unemployment insurance for those between jobs; and stricter child-support enforcement, expanded tax policies such as the Earned Income Tax Credit, and adequate mortgage subsidies to help low-income working families make ends meet (Jenks 1992, 226–235; McLanahan and Sandefur 1994, chap. 8; Wilson 1996, chap. 8). In this way, providing more and better jobs with increased public sector support for those who hold them can not only help move single-parent families off public assistance, but it can also help ease much of the pressure on the structure of the black family by making decent employment opportunities available to both black men and women.

Addressing the crisis of black employment and the barriers to autonomy that it raises means the state must embrace public policies that move the country closer to a full employment economy and are more favorable to the interests of workers across the board.[8] Such policies must include measures like a higher minimum wage, more generous benefits such as health and child care, and a shorter work week. They must facilitate more union organizing and provide a greater role for labor in the policy process. They must concern themselves with corporate wage levels as much as profit levels. They must boost levels of public investment in such things as education, job training, and unemployment insurance, as well as in public works projects that both build infrastructure and provide jobs. John Jacob (1994), for example, argues that increasing public investment in rebuilding the country's infrastructure—roads, bridges, parks, communications networks, public transportation systems, and so on—can not only spur long-term economic growth, but also provide jobs for those most in need, especially black Americans. Indeed, both William Julius Wilson (1996, chap. 8) and Mikey Kaus (1992, chap. 8) offer compelling proposals to replace most antipoverty programs in the United States with a single New Deal WPA-style jobs program targeted at restoring and maintaining the country's public spaces and economic infrastructure—thereby improving civic life and spurring economic growth throughout the nation, as well as attacking poverty and its attendant social problems. Such a program would offer guaranteed employment to all able-bodied adults at a wage high enough to support an average size family above the poverty line (one set just below a higher minimum wage for private employment) and come with adequate health and child-care benefits. Such jobs would address the scourge of unemployment and the host of social ills it breeds in a comprehensive way, especially in our central cities; they would offer the dignity of earning a living wage through one's own hard work; and they would provide employment skills and references for those who want to move on to better jobs in the private sector. In short, such a program would offer all Americans the chance to join the working class, and it would provide adequate wages and benefits so that individuals and families in the working class could avoid poverty and lead lives of dignity. It is just this kind of comprehensive policy proposal that, while formally race-neutral, could have an enormous impact on black Americans and their ability to carve out autonomous lives for themselves, since they suffer so disproportionately from the economic and social hardships it seeks to alleviate.

## Social Welfare Policy and Black Civil Society

As I have argued, color-blind considerations are important in a liberal understanding of race that is informed by autonomy, but they are not sufficient. They provide a focus on such things as citizenship rights, nondiscrimination, more opportunities for black citizens, and social and economic equality that are necessary for guiding certain kinds of policies that contribute to the autonomy of black men and women. But in other areas group-conscious considerations are necessary. Public policy must also account for the importance of cultural groups and their role in making autonomy possible in American civil society. This means that since black civil society carries such a heavy burden in providing resources necessary for African American autonomy, as well as in struggling against forces that threaten it, a public policy approach to enhancing black autonomy must pay particular attention to ways it can help support and revitalize black civil society, and one of the most important of these is through its social welfare spending. By channeling more resources through institutions in black civil society committed to social outreach and mutual aid, the state can help strengthen black civil society as well as deliver social services more effectively to those in black communities most in need of them.

The issue of the state's taking action to revitalize the institutions of American civil society generally has become increasingly important in recent years. Many people are alarmed by what they see as a decline in the health of civil society, an alarm that is supported by research in the area.[9] This has sparked cries for the strengthening of civil society from a variety of quarters, many of them calling on the state to aid in such efforts through its public policies, including social welfare spending. Indeed, as long as two decades ago, Peter Berger and Richard Neuhaus (1977) argued that social policies could strengthen and more effectively work through what they called "mediating structures" such as families, churches, and neighborhoods that stand between individuals and large megainstitutions like the state or corporations. On their account, it is through such structures that individuals can gain more control over the course of their own lives in the face of social isolation on the one hand and impersonal, overwhelming bureaucratic power on the other. Many on the right have come to endorse this kind of policy approach, because they see it as a move away from big government and the bureaucratic welfare state. President Reagan made taking social-welfare power and resources away from the federal bureaucracy and passing them down to voluntary groups on the local level an important part of his public rhetoric, though not necessarily of his actual policy initiatives, and today within the Republican Party, leaders such as Senator Dan Coats of Indiana and William Bennett push for legislation to channel more public money away from direct government assistance and into social outreach efforts within civil society (Coats 1996; Bennett and Coats 1995; Dewar 1996). There is also, however, significant support on the left for directing social welfare spending through institutions in civil society. John Keane, for example, points out that socialist parties in Europe have consistently pushed for state policies that strengthen labor unions, facilitate more investment in worker collectives, and provide more public funding to child care cooperatives (1988a, 15–20). According to Keane, funneling state money through institutions in civil society often provides social services more efficiently than the state bureaucracy, and at the same time it empowers people by involving them in collective, community projects rather than their simply being the passive beneficiaries of state largesse (1988a, chap. 1). Similarly, Frank Riessman (1986) calls for encouraging a spirit of "self-help populism" by empowering associations in civil society that deliver social outreach and mutual aid in a more cooperative, personal, and empowering way than hierarchical, impersonal, and expert-driven state agencies that often treat recipients as powerless and interchangeable supplicants.

The voice on the left making what I consider the strongest case for the role of the state in supporting the institutions of civil society belongs to Michael Walzer. He writes: "Civil society is for us the ground of democratic politics, and this is ground that must be tended by the state. Regulation and subsidy are both necessary, but so is active cooperation of a sort that might be inappropriate in a less divided society" (1992a, 18). For Walzer, the diverse voluntary associations that constitute civil society are able to protect Americans from becoming too atomistic and isolated from their fellow citizens, but this function is threatened by their increasing fragility. He writes that "weakness is a general feature of associational life in America today. Unions, churches, interest groups, ethnic organizations, political parties and sects, societies for self-improvement and good works, local philanthropies, neighborhood clubs and cooperatives, religious sodalities, brotherhoods and sisterhoods: this American civil society is wonderfully multitudinous. Most of the associations, however, are precariously established, skimpily funded, and always at risk. They have less holding power than they once did" (1994, 187). While this decline of civil society is a cause for concern, it is not too late to do something about it. Walzer says, "We are at the point where we can still safely bring the pluralism of groups to the rescue of the pluralism of dissociated individuals" (1994, 189). This is important, because American society "requires not only individual rights but group solidarities and the pluralist and democratic politics that groups make possible." The state must therefore not only concern itself with the extension and protection of the "regime of rights," but also with finding ways to "strengthen the internal life, the jurisdictional reach, and the cohesiveness of secondary associations" (Walzer 1992a, 122). Walzer argues that "it makes sense to call the state to the rescue of civil society and then search for effective means of rescue" through its public policies (1992a, 123). On his account, the state can work to revitalize civil society by facilitating the organization of voluntary groups in ways similar to the Wagner Act in the 1930s, legislation that helped support the organization of labor unions. It can do this by fostering the growth of things like experimental charter schools, tenant-owned or run public housing, and neighborhood crime-control organizations, as well as by providing more public funding to groups, especially religious ones, that provide social welfare services such as hospitals, day-care centers, nursing homes, and so on (Walzer 1994, 189–190; 1992a, 122–123; 1990, 15–18).

As we have seen, many of the groups that structure civil society are those based on race or ethnicity, and Walzer argues that while such groups should not be fixed in any formal way by the state, it is possible to let public funds seep across the border between the state and civil society to these groups' own distinct institutions (1992a, 74–76; 1982, 26–28). Membership in these kinds of cultural groups is a significant public good, so it is reasonable to provide some level of public support to their organization in civil society. According to Walzer, such a public-policy approach recognizes and encourages the pluralism of American life, even while avoiding the mistake of locking it into a rigid and formalized scheme of group-differentiated citizenship. This kind of public support for the institutions of various cultural groups that Walzer advocates becomes even more important when such groups are cultural minorities and when their distinct institutions carry a particularly heavy burden in providing a foundation for the autonomy of group members. As Joseph Raz argues, since membership in a cultural group is so important to autonomy, public support for that group's institutions in civil society is often appropriate in order to help develop an autonomy-enhancing environment for its members. Furthermore, this becomes particularly critical when the group in question is a cultural minority that does not draw on the mainstream institutions of civil society in the same way as the majority. On Raz's account, such a group often requires significant public support for its own institutions to help make the autonomy of its members possible (1994, 78–79).

African Americans are a prime example of this kind of cultural minority, one whose distinct institutions in civil society public policy should help support, because they are so important to the autonomy of black men and women. Public policy can do this by channeling more social welfare spending through the social outreach and mutual aid institutions of black civil society. These can range from historically black colleges and universities to ecumenical religious groups to local community centers. An important part of the state's child care and health care policies, for example, can focus on providing resources to locally run, nonprofit day care centers and medical clinics in black communities. And as part of its efforts to fight things like hunger, homelessness, crime, and drug abuse, it can direct more funds to local churches, mosques, neighborhood associations, and other groups in black civil society that are battling the same problems by establishing shelters, soup kitchens, job training programs, mentoring networks, sports leagues, drug counseling meetings, neighborhood watch groups, antiviolence campaigns, and so on. The state, in short, can pursue many of its existing policy goals by providing much more support to ongoing efforts within black civil society to address the same kinds of problems.

This policy approach has several benefits. First, it strengthens institutions within black civil society by providing them with more financial resources, by increasing their public importance in the life of black communities, and by bringing more people in need to the institutions of their own communities rather than directly to the state for help. As such, it is an approach that does not simply support black individuals, but the institutional base of entire black communities as well. Second, such an approach contributes to black political empowerment by giving black men and women in black institutions more control over the delivery of public assistance. It puts black civil society in a stronger position in the policy process, allowing black-controlled institutions to gain and use political leverage. Rather than making African Americans passive aid recipients in a routinized and distant state bureaucracy, it helps strengthen the black self-help tradition within those institutions that provide social services in a context that also cultivates political solidarity and cultural consciousness among group members (Pope 1992; Hamilton 1976). Finally, such an approach can boost the effectiveness of social welfare efforts. For generations institutions within black civil society have proven their potential to provide effective aid to group members in need, to fight the forces of hopelessness and despair, and to struggle against a host of social problems such as crime, drug and alcohol abuse, and family disintegration. These institutions provide grassroots and black-controlled settings in which African Americans can provide effective social support to group members in need.

This potential for institutions in black civil society to more successfully attack a variety of social problems than government-run efforts alone has attracted the attention of a host of scholars and activists in recent years. Michael Rice and Woodrow Jones (1994), for example, point to the important role of historically black hospitals in delivering health care services to African Americans; Janie Ward (1995) argues that violence-prevention programs are more effective among black youth when run by organizations within black communities that stress group consciousness and an ethic of intragroup cooperation, solidarity, and care; and Jacqueline Pope (1992) points to the success of antidrug initiatives that emphasize black group-consciousness and cultural awareness.[10] Much of this recent attention to the potential of institutions in black civil society to effectively deliver social services has centered on black churches. Especially following the Supreme Court's 1988 decision in *Bowan v. Kendrick*, in which the Court stated that religious groups can receive certain kinds of government funding to help provide social welfare services, many people have called for an increase in public funding to black churches engaged in fighting various social problems in black communities.[11] Howard Stevenson (1990), for instance, argues that black churches provide an excellent institutional context for programs aimed at reducing teenage pregnancy, and John Morrison (1991) highlights the potential of black churches to deliver services to the elderly. Similarly, John Hatch and Steve Derthick (1992) and Stephen Thomas and his colleagues (1994) point to the need for more government support of public health programs sponsored by black churches across the country. Finally, Lincoln and Mamiya report that these are the kinds of policy roles black churches are increasingly willing to fill as greater numbers of them seek government funding to help start or expand social-outreach programs like Head Start, day care centers, food banks, homeless shelters, nursing homes, antidrug counseling, and so on (1990, chap. 6).

This growing awareness of the important background role public policy can take in supporting social outreach and mutual aid efforts within black civil society is supported by an increasing number of successful initiatives across the country. For example, the Rheedlen Centers for Children and Families in New York City relies on both private and government funding to help provide a safe and enriching haven for urban children and their families struggling to live in an environment often characterized by extreme poverty, crime, violence, drug abuse, fear, and hopelessness. Rheedlen Centers organize afterschool activities, mentoring programs, academic tutoring, recreation programs, and perhaps most importantly provide a strong network of concerned members of local communities taking an active interest in vulnerable children and their families (Canada 1995; Holmstrom 1995). Harry Boyte (1984) describes the transformation of a public housing complex in St. Louis after local residents wrested control of its operation from the city. While the city, state, and federal governments continued to provide funding and logistical support, the residents organized themselves to manage the complex. As Boyte reports, in a few years the complex went from a crime-ridden, violence-plagued, and dilapidated set of buildings dominated by a pervasive sense of fear and powerlessness to a secure, carefully landscaped, well-maintained, and stable community with an active schedule of neighborhood cultural and social activities. Building on their new-found empowerment and achievements, the residents also established a community center, child care services, and a host of small businesses. As Boyte points out, it was the critical combination of government background support and local neighborhood control that made such a transformation in the lives of these residents possible (1984, 95–114).

Robert Halpern (1995) discusses even larger efforts at urban renewal along the same lines in Boston and Baltimore. In both cities, local neighborhood groups and churches have organized to win special grants, zoning changes, and logistical support from city, state, and federal agencies to rebuild decaying neighborhoods by attracting businesses and jobs, constructing community centers, improving schools, and rehabilitating housing stock for ownership by local residents through mortgage assistance programs. Again, the driving force behind such initiatives is control by local residents with responsive background support by several government agencies (Halpern, chap. 7). These kinds of renewal initiatives are becoming more common across the country, and as Lloyd Gite (1993) points out, it is black churches that are increasingly drawing on their institutional resources to spearhead them. For example, in his study of one black church in Brooklyn, Samuel Freedman (1993) describes its contributions to an organization called the East Brooklyn Congregations. This group has managed to use its collective resources to pressure local supermarkets to improve service and lower prices, to demand better police protection and less harassment, to force local officials to maintain area streets and parks and to tear down abandoned buildings, and to convince local hospitals to provide better health care facilities to area residents through branch clinics. Perhaps its most successful effort, however, has been its Nehemiah program, which has provided thousands of new single-family homes to low-income buyers. With land, low-interest mortgages, special tax exemptions, utility improvements, and construction loans the group had won from city, state, and federal agencies, East Brooklyn Congregations raised enough money from private sources, mainly national religious denominations, to build several new neighborhoods with high-quality homes and mortgage programs making them affordable to buyers with an average household income of only $25,000, almost half of whom moved in directly from crumbling housing projects (Freedman 1993, chap. 11; Prokesch 1992). The program has been so successful in raising local property values, attracting more businesses, and giving thousands of low-income residents a secure stake in owning their own homes for a lower cost than they would pay to endure the indignity of renting poor quality, crowded, and often dangerous public housing units, that it is being replicated by local religious and neighborhood groups in other parts of New York, as well as in Washington, D.C., and Los Angeles among other cities (Oser 1994; Kaggwa 1993; Stewart 1990).

As these and many other examples show, public policy can support in valuable and creative ways the initiatives launched and run by institutions within black civil society to give more African Americans greater control over their own lives. Through its social welfare spending, the state can in fact help strengthen black civil society and its ability to enhance the autonomy of black men and women. I think it is important, however, to keep several points in mind with such an approach. First, the United States already channels a considerable part of its budget for social provision through nonprofit organizations, making the nonprofit sector one of the most important elements of its modern welfare state (Salamon 1995; Smith and Lipsky 1993; Kramer 1981). So providing public funds to social outreach institutions in civil society is nothing new. The need, rather, is to expand and strengthen this policy approach, particularly when it comes to those institutions controlled by African Americans. Second, we must be wary of proposals, coming most frequently from the right, to shift social welfare spending away from government programs and toward the nonprofit sector. Such proposals can actually result in drastic cuts to government safety net programs and little or no increase in state funding to social outreach organizations in civil society. The Reagan administration's dramatic cuts in social welfare spending, for example, hurt the nonprofit sector as much as they did government-run programs (Salamon 1995, chaps. 10–12). As I argued in the previous section, it is still important to maintain and even increase spending on government safety net programs. So proposals to increase support for institutions in black civil society must be clear that such support is in addition to fully funded safety net policies by the government, not a replacement for them.

Third, research shows that simply channeling more social welfare spending through the nonprofit sector does not necessarily insure that it will reach those most in need. Indeed, the majority of nonprofit organizations, including those that make delivering social services their main activity, do not provide benefits primarily to the poor, though there is evidence that those receiving more government aid are more likely to deliver a higher percentage of their services to poor clients (Salamon 1995; Clotfelter 1992). In providing more support to institutions in black civil society, then, public policy should be careful to favor organizations and programs that make serving those most in need their top priority. Fourth, this requirement for some level of government oversight brings up the issue of protecting the independence of those institutions receiving aid. It is particularly important that institutions in black civil society maintain their independent character and that they remain distinctly black-defined and black-dominated in order for them to support the autonomy of black men and women as they are capable of doing. The state, therefore, should not try to mandate the character and content of black civil society itself, but only take a background role in supporting many of its institutions through funding and logistical support when needed. The institutions themselves must remain firmly in control of their own programs. Indeed, there is strong evidence that even providing funds to organizations in civil society does not give the state any real leverage over the operation, objectives, or character of such organizations, except that they do feel somewhat more pressure to deliver a greater proportion of their services to the poor (Salamon 1995, chaps. 8–9; Kramer 1981).

Finally, it should be clear that channeling more funds to social outreach and mutual aid efforts in black civil society is not a miracle cure for all the social and economic problems plaguing many black communities. Such efforts can do much good, but they have their limits. They must take their place beside rather than replacing policies that address larger systemic and structural forces outside of black civil society. Furthermore, while in some ways superior to state-run programs, such organizations are not flawless delivery systems for social services either. They too can sometimes seem bureaucratic and impersonal, they too can be underfunded and understaffed, and they too can suffer from problems such as incompetence or paternalism. So while strengthening institutions in black civil society through social welfare spending is an important part of a public policy approach to enhancing black autonomy, and one that should be dramatically expanded, it is not by itself a miracle solution to the many barriers to black autonomy that remain.

*Economic Development*

As I argued in chapter 5, the economic space of black civil society is an important foundation for the autonomy of black men and women. It is where African Americans as a distinct cultural group develop and maintain the kinds of economic resources group members can draw upon in constructing autonomous lives for themselves. This is a space, however, that is still dramatically underdeveloped and insecure. It remains far too narrow and too weak, and it still sees too much money pass through it without being trapped and circulated for group members to build and use as capital. Almost twenty-five years after the passage of the Civil Rights Act of 1964, black-owned firms accounted for only one percent of all business sales in the United States (Samuelson 1995). Indeed, as recently as 1989 every single black-owned business in the United States could have been bought out with only the liquid assets of one or two of the country's largest corporations like Mobil Oil or General Electric (Cotton 1992, 14). As William Bradford (1994) reports, in 1993 there were seventy-seven black-owned banks, Savings and Loans, and insurance companies, accounting for only half of one percent of all such institutions in the country and holding only .06 percent of the assets in these institutions. Finally, as Marcus Alexis and Geraldine Henderson (1994) point out, while each dollar changes hands seven times in white communities, it only does so 1.5 times in black ones. There continues, then, to be a serious need for more and stronger economic institutions in black civil society—things like black-owned and operated firms, small businesses, banks, credit unions, and so on. Given this fragile condition of black economic space and its importance to the autonomy of African Americans, the state can and should use its public policies to help expand and strengthen it. In today's modern welfare state, the government is a key player in the economy, and it is able to promote development in certain sectors through its economic policies. Black civil society should be one such sector. So in addition to the race-neutral safety net policies designed to alleviate economic hardship generally that I considered earlier in this chapter, the state should also embrace an explicitly group-conscious approach in its economic policies, one that works to strengthen the economic space of black civil society in order to help it better provide resources so important to the autonomy of black men and women.

The state can do this in several ways. As we saw in the last section, it can provide background support to certain institutions in black civil society, in this case those that work to foster black economic development. In his research, John Butler (1991) details a long and influential entrepreneurial tradition among African Americans, one that when not crushed by the forces of segregation, discrimination, and outright violence against black business owners can provide a solid foundation for development efforts. As Butler and others point out, this is a tradition in black civil society that must be strengthened by revitalizing the kinds of institutions in black communities that provide business-information programs, classes in entrepreneurial skills, networking opportunities, professional degrees, capital assistance, technical advice, rotating credit arrangements, and similar services (Butler 1991, chap. 9; Oliver and Shapiro 1995, chap. 7; Henderson 1984, 66–67). Indeed, Jeremiah Cotton suggests that these kinds of institutions might even provide the basis for the creation of a national corporation in which black Americans could pool their resources by buying shares to make investment funds available for black businesses and community development efforts (1992, 29). As usual, black churches and ecumenical religious organizations are at the forefront of these kinds of efforts. They are increasingly using both private funds and government grants to start development foundations, provide credit, invest in real estate, open businesses, run entrepreneurial skills and technical assistance seminars, begin job training workshops, and sponsor business networking meetings.[12] It is just this kind of institution building and strengthening within black civil society that the state should support with more public funding in order to help foster black economic development.

Beyond providing background support to institutions in black civil society working for economic development, of course, the state can also expand programs aimed at assisting black business formation directly through policies that provide or guarantee credit, sponsor business partnerships, foster investment through tax incentives, set aside parts of government contracts, and provide small business services and technical assistance. As Billy Tidwell, Karen Hill, and Lisa Malone (1988) and Lenneal Henderson (1984) point out, these kinds of efforts were tried in a modest way in the 1970s, but since the early 1980s they have been cut back drastically. As part of a public policy committed to black economic development, however, they should be expanded. One of the most important policies of this kind is minority set-asides in government procurement programs that direct agencies to reserve a certain part of government contracts for minority firms. While the Supreme Court has recently struck down such programs in cases such as *Croson* and *Adarand*, it has nonetheless continued to leave some constitutional room for them, however narrow. It is important that governments at all levels—city, state, and federal—continue to push for such programs as a significant source of support for black-owned businesses. In doing so, they must aggressively gather the evidence of past discrimination that the courts require in such cases, as well as working through the courts to win greater scope for such programs than they currently allow (Bates 1993, chap. 7).

Another policy tool for supporting black economic development is the use of enterprise zones in ghetto neighborhoods. For such zones to be effective, however, they must go beyond simple tax breaks to those maintaining a business address in the neighborhood. As Timothy Bates argues, they must include infrastructure improvements for things like utilities, building renovation, street repair, and communications. They must include programs like low-interest loans, start-up assistance, and set-asides for businesses operating in the zone. And perhaps most importantly, they must carry the requirement that businesses benefiting from such programs draw a significant number of their employees from within that zone (Bates 1993, chap. 7). These kinds of requirements help deliver more of the development benefits of enterprise zones to those actually living in the neighborhoods they cover. Furthermore, insuring that such urban development efforts actually benefit the residents of targeted areas also requires the political mobilization of the local community. This gives residents more control over the course of the development project, allowing them to shape it in ways that most effectively help the neighborhood (Fletcher and Newport 1992). This important role for political mobilization is part of the reason Bates finds that cities with higher levels of black political empowerment, represented by those electing black mayors, provide more hospitable environments for successful black economic development initiatives (1993, chap. 6).

Finally, efforts to foster economic development in black civil society through public policy must make the kinds of enterprises with the best chances for success their primary focus. What Lenneal Henderson wrote more than a decade ago is still largely true today: "Although blacks are no longer captives of black business, black business remains captive to blacks" (1984, 61). The end of segregation meant black consumers could shop at white businesses, but it has not led to many white consumers shopping at black businesses. Black businesses still have had a great deal of difficulty attracting white customers and clients, and this is a problem since a critical part of successful economic development among ethnic or racial minorities is filling market niches serving nongroup consumers (Butler 1991). Not only Greeks eat at Greek diners, and not only Koreans shop at Korean markets. This is why black businesses most likely to attract customers and clients outside as well as within black communities have the most promise and should receive significant support through public policy. Bates (1993) makes a compelling case for this kind of policy approach. He argues that traditional mom-and-pop type businesses with an exclusively black clientele—small food stores, beauty parlors, and so on—hire few if any employees, bring little capital into black communities, and have a high failure rate. On the other hand, an emerging kind of larger and better capitalized black-owned firm that has many employees, higher profits, and clients outside of black communities shows more promise. Such firms in areas like contracting, finance, wholesale, and business and professional services are better able to take advantage of government set-aside programs and enter high-growth sectors of the economy. Their owners tend to have higher incomes and education levels, and they have more start-up capital on hand to establish their businesses in more profitable markets, making their chances for success much higher. They also tend to hire black employees at much higher rates than white businesses that overwhelmingly hire white workers and traditional black family businesses that often have no employees at all. Bates argues that these kinds of emerging black businesses can benefit the most from public policies designed to foster black economic development, and that they in turn can provide more jobs, entrepreneurial leadership, and stable economic institutions for black communities. So while public policy should aim to support economic development within black civil society generally, it should pay particular attention to those areas in which it can have the greatest impact.

*Education*

While the state can play an important role in helping to strengthen the institutions of black civil society through its pubic policies, some of its own institutions are themselves significant contributors to the shape of black civil society, and so policies tied to such institutions must also rely on group-conscious considerations at times. While the basic rights of citizenship that individuals hold from the state should remain grounded in color-blind principles, this does not mean that all state institutions must do so as well, especially those having a large impact within black communities. Public schools are perhaps the best example of this kind of state institution, one that clearly has a significant influence on the shape of black civil society and hence on the autonomy of black Americans. Predominately black primary and secondary schools are institutions that help provide critical cultural, social, and economic resources to group members. They are places where black children interact with each other and with adult role-models, form relationships, pick up cultural meanings and values, and learn social skills. They equip black children to go to college or professional school or directly into the workplace. Predominately black public schools, then, even though organs of the state, serve as important institutions that help define the distinctly black cultural, social, and economic space so critical to autonomy. They are important in group-specific ways, and so group-conscious considerations in designing policies for them are often appropriate.

This is not to say that color-blind considerations are not also important in some areas of education policy. As Jonathan Kozol (1991) points out, a system of funding public education in this country that relies on local property taxes means that predominately black urban schools frequently have far fewer resources than do predominately white suburban ones. Compared to their suburban counterparts, such schools are drastically underfunded and understaffed, they exist in decaying and often dangerous buildings, and they have outdated texts, fewer course offerings, oversized classes, and scarce educational materials. According to Kozol, treating children this unequally in an area as critical to the course of their entire lives as is education, should shock the moral conscience of all citizens. The state mandates that all children go to school, but it does not ensure that the schools they attend will be anything approaching equal: "Thus the state, by requiring attendance but refusing to require equity, effectively requires inequality. Compulsory inequity, perpetuated by state law, too frequently condemns our children to unequal lives" (1991, 56). Kozol is correct. Dramatically unequal support for the education of black and white children effectively reproduces racial inequality across generations by helping to ensure that they will face unequal social and economic opportunities for the rest of their lives. This is why making the amount of time, attention, and resources devoted to educating all children, regardless of race, more equitable should be a primary aim of education policy. The most effective way to do this is also the most overdue reform in American education: abandoning local financing of schools for equal levels of funding across all the districts in a state. The fact that this reform, which seems so obvious since Americans almost universally say educational opportunity should be equally available to all children, is so bitterly resisted by white suburban parents is the strongest testament to its potential to undermine the existing reproduction of economic and social inequality that benefits their children at the expense of poor black children.

The state can also pursue other color-blind educational policies to attack the economic hardship and attendant social problems that disproportionately burden black Americans. These include more funding for efforts such as Head Start, school breakfasts and lunches, tutoring for at-risk students, and afterschool mentoring programs. Urban schools with high numbers of disadvantaged students must also do a much better job expanding and strengthening courses that teach computer, mathematic, language, and critical-thinking skills if their students are to survive in the changing American economy (Wilson 1996, chap. 8; Jones, Chunn, and Robinson 1988). Furthermore, we can only demand and measure progress in these and other academic areas by establishing national education standards with corresponding tests, and by requiring all schools, urban as well as suburban, to meet them. This will allow officials to identify schools that are not doing an adequate job and target them for reform—including firing incompetent teachers and administrators—and additional resources—including more and higher priced teachers, counselors, facilities, and equipment. Finally, education policy must also include stronger efforts to reduce discrimination within schools, discrimination that more frequently makes black students the target of disciplining measures, places them in lower-ability groupings, and channels them into vocational rather than college curriculum tracks (Meier, Stewart, and England 1989a and 1989b; Reed 1988). In all of these areas, then, there continues to be an important role for education policies guided by color-blind principles such as fairness, equality of opportunity, and nondiscrimination. These, however, must also take their place beside policies guided by group-conscious considerations.

Part of the reason for the persistent problems in black education goes beyond funding disparities and similar issues to cultural factors as well. Too often black students do not find the cultural norms and practices of public schools their own, but rather those of white Americans (Brown 1993; Beckman 1995; Schofield 1986). As Janice Hale-Benson argues, black children "participate in a coherent culture that shapes their cognitive development and affects the way they approach academic tasks and the way they behave in traditional academic settings" (1986, 21). In her research, she finds that black and white students tend to have different cognitive and expressive learning styles provided by their cultural backgrounds, and too often schools are exclusively built around and celebrate those of white children, putting black children at a disadvantage and often contributing to their growing discomfort, disinterest, and alienation in academic settings. According to Hale-Benson, black children need the kind of educational environment that accounts for and builds on the strengths of their own cultural experience, one that incorporates norms of achievement, learning, behavior, and communication provided by black culture. This is the kind of approach that education policy should take account of and support if it is to help strengthen the contributions public schools can make within black civil society.

One of the most important ways it can do this is by increasing the number of black teachers and administrators in predominately black schools. One of the consequences of desegregation, especially in the South, was the firing of thousands of black teachers, principals, and other school administrators as separate school systems were merged into single ones (Meier, Stewart, and England 1989a, 17; Blackwell 1985, 158–160). This deprived many black children of a valuable resource in their education by taking away black educators, role-models, and disciplinarians. It is a loss that still needs reversing. Black teachers and administrators help create an educational environment more sensitive to black cultural norms and styles, one that helps black children feel more at home in their own schools rather than like strangers. Such an environment is more challenging and engaging for black children, and as such it can help keep them in school and improve their academic performance. Increasing the number of black teachers and administrators gives more control over black education to African American men and women, it allows black children to see and interact with black adults in positions of authority and responsibility, and research shows it reduces the discriminatory treatment of black children within schools in areas such as disciplining and curriculum tracking (Foster 1994; Hale-Benson 1986, chap. 7; Meier, Stewart, and England 1989a, 31–34, 140–142). Of course, an additional economic and social advantage of hiring more black teachers and administrators is that it opens up more secure and relatively well-paying middle-class jobs for black men and women. Districts with predominately black schools, therefore, should make aggressive efforts to hire more African Americans to staff them, something a politically empowered local black community can effectively push by electing more black school board members (Meier, Stewart, and England 1989a). Such districts will have a difficult time finding enough qualified applicants, however, unless both the federal and state governments join in these efforts and help increase the applicant pool through such measures as special minority scholarships for black undergraduate and graduate students working toward education degrees.

Along with more black teachers and administrators, predominately black schools also need a curriculum that reflects black experiences and accomplishments, one that provides children with the kinds of cultural meanings that affirm black possibility. As Hale-Benson points out, such a curriculum must emphasize academic rigor in traditional subjects like mathematics, writing, and language skills, but it should also draw on the history of African peoples in the United States and the world, as well as the rich traditions of African American literature, art, and music in doing so (1986, chaps. 5–7). Incorporating African American history and culture into the curriculum in this way can help engage black students, make their education more relevant to their own experiences, and better equip them to construct their own lives in civil society (Shujaa 1994a; Brown 1993; Arnez 1993).

In addition to internal changes, predominately black schools must also establish closer ties to the local communities they are a part of. They should be subject to more community involvement and control, allowing black families in black neighborhoods to exercise more of a role in shaping policy at their local schools. This can help establish schools as more influential institutions in black civil society. A closer link between schools and local communities can also expand the role schools play in providing facilities for other activities in black civil society. They can be used for child care in the mornings and afternoons, job training and adult education classes in the evenings and on weekends, sports leagues in the summer, and after-hours meetings by a host of voluntary associations. In this way, they can provide an institutional foundation for many important activities in black civil society that go beyond traditional education, increasing their potential to serve as focal points for the cultural, social, and economic life of their communities.

One recent trend in education policy in which these kinds of efforts—more black teachers and administrators, curriculum changes, closer community ties, and so on—might be more effectively implemented is charter schools. In the last several years, an increasing number of states have drafted legislation allowing community groups to open and operate their own public schools with state funding, usually on a per-pupil basis equal to what the state spends on each student in its traditional public schools. These groups are generally given considerable discretion over how they design, staff, and run each school, as long as they have an open-admissions policy, charge no additional tuition, and observe such things as basic health and safety requirements (Koprowicz and Gordon 1996; Medler 1996; Wohlstetter, Wenning, and Briggs 1995). With the proviso that the state require them to meet the same minimum levels of academic achievement set by the national education standards I advocated above, these kinds of charter schools are an excellent opportunity for groups in black civil society to establish alternative schools offering more creative and engaging programs, more black teachers and administrators, more culturally appropriate curriculums, and higher expectations for parental and community involvement. They provide a way to expand and accelerate the recent and promising trend toward establishing Afrocentric or black-immersion academies, either single sex or coeducational, that provide a culturally supportive environment with a more comprehensive, intensive, and disciplined approach to educating black students, an approach that polls show enjoys a high level of support among black Americans, as well as among a significant number of white Americans (Houppert 1994; Leake and Faltz 1993; Herring 1994, 85–86).

Another policy that can help support these kinds of Afrocentric or black-immersion schools is one providing state vouchers for use by parents at private schools, frequently called a school choice program. Such proposals have attracted praise from many on the right for some time, but they also have supporters across the political spectrum (Nord 1995, chap. 12). Some on the left view these proposals with suspicion, seeing them as attacks on public education that will lead to a grossly unequal two-tiered system with the best students attending secure private schools at government expense and the rest stuck in public schools in even worse shape than today.[13] As people like Josh Clarke (1994) argue, however, the wealthy already enjoy the choice of whether to send their kids to public or private schools, and voucher programs can empower poor urban parents by giving them this same choice, thereby helping to eliminate a two-tiered and unequal system rather than perpetuating it. Indeed, polls show that almost half of all African Americans support vouchers for private schools (Fletcher 1996). Part of this is due to the dismal state of many urban public schools and the fairly successful job many private schools, especially urban Catholic schools that serve increasing numbers of black students, are doing in providing an alternative education (Polite 1992; Chubb and Moe 1990). School-choice plans, then, can provide more black students with a better education while putting pressure on the public schools to also improve in order to attract students and survive.

Perhaps the most promising potential of school-choice plans is to allow more black parents to send their children to independent black private schools. Such schools have been an important part of black civil society for generations. They tend to be small and financially fragile, but they are also able to deliver a quality education in a cultural environment more supportive of black students, one that includes black teachers and administrators as role models and disciplinarians, close ties to other institutions in black communities such as churches, and an increasingly Afrocentric focus in their curriculums.[14] Voucher plans, as well as charter school opportunities, can be an important source of funding for these kinds of schools. Such policies can also spark the financial investment necessary to start many more of them. Black churches, for example, are already often the most financially and socially powerful institutions in many black communities, and with more resources available from the state under these kinds of policy proposals, they have the potential to open and sustain many more black independent schools. Just as urban immigrant Catholics built a vast network of church-based parochial schools as a more secure and culturally appropriate alternative to public schools, black churches can take advantage of voucher and charter policies to begin building such a network for African American children and their parents. This can help dramatically expand the number, scope, and influence of educational institutions in black civil society striving to meet the educational needs of African American students.

## The Police

Police forces are another example of state institutions that have a critically important impact within black civil society and hence on conditions vital to black autonomy. In many ways, the cultural, social, and economic space that constitutes black civil society depends upon police protection for its security. But historically police forces have done a poor job of providing such security, many of them instead posing a serious threat to persons within this space. Rather than providing a secure context in which autonomy becomes possible, police forces themselves in the United States have too often been a severe threat to black autonomy. While modern policing is often traced to Robert Peel's establishing a force in London in the early nineteenth century, it also has deep American roots in the antebellum slave patrols organized in Southern cities and towns to keep slaves from congregating together unless working, to search their quarters for arms, to restrain those acting in any way disruptive, to check them for proper papers when traveling on their owners' business, and to track runaways (Dulaney 1996, chap. 1; Peak and Glensor 1996, 20–21). This pattern continued following the Civil War and up through to the modern civil rights era, as the job of police forces in the United States was less often to protect black citizens than to enforce their subordination through violence and intimidation. This is why protest against police brutality and mistreatment has always been a central part of the quest for freedom by black Americans. Indeed, the riots that rocked many cities across the country in the 1960s were often sparked by incidents of police brutality (Rosentraub and Harlow 1984). Furthermore, this is a pattern that is still powerful today, as the more recent Los Angeles riots in the wake of the Rodney King beating and his attackers' initial acquittal show. There is still considerable evidence that black citizens have much less favorable impressions of the police and their job performance, and that they are far more often the victims of verbal abuse, harassment, brutality, and deadly force at the hands of the police as well.[15]

A police force is at its best when it is part of a community, protecting and strengthening it from within. Too frequently, however, this is not the case in black communities, where the police often continue to be an outside force exercising control and intimidation rather than providing protection and cooperation. This is why police policy must rely on group-conscious considerations at times. It needs to recognize the importance of the police to the security and stability of black civil society, and how this role still goes unfulfilled far too often. In order to help enhance the ability of black civil society to support the autonomy of black men and women, then, police policy must find ways to protect and strengthen this space rather than threatening or neglecting it.

One of the most critical ways it can do this is to increase the number of black officers and commanders in predominately black neighborhoods. It is certainly reasonable to insist that an institution so important to the security of black civil society have a significant black presence. Having group members as officers and in positions of power within the police-command structure can help minimize the abuse of black citizens and reduce the feeling in black communities of being controlled by an outside force. It provides the community, particularly its young people, with black role-models in positions of power, authority, and responsibility. It also helps build trust between the police and local residents, something vital to the ability of the police to effectively fight crime (Ackerlof and Yellen 1994). Increasing the numbers of black Americans in police forces also has economic advantages for group members. In an era of shrinking blue-collar employment, such positions provide stable jobs with decent benefits and relatively good incomes. Indeed, Irish Americans showed a century ago how police jobs can help many group members climb into solid places in the middle or lower-middle class. These social and economic advantages become even more pronounced with policies that give officers financial and promotion incentives to live in the same neighborhoods in which they work. This helps establish greater economic and social stability in such neighborhoods, makes police officers neighbors with a stake in the community rather than strangers, and provides group members in positions of power and authority who can furnish local leadership and inspiration.

It is not enough, however, to simply put more black officers on the streets and in police-command positions. As several researchers point out, African American officers can be just as abusive, corrupt, and neglectful as white officers (Mann 1993, chap. 4; Walker, Spohn, and DeLone 1996, chap. 4; Leinen 1984). It is also necessary to change the structure of traditional policing in black communities. A promising trend in this direction is the recent movement toward community and problem-oriented policing.[16] Both of these reforms move away from the traditional police practice of officers in squad cars responding to emergency calls. Instead, they take a more comprehensive and proactive approach by having officers get to know and work with citizens (not just criminals and their victims) as well as other agencies (utilities, refuse collection, building inspection, and so on) in communities to identify and solve problems as they arise, rather than just coming in to clean up after the fact. Their duties can range from preventing actual lawbreaking to other activities such as helping coordinate neighborhood clean-up, running youth sports leagues, intervening on behalf of tenants with a negligent landlord, and so on. By forming a closer relationship with the communities they protect, such officers are in a better position to work with neighborhood-watch groups, churches and schools, and other voluntary associations trying to fight crime and its roots in more comprehensive and imaginative ways. This style of policing puts an emphasis on combating quality-of-life crimes such as vandalism and disorderly behavior, as well as more violent crimes, in order to reduce fear and to restore a sense of control and stability within neighborhoods. Community and problem-oriented policing, in short, integrates officers into a community to a much greater extent, and it gives them the resources, discretion, and flexibility they need to serve that community once they have gotten to know its residents and their problems in more comprehensive and creative ways.

Much of the momentum for these kinds of policing reforms has come out of problems that African American and other minority neighborhoods have had with the police, and they offer the potential for real improvement (Peak and Glensor 1996, chap. 8). Furthermore, research conducted by Donald Yates and Vijayan Pillai (1992–93) shows that black police officers tend to be more receptive to such innovations in policing than their white colleagues. Combining more black officers and commanders with these kinds of policing reforms, then, has considerable promise. Such an approach to police policy in black neighborhoods can begin to make officers important actors within black communities, ones having the power and expertise to help solve a wide array of problems. It can, in short, begin to draw on the police to help strengthen black civil society rather than threatening it.

### The Potential and the Limits of Public Policy

I have argued in this chapter that public policy can help enhance the autonomy of black men and women in a variety of areas and in a variety of ways. Policies that aggressively enforce nondiscrimination rights, that provide assistance to the economically and socially vulnerable, that foster greater economic and social equality, that open more opportunities in American life for black men and women, that help strengthen institutions in black civil society, that foster black economic development, and that give black citizens greater control over the schools and police forces in their own neighborhoods all contribute to the kind of cultural, social, economic, and political environment that supports the autonomy of black Americans. The different kinds of policies I point to in each of these areas are not new. Most of them have had proponents among scholars, activists, and politicians for some time. What I have tried to show, however, is how these various policy proposals can fit together into a broader approach, one that recognizes the need for a more complex normative framework provided by autonomy.

As I have claimed throughout this book, race is a phenomenon in American life with many dimensions, and so any compelling normative understanding of it must be multidimensional as well. This is also why no single kind of policy is an adequate response to the tangle of issues tied to race. Different kinds of policies are called for in different spheres of American life. What is able to unite these different kinds of policies into a coherent framework, however, is autonomy, itself a complex and multidimensional concept. Too often our policy debates over race are fragmented and narrow, as if a single kind of policy—affirmative action, reducing unwed teenage pregnancy, lowering unemployment, and so on—holds all the answers. Too often we look at race and public policy as a set of discrete, unrelated, and competing proposals. But a concept like autonomy provides a way to unite different kinds of promising policy ideas into a larger and multidimensional theoretical approach. Such an approach is able to grasp the interrelated nature of such policies, showing how taken together they can address the many different dimensions of race in the United States. Autonomy uncovers how we do not face a simple choice between either color-blind or group-conscious policies, because both kinds are necessary. It shows how we do not face a choice between focusing solely on structural economic issues or on so-called values-related issues, but rather how we need to think about both. And autonomy does something more. It grounds this kind of multidimensional policy framework firmly in one of the core values of American liberalism, giving it a normative force and urgency that policy programs too often lack. It is able to give policy debates over race a greater normative as well as theoretical coherence, a coherence that promises to bring more focus and more vitality to liberal policy proposals. Autonomy, therefore, is a powerful way to collect a host of existing policy proposals into a fresh, compelling, and multidimensional framework for addressing issues tied to race in contemporary American life.

In spite of this potential for public policy, however, I think it is critical to remember that there are also limits to what the state can accomplish through its policies when it comes to race. As I have argued, a liberal understanding of race informed by autonomy must recognize the importance of things like informal social practices, cultural meanings, and membership in cultural groups, things that are often beyond the reach of public policy. While the state can help create conditions more supportive of autonomy, it can do so only in a partial way. In a liberal regime, the state has substantial limits; it does not encompass the whole of civil society itself, as in totalitarian regimes. In the United States, then, many of the conditions upon which the autonomy of black men and women hinges exist in civil society beyond the reach of state action. This is why people, both black and white, concerned with autonomy must also work within the institutions, practices, and meanings of civil society themselves, without always turning to the state for help. Focusing attention and effort exclusively on the state falls into color-blind liberalism's error of not paying enough attention to what goes on within civil society; it narrows the possibility of finding ways to address issues tied to race within civil society itself. If autonomy hinges in large part on cultural membership and its influence within the institutions, practices, and meanings of civil society, then that is where those concerned with its promotion must focus more time, money, and energy. This means that efforts to strengthen the institutions of black civil society and to fight discrimination and open up more opportunities in American life generally, independent of any state action, are also critically important to the creation of an autonomy-enhancing environment for black men and women. In short, while recognizing the vital role of public policy in these areas, we must also recognize its limits.

## CONCLUSION

Sometimes public policy is helpful, but sometimes it is not. Just as sometimes color-blind considerations are appropriate, but sometimes group-conscious ones are necessary. This kind of approach to race is full of tensions; it contains different elements pulling it in different directions. Sometimes it demands treating people as individuals without regard to their race, but sometimes it demands treating them differently based on their membership in particular cultural groups. But this is how an understanding of race in the United States should look. Race is a multidimensional phenomenon, one that necessitates a multidimensional normative approach. I think something as complex and full of difficult tensions as race in American life demands a liberal understanding that is also complex and full of difficult tensions. This is what color-blind liberalism has often failed to grasp over the last five decades, causing it to overlook as much as it perceives. The liberal understanding of race I develop in this book is not as neatly unified as the color-blind paradigm I critique, but it does open up the liberal dialogue about race to the kinds of issues color-blind liberalism leaves largely unexamined, issues that turn out to be critical.

It is difficult to try and move beyond color-blind liberalism in this way, because it offers such a powerful moral vision of a society in which people are treated fairly regardless of their race, one in which the color of their skin does not matter to their prospects in life. This is why many people respond with deep suspicion to arguments like the ones I have offered here. They see them as giving up on the promise of our being one common people, of encouraging destructive fragmentation and balkanization in the United States. But for political communities with several distinct cultural groups, the problem should not be how to minimize or eliminate this fact, but rather how to deal with it as a public reality in just and nonviolent ways. The problem with the Balkans being so balkanized is not that it is a region with several distinct cultural groups, but rather that these groups are in the habit of slaughtering each other every so often. Citizens of the United States have never been one common people if this is taken to mean that membership in various and distinct cultural groups is not a critically important part of the country's public life. But this is the wrong way to define national unity. The correct way is to recognize that Americans have always been a common people with a common cultural, social, economic, and political life, but nested within this unity they have also always existed as members of many distinct cultural groups, a fact that is best accommodated and managed rather than suppressed or ignored (Cochran 1995–96). A liberal approach to multiculturalism, then, should not be about a false choice between an American people divided or unified, but rather about how to respond to the reality of cultural diversity within the country's common public life in ways that best uphold our common liberal values, values such as freedom.

While some people are uncomfortable with the idea of trying to move beyond color-blind liberalism, others are uncomfortable with trying to salvage liberalism at all. On their account, liberalism is inescapably infected by its racist past in the United States, and racial justice can only come when liberalism finally goes. I think this objection is also misguided. As the country's primary political language, liberalism certainly bears much of the burden for its political legacy of racism, but, as I have argued, liberalism has the resources to heal itself. Indeed, precisely because it is the country's primary political language, it has the most promise for coming to terms with our persistent "American dilemma." Working within liberalism, and drawing on its core values, like autonomy, is the most fruitful way to find realistic *political* solutions to pressing public problems tied to race in the post–civil rights era. I use the word *political* to indicate that such solutions necessarily lack the refined elegance of abstract political theory. They will not be perfect in the sense of having any measure of postliberal theoretical purity. They are, however, possible in the context of American politics; they hold the promise of real and significant, albeit partial and incomplete, progress.

This emphasis on the *political* flows from my effort to develop an argument at the intersection of theory and practice. I have tried to uncover how liberal political theory has very real applications for one set of political problems—those tied to race—in a single historical and national setting—the postwar United States. Positioning the argument in this way allows it to address some of the central debates within liberal theory by looking at their relevance in a particular and concrete context. The issue of race in the postwar United States shows how the communitarian and politics-of-difference critiques of liberalism both have important applications to very real problems in political life, and it also shows how liberalism can strengthen its ability to respond to these same problems by taking account of both critiques. More specifically, this approach shows how work such as Will Kymlicka's on liberalism and multiculturalism has a concrete relevance in the postwar United States when it comes to race, but that the solutions offered by those like Kymlicka are also not appropriate in this setting. On the other side of the theory-practice divide, my approach shows how normative political thinking can provide a coherent guide for political action. It uncovers the importance of thinking about how we think about race in a moral way, and how abstract theoretical concepts like autonomy can help us do so more fruitfully. This can lay the foundation for a deeper understanding of race and the tangle of issues bound up with it in American life, an understanding that I think ultimately can furnish a better guide for our policy responses. Working at the intersection of theory and practice in this way, then, informs and strengthens both of them, and this is especially important when trying to come to grips with such a pressing and persistent dilemma like race. The intersection of race, liberalism, and freedom in the United States today is necessarily the intersection of theory and practice as well, and this remains a critical intersection to explore as long as we remain a nation defined the way we are by the reality of black and white.

# NOTES

## CHAPTER 1. INTRODUCTION

1. For general overviews of these radical and nationalist traditions in African American thought and practice, see Fredrickson 1995; Marable and Mullings 1994; and Omi and Winant 1994, chapters 3 and 4.

2. See Ignatiev 1995 for a discussion of the Irish and this process.

3. Jenks (1993) and Sewell (1992) both provide useful discussions of how culture can be defined in different ways, including the broad sense that I rely upon here. The view of culture I take is similar to Kymlicka's notion of "societal cultures," which "involve not just shared memories or values, but also common institutions and practices" (1995a, 76–80). I do, however, go beyond Kymlicka's definition of societal culture by claiming that different societal cultures can overlap significantly and that various distinct societal cultures can come nested within larger common ones.

## CHAPTER 2. COLOR-BLIND LIBERALISM

1. As a central feature of the color-blind paradigm, the concept of *discrimination* traditionally refers to practices designed to treat people in such a way as to keep them in a subordinated social, cultural, economic, or political position. Its primary meaning, then, is pejorative, in that it is intended to produce and protect an unjust pattern in which members of a dominant racial group maintain a position of arbitrary privilege at the expense of those belonging to a subordinated group. The concept becomes more complicated, however, with policies such as busing or affirmative action that take explicit account of race in an effort to reverse this pattern of racial subordination. This has lead some within the color-blind paradigm to argue for a distinction between "invidious" discrimination of the traditional kind and "benign" discrimination designed to actually promote racial equality. So while opposition to traditional forms of discrimination designed to enforce racial subordination is at the heart of color-blind liberalism, the issue of race-conscious public policies designed to remedy such subordination has sparked intense internal conflicts within the color-blind paradigm itself, internal conflicts that I examine later in this chapter. In my discussion of color-blind liberalism, then, I use the term *discrimination* in its usual sense to indicate the traditional or "invidious" kind. When I refer to race-conscious policies designed to fight racial subordination, or discrimination with a "benign" intent, I do so explicitly.

2. My discussion of their thought draws primarily on Rawls 1971; Ackerman 1980; and Dworkin 1978a, 1978b, and 1981.

3. Notice that membership in any kind of expressive or cultural group is not one of the two morally relevant positions Rawls considers.

4. For historical accounts of the book's reception and social significance, see Jackson 1990 and Southern 1987.

5. *Brown v. Board of Education*, 347 U.S. 483, 494–495 (1954).

6. King is quoted in Branch 1988, 138–139.

7. Branch (1988 and 1998) and Sitkoff (1993) both provide excellent overviews of the civil rights movement and the resistance to its demands offered by government officials at all levels.

8. The students are quoted in Sitkoff 1993, 70–71.

9. Good discussions of the courts and issues of race can be found in Kull 1992, Lively 1992, and Davis and Graham 1995.

10. *Plessy v. Ferguson*, 163 U.S. 537, 559 (1896).

11. Marshall is quoted in Kull 1992, 146.

12. See her opinions for the Court in decisions such as *City of Richmond v. J. A. Croson Co.*, 488 U.S. 469 (1989); *Adarand v. Pena* 115 S.Ct. 2097 (1995); and *Shaw v. Reno*, 113 S.Ct. 2816 (1993).

13. For an account of the parties and their positioning on racial issues in the postwar period, see Carmines and Stimson 1989.

14. Johnson is quoted in Piven and Cloward 1977, 246.

15. Reagan is quoted in Carmines and Stimson 1989, 54.

16. See Page and Shapiro 1992, 68–75; Sniderman, Tetlock, and Carmines 1993, chap. 10; Sniderman and Piazza 1993; and Sniderman and Hagen 1985.

17. For the records of Republican administrations on these issues, particularly under Reagan, see Shull 1993; Guinier 1994, chap. 2; Carnoy 1994; Days 1984; Barker 1987; Sitkoff 1993, chap. 8; and Franklin 1993, 15–25.

18. For examples of these kinds of arguments within the left interpretation of color-blind liberalism, see Carnoy 1994; Orfield 1988 and 1986; J. Williams 1991; National Urban League 1988; the essays in Gibbs 1988b; and Franklin 1993, chap. 2.

19. See Kull 1992 for a critique of the *Brown* decision on these grounds.

20. The 1972 Democratic Party platform endorsed busing as a way to "eliminate legally imposed segregation." See Carmines and Stimson 1989, 51–52.

21. See several of the essays in Collier and Horowitz 1991 for these kinds of arguments.

22. *Richmond v. Croson*, 488 U.S. 469, 520–521 (1989).

23. Clinton is quoted in "The End of Affirmative Action," *The New Republic*, 3 July 1995.

24. *Regents of the University of California v. Bakke*, 438 U.S. 265 (1978).

25. Ibid., 369.

26. Ibid., 374.

27. Ibid., 401–402.

28. For a good example of how sports metaphors and the language of individual fairness often frames affirmative action debates, see the exchange between Raspberry (1995) and Chavez (1995).

29. Taylor contrasts this view with an exercise-concept of freedom that incorporates some elements of Berlin's positive liberty. It is a version of freedom that will play an important role in my discussion of liberal autonomy in chapter 4.

## CHAPTER 3. THE LIMITS OF COLOR-BLIND LIBERALISM

1. See, for example, Carmichael and Hamilton 1967; Carson 1981; Malcolm X 1970; Lester 1992; Haines 1988; and Sitkoff 1993, chap. 7.

2. For these and related figures on the economic status of African Americans, see Tidwell 1994, appendix; Walker, Spohn, and DeLone 1996, chap. 3; Barker and Jones 1994, 34–41; Hacker 1992, chaps. 6–7; Sitkoff 1993, chap. 8; Jenks 1992, chap. 1; Jacob 1994; and Pennick 1990.

3. For these and related figures on the social burdens disproportionately born by African Americans, see Tidwell 1994, appendix; Walker, Spohn, and DeLone 1996, chaps. 2–3; Blake and Darling 1994; Chiricos and Crawford 1995; McKean 1994; Oliver 1994; Polite 1994; Smith 1995, 69–73; Majors and Billson 1992, chap. 2; Hale-Benson 1986; Farley and Bianchi 1991; Dickson 1993; Massey and Denton 1993; Sitkoff 1993, chap. 8; and the essays in Gibbs 1988b.

4. *Washington v. Davis*, 426 U.S. 229 (1976); *McCleskey v. Kemp*, 481 U.S. 279 (1987); *St. Mary's Honor Center v. Hicks*, 113 S.Ct. 2742 (1993).

5. *Milliken v. Bradley*, 418 U.S. 717 (1974).

6. See *City of Richmond v. J. A. Croson Co.*, 488 U.S. 469 (1989); and *Adarand v. Pena* 115 S.Ct. 2097 (1995).

7. See, for example, Sandel 1996, 1984a, 1984b, and 1982; MacIntyre 1984; Walzer 1990, 1983, and 1992b; Taylor 1993, 1989a, 1989b, and 1985b; Galston 1991, 1988, 1982, and 1980; Bellah et al. 1985; and Glendon 1991.

8. See, for example, Young 1990 and 1989, Kymlicka 1995a and 1989, Okin 1991 and 1989, Pateman 1991, Williams 1995, MacKinnon 1989, Rickard 1994, Taylor 1992, Spinner 1994, Hirshman 1992, Hirshmann 1996, and Gould 1993.

9. This may be part of the reason that the courts, one of color-blind liberalism's most visible forums for developing formal nondiscrimination rights and procedural protections, have had only limited success in fighting discrimination in American public life. See Rosenberg 1991, part 1; Spann 1993; and Bell 1987, chap. 2.

10. See Schofield 1986; Majors and Billson 1992, 13–15; Beckman 1995; and Hale-Benson 1986.

## CHAPTER 4. LIBERAL AUTONOMY

1. It is also why color-blind liberalism's focus on rights, procedural fairness, and equal protection of the laws is still of great value and remains in the autonomy-based liberal understanding of race that I outline in chapter 5.

2. Terry Hoy (1990) argues that Taylor's is a "moral ontology."

3. See Crittenden 1993 for an argument about liberalism and autonomy along these lines.

4. This is a proposal that I consider and reject in the case of race in the United States in chapter 5.

5. Indeed, some might argue that African Americans have demonstrated a deeper commitment to these values, if only because so many white Americans have shown such little regard for them in their racist attitudes and actions throughout American history.

## CHAPTER 5. EXPANDING THE
## LIBERAL UNDERSTANDING OF RACE

1. See Hirshmann 1996 for a similar argument about how a broader notion of autonomy provides the basis for an expanded understanding of gender and freedom in the contemporary United States, one that goes beyond negative liberty to include issues of culture, informal social practices, and group membership in civil society.

2. *Scott v. Sandford*, 60 U.S. (19 How.) 393 (1857).

3. See, for example, Kymlicka 1995a, 1995b, 1993, and 1989; Young 1990 and 1989; Baker 1994; and Svensson 1979. For a general case against such group rights, see Kukathas 1992.

4. See also Frances Svensson's (1979) argument that indigenous Americans deserve communal group rights and a special constitutional status precisely because they are very different from African Americans who pushed for universal rights and the equal protection of the laws during the civil rights movement.

5. For an argument about the importance of this kind of space to the political history of European ethnic groups in the United States, especially that of Irish Americans, see Cochran 1995–96.

6. One may even be both a black American and an Irish American, though an ethnic group that considers itself a part of white America may be rather unwilling to accept its members who are also black.

7. See, for example, Baldwin 1990; Allen, Dawson, and Brown 1989; Hale-Benson 1986, 14–19, 61–62, chap. 2; Mitchell 1994; and Majors and Billson 1992, chap. 5.

8. See, for example, Frankenberg 1993, Roediger 1991 and 1994, Ignatiev 1995, Haney-Lopez 1996, and Allen 1994.

9. See Littlejohn-Blake and Darling 1993; Hale-Benson 1986, chap. 3; Stack 1991; and Flaherty, Facteau, and Garver 1991.

10. See Darling 1994; Butler 1991; Lincoln and Mamiya 1990, chap. 9; and Taylor 1994, 14–20.

11. See, for example, Olsen 1970, Miller et al. 1981, London and Giles 1987, Ellison and London 1992, and Whittler, Calantone, and Young 1991.

12. I take at detailed look at such policies in the next chapter.

13. See, for example, Olsen 1970, McPherson 1977, Miller et al. 1981, Shingles 1981, London and Giles 1987, and Ellison and London 1992.

14. These denominations are the African Methodist Episcopal Church; the African Methodist Episcopal Zion Church; the Christian Methodist Episcopal Church; the National Baptist Convention, U.S.A.; the National Baptist Convention of America; the Progressive National Baptist Convention; and the Church of God in Christ (Lincoln and Mamiya 1990, 1).

15. See Lincoln and Mamiya 1990, chap. 1; Wilmore 1983; Lincoln 1983; and Baer and Singer 1992, chap. 1.

16. It has, however, rarely been a position open to young black women of ambition and talent (Lincoln and Mamiya 1990, chap. 10).

17. Samuel Freedman (1993) provides a particularly detailed portrait of this kind of extended social network serving the needs of members of a large black church in Brooklyn.

18. See Lincoln and Mamiya 1990, Freedman 1993, Baer and Singer 1992, Taylor 1994, and Harris 1993.

19. See Lincoln and Mamiya 1990, Freedman 1993, Baer and Singer 1992, Taylor 1994, and Harris 1993.

20. For evidence of this trend with many local examples, see Richardson 1994; Gite 1993; Freedman 1993; and Lincoln and Mamiya, chap. 9.

21. Branch (1988 and 1998) provides perhaps the best recent account of the contributions of black churches to the civil rights movement.

22. See p. 51.

23. See Wilson 1987 and 1996; Smith 1995, chap. 6; K. Jennings 1992; Crutchfield 1995; and many of the essays in Lawson 1992 and Gibbs 1988b for examples of scholars who focus on the structural causes of social problems in black communities, though they often disagree sharply over what kinds of structural factors are most decisive, as the debate over Wilson's (1987) work indicates.

24. Harris (1993) provides the best general description of this kind of potential within the black church, while Freedman (1993) provides the best description of it in action.

## CHAPTER 6. PUBLIC POLICY

1. See, for example, Ignatiev's (1995) study of this process and Irish Americans.

2. *Griggs v. Duke Power Co.*, 401 U.S. 424 (1971); *McDonnell Douglass Corp. v. Green*, 411 U.S. 792 (1973).

3. *Washington v. Davis*, 426 U.S. 229 (1976).

4. *Pullman-Standard v. Swint*, 456 U.S. 237 (1982); *Firefighters v. Stotts*, 467 U.S. 561 (1984); *Wygant v. Jackson Board of Education*, 476 U.S. 267 (1986); *St. Mary's Honor Center v. Hicks*, 113 S.Ct. 2742 (1993); *McCleskey v. Kemp*, 481 U.S. 279 (1987).

5. *Wards Cove Packing, Co., Inc. v. Antonio*, 490 U.S. 642 (1989).

6. *City of Richmond v. J. A. Croson Co.*, 488 U.S. 469 (1989); *Adarand v. Pena*, 115 S.Ct. 2097 (1995).

7. For evidence of this comparative underdevelopment and various explanations for it, see Esping-Anderson 1990a and 1990b, Skocpol 1992, Amenta

and Skocpol 1988 and 1989, Orloff 1988, Weir and Skocpol 1985, Katz 1986 and 1989, and Brinkley 1994.

8. See, for example, Carnoy 1994, chap. 9; K. Jennings 1992; Marable 1991b; Larson 1988; and Watson, Austin, and Reed 1988.

9. See, for example, a recent series of articles by Robert Putnam (1995a, 1995b, 1995c).

10. Indeed, as C. Eric Lincoln claims, few programs can match the success of the highly nationalistic Nation of Islam in helping individuals turn away from a life of crime, drug abuse, and alienation (1994, 24, 28–30).

11. *Bowan v. Kendrick* , 108 S.Ct. 2562 (1988).

12. See, for example, Richardson 1994; Gite 1993; Lincoln and Mamiya 1990, chap. 8; and Sawyer 1994, chap. 7.

13. See, for example, Greider 1992; Carnoy 1994, 226–228; and Kozol 1991, 61–63.

14. For discussions of black independent schools and their potential benefits, see Ratteray 1994 and 1992; Foster 1992; Jones-Wilson, Arnez, and Asbury 1992; Lee 1992; and Shujaa 1994b.

15. See, for example, Walker, Spohn, and DeLone 1996, chap. 4; Mann 1993, chap. 4; McKean 1994; Browning et al. 1994; Webb and Marshall 1995; Smith 1995, chap. 3; Peak and Glensor 1996, chap. 8; and Davis and Graham 1995, 397–407.

16. For discussions of both these approaches, see Peak and Glensor 1996, Goldstein 1990, Eck 1993, Mastrofski and Green 1993, and Buerger 1993.

# REFERENCES

Ackerlof, George, and Janet L. Yellen. 1994. "Gang Behavior, Law Enforcement, and Community Values." In *Values and Public Policy*, ed. Henry J. Aaron, Thomas E. Mann, and Timothy Taylor. Washington, D.C.: Brookings.

Ackerman, Bruce A. 1980. *Social Justice in the Liberal State*. New Haven, Conn.: Yale University Press.

Alexis, Marcus, and Geraldine R. Henderson. 1994. "The Economic Base of African-American Communities: A Study of Consumption Patterns." In *The State of Black America 1994*, ed. Billy J. Tidwell. New York: National Urban League.

Allen, Richard L., Michael C. Dawson, and Ronald E. Brown. 1989. "A Schema-Based Approach to Modeling an African-American Racial Belief System." *American Political Science Review* 83:421–441.

Allen, Theodore W. 1994. *The Invention of the White Race*. Vol. 1: *Racial Oppression and Social Control*. London: Verso.

Amenta, Edwin, and Theda Skocpol. 1988. "Redefining the New Deal: World War II and the Development of Social Provision in the United States." In *The Politics of Social Policy in the United States*, ed. Margaret Weir, Ann Shola Orloff, and Theda Skocpol. Princeton, N.J.: Princeton University Press.

———. 1989. "Taking Exception: Explaining the Distinctiveness of American Public Policies in the Last Century." In *The Comparative History of Public Policy*, ed. Francis G. Castles. New York: Oxford University Press.

Arnez, Nancy L. 1993. "Equity and Access in the Instructional Materials Arena." *Journal of Black Studies* 23:500–514.

Asante, Molefi Kete. 1987. *The Afrocentric Idea*. Philadelphia: Temple University Press.

———. 1990. *Kemet, Afrocentricity, and Knowledge*. Trenton, N.J.: Africa World Press.

Baer, Hans A., and Merrill Singer. 1992. *African-American Religion in the Twentieth Century: Varieties of Protest and Accommodation*. Knoxville: The University of Tennessee Press.

Bailyn, Bernard. 1967. *The Ideological Origins of the American Revolution*. Cambridge: Harvard University Press.

Baker, Judith, ed. 1994. *Group Rights*. Toronto: University of Toronto Press.

Baldwin, Joseph A. 1990. "African-American and European-American Cultural Differences as Assessed by the Worldviews Paradigm: An Empirical Analysis." *The Western Journal of Black Studies* 14:38–52.

Banfield, Edward C., and James Q. Wilson. 1966. *City Politics*. Cambridge: Harvard University Press.

Barker, Lucius J. 1987. "Ronald Reagan, Jesse Jackson, and the 1984 Presidential Election: The Continuing American Dilemma of Race." In *The New Black Politics: The Search for Political Power*, ed. Michael B. Preston, Lenneal J. Henderson Jr., and Paul L. Puryear. 2nd ed. New York: Longman.

Barker, Lucius J., and Mack H. Jones. 1994. *African Americans and the American Political System*. Englewood Cliffs, N.J.: Prentice Hall.

Bates, Timothy. 1993. *Banking on Black Enterprise: The Potential of Emerging Firms for Revitalizing Urban Economies*. Washington, D.C.: Joint Center for Political and Economic Studies.

Beckman, Walter F. 1995. "Race Relations and Segregation in the United States." In *Class, Culture, and Race in American Schools: A Handbook*, ed. Stanley William Rothstein. Westport, Conn.: Greenwood Press.

Bell, Daniel. 1975. "Ethnicity and Social Change." In *Ethnicity: Theory and Experience*, ed. Nathan Glazer and Daniel P. Moynihan. Cambridge: Harvard University Press.

Bell, Derrick. 1987. *And We Are Not Saved: The Elusive Quest for Racial Justice*. New York: Basic Books.

Bellah, Robert N., et al. 1985. *Habits of the Heart: Individualism and Commitment in American Life*. New York: Harper & Row.

Bennett, William J., and Dan Coats. 1995. "Moving Beyond Devolution." *The Wall Street Journal*, 5 September, A14.

Berger, Peter L., and Richard John Neuhaus. 1977. *To Empower People: The Role of Mediating Structures in Public Policy*. Washington, D.C.: American Enterprise Institute.

Berlin, Isaiah. 1969. *Four Essays on Liberty*. London: Oxford University Press.

Bernstein, Blanche. 1991. "Since the Moynihan Report." In *The Black Family: Essays and Studies*, ed. Robert Staples. 4th ed. Belmont, Calif.: Wadsworth.

Blackwell, James E. 1985. *The Black Community: Diversity and Unity*. 2nd ed. New York: Harper & Row.

Blake, Wayne M., and Carol A. Darling. 1994. "The Dilemmas of the African American Male." *Journal of Black Studies* 24:402–415.

Bolick, Clint. 1995. "Fulfilling the Promise of Equal Opportunity." *The Responsive Community* 5(2):54–58.

Boxhill, Bernard R. 1984. *Blacks and Social Justice*. Totowa, N.J.: Rowman & Allanheld.

Boyte, Harry C. 1984. *Community is Possible: Repairing America's Roots*. New York: Harper & Row.

Bradford, William D. 1994. "Dollars for Deeds: Prospects and Prescriptions for African-American Financial Institutions." In *The State of Black America 1994*, ed. Billy J. Tidwell. New York: National Urban League.

Branch, Taylor. 1988. *Parting the Waters: America in the King Years, 1954–1963*. New York: Simon & Schuster.

———. 1998. *Pillar of Fire: America in the King Years, 1963–1965*. New York: Simon & Schuster.

Brinkley, Alan. 1994. "For Their Own Good." *The New York Review of Books*, 26 May, 40–43.

Brooks, Roy L. 1990. *Rethinking the American Race Problem*. Berkeley, Calif.: University of California Press.

Brown, Kevin. 1993. "Do African-Americans Need Immersion Schools? The Paradoxes Created by Legal Conceptualization of Race and Public Education." *Iowa Law Review* 78:813–881.

Browning, Sandra Lee, et al. 1994. "Race and Getting Hassled by the Police." *Police Studies* 17(1):1–11.

Buerger, Michael E. 1993. "The Challenge of Reinventing Police and Community." In *Police Innovation and Control of the Police: Problems of Law, Order, and Community*, ed. David Weisburd and Craig Uchida. New York: Springer-Verlag.

Butler, John Sibley. 1991. *Entrepreneurship and Self-Help among Black Americans: A Reconsideration of Race and Economics*. Albany: State University of New York Press.

Canada, Geoffrey. 1995. *Fist, Stick, Knife, Gun: A Personal History of Violence in America*. Boston: Beacon Press.

Carmichael, Stokely, and Charles V. Hamilton. 1967. *Black Power: The Politics of Liberation in America*. New York: Random House.

Carmines, Edward G., and James A. Stimson. 1989. *Issue Evolution: Race and the Transformation of American Politics*. Princeton, N.J.: Princeton University Press.

Carnoy, Martin. 1994. *Faded Dreams: The Politics and Economics of Race in America*. Cambridge: Cambridge University Press.

Carson, Clayborne. 1981. *In Struggle: SNCC and the Black Awakening of the 1960s*. Cambridge: Harvard University Press.

Chavez, Linda. 1995. "Specific Remedies for Specific People." *The Washington Post*, 4 July, A21.

Chiricos, Theodore G., and Charles Crawford. 1995. "Race and Imprisonment: A Contextual Assessment of the Evidence." In *Ethnicity, Race, and Crime: Perspectives across Time and Place*, ed. Darnell F. Hawkins. Albany: State University of New York Press.

Chubb, John E., and Terry M. Moe. 1990. *Politics, Markets, and America's Schools*. Washington, D.C.: Brookings.

Clark, Josh. 1994. "Offer Competition in the Form of Choice and Charter Schools." *Utne Reader* 61:85–87.

Clarke, Stuart Alan. 1989. "Liberalism and Black Political Thought: The Afro-American Dilemma." *National Political Science Review* 1:5–14.

Clotfelter, Charles T., ed. 1992. *Who Benefits from the Nonprofit Sector?* Chicago: University of Chicago Press.

Coats, Dan. 1996. "Can Congress Revive Civil Society?" *Policy Review* 75:24–28.

Cochran, David Carroll. 1995–96. "Ethnic Diversity and Democratic Stability: The Case of Irish Americans." *Political Science Quarterly* 110:587–604.

Cohen, Richard. 1995. "Affirmative Action under the Gun." *The Washington Post*, 31 January, A15.

Collier, Peter and David Horowitz, eds. 1991. *Second Thoughts about Race in America*. Lanham, Md.: Madison Books.

Cotton, Jeremiah. 1992. "Towards a Theory and Strategy for Black Economic Development." In *Race, Politics, and Economic Development: Community Perspectives*, ed. James Jennings. London: Verso.

Crittenden, Jack. 1993. "The Social Nature of Autonomy." *The Review of Politics* 55:35–65.

Crutchfield, Robert D. 1995. "Ethnicity, Labor Markets, and Crime." In *Ethnicity, Race, and Crime: Perspectives across Time and Place*, ed. Darnell F. Hawkins. Albany: State University of New York Press.

Darling, Marsha Jean. 1994. "We Have Come this Far by Our Own Hands: A Tradition of African American Self-Help and Philanthropy and the Growth of Corporate Philanthropic Giving to African Americans." In *African Americans and the New Policy Consensus: Retreat of the Liberal State?*, ed. Marilyn E. Lashley and Melanie Njeri Jackson. Westport, Conn.: Greenwood Press.

Davis, Abraham L., and Barbara Luck Graham. 1995. *The Supreme Court, Race, and Civil Rights*. Thousand Oaks, Calif.: Sage Publications.

Dawson, Michael C. 1994. *Behind the Mule: Race and Class in African-American Politics*. Princeton, N.J.: Princeton University Press.

Days, Drew S. III. 1984. "Turning Back the Clock: The Reagan Administration and Civil Rights." *Harvard Civil Rights–Civil Liberties Law Review* 19:309–347.

Dewar, Helen. 1996. "Coats Seeks to Warm GOP Image through 'Poverty Tax Credit' Plan." *The Washington Post*, 25 February, A4.

Dickson, Lynda. 1993. "The Future of Marriage and Family in Black America." *Journal of Black Studies* 23:472–491.

Dolbeare, Kenneth M. 1984. Introduction to *American Political Thought*. Rev. ed. Chatham, N.J.: Chatham House.

D'Souza, Dinesh. 1995. *The End of Racism: Principles for a Multiracial Society*. New York: The Free Press.

Dulaney, W. Marvin. 1996. *Black Police in America*. Bloomington, Ind.: Indiana University Press.

Dworkin, Gerald. 1988. *The Theory and Practice of Autonomy*. Cambridge: Cambridge University Press.

———. 1989. "The Concept of Autonomy." In *The Inner Citadel: Essays on Individual Autonomy*, ed. John Christman. New York: Oxford University Press.

Dworkin, Ronald. 1977. "Social Sciences and Constitutional Rights." *The Educational Forum* 41:271–280.

———. 1978a. "Liberalism." In *Public and Private Morality*, ed. Stuart Hampshire. Cambridge: Cambridge University Press.

———. 1978b. *Taking Rights Seriously*. Cambridge: Harvard University Press.

———. 1981. "What Is Equality? Part 2: Equality of Resources." *Philosophy and Public Affairs* 10:283–345.

———. 1985. *A Matter of Principle*. Cambridge: Harvard University Press.

———. 1986. *Law's Empire*. Cambridge, MA: Harvard University Press.

Eck, John E. 1993. "Alternative Futures for Policing." In *Police Innovation and Control of the Police: Problems of Law, Order, and Community*, ed. David Weisburd and Craig Uchida. New York: Springer-Verlag.

Eisenhower, Dwight D. 1992. "Address on Little Rock." In *Documentary History of the Modern Civil Rights Movement*, ed. Peter B. Levy. New York: Greenwood Press.

Ellison, Christopher G., and Bruce London. 1992. "The Social and Political Participation of Black Americans: Compensatory and Ethnic Community Perspectives Revisited." *Social Forces* 70:681–701.

Esping-Anderson, Gosta. 1990a. *The Three Worlds of Welfare Capitalism.* Princeton, N.J.: Princeton University Press.

———. 1990b. "The Three Political Economies of the Welfare State." *International Journal of Sociology* 20(3): 92–123.

Farhi, Paul. 1994. "A Television Trend: Audiences in Black and White." *The Washington Post*, 29 November, A1, 20.

Farley, Reynolds, and Suzanne M. Bianchi. 1991. "The Growing Racial Difference in Marriage and Family Patterns." In *The Black Family: Essays and Studies*, ed. Robert Staples. 4th ed. Belmont, Calif.: Wadsworth.

Feagin, Joe R. 1991. "The Continuing Significance of Race: Anti-Black Discrimination in Public Places." *American Sociological Review* 56:101–116.

Feagin, Joe R., and Melvin P. Sikes. 1994. *Living with Racism: The Black Middle-Class Experience.* Boston: Beacon Press.

Feinberg, Joel. 1989. "Autonomy." In *The Inner Citadel: Essays on Individual Autonomy*, ed. John Christman. New York: Oxford University Press.

Fields, Barbara Jeanne. 1990. "Slavery, Race and Ideology in the United States of America." *New Left Review* 181:95–118.

Fix, Michael, and Raymond J. Struyk, eds. 1992. *Clear and Convincing Evidence: Measurement of Discrimination in America.* Washington, D.C.: Urban Institute Press.

Flaherty, Sr. Mary Jean, Lorna Facteau, and Patricia Garver. 1991. "Grandmother Functions in Multigenerational Families: An Exploratory Study of Black Adolescent Mothers and their Infants." In *The Black Family: Essays and Studies*, ed. Robert Staples. 4th ed. Belmont, Calif.: Wadsworth.

Fletcher, Michael A. 1996. "Study Tracks Blacks' Crime Concerns." *The Washington Post*, 21 April, A11.

Fletcher, William, and Eugene Newport. 1992. "Race and Economic Development: The Need for a Black Agenda." In *Race, Politics, and Economic Development: Community Perspectives*, ed. James Jennings. London: Verso.

Foley, Michael. 1991. *American Political Ideas: Traditions and Usages.* Manchester, England: Manchester University Press.

Fordham, Signithia, and John U. Ogbu. 1986. "Black Students' School Success: Coping with the 'Burden of "Acting White."'" *The Urban Review* 18:176–206.

Foster, Gail. 1992. "New York City's Wealth of Historically Black Independent Schools." *The Journal of Negro Education* 61:186–200.

Foster, Michele. 1994. "Educating for Competence in Community and Culture: Exploring the Views of Exemplary African-American Teachers." In *Too Much Schooling, Too Little Education: A Paradox of Black Life in White Societies*, ed. Mwalimu J. Shujaa. Trenton, N.J.: Africa World Press.

Frankenberg, Ruth. 1993. *White Women, Race Matters: The Social Construction of Whiteness.* Minneapolis: University of Minnesota Press.

Frankfurt, Harry G. 1988. *The Importance of What We Care About: Philosophical Essays*. Cambridge: Cambridge University Press.

Franklin, John Hope. 1993. *The Color Line: Legacy for the Twenty-First Century*. Columbia: University of Missouri Press.

Fredrickson, George M. 1995. *Black Liberation: A Comparative History of Black Ideologies in the United States and South Africa*. New York: Oxford University Press.

Freedman, Samuel G. 1993. *Upon This Rock: The Miracles of a Black Church*. New York: HarperCollins.

Gaertner, Samuel L., and John F. Dovidio. 1986. "The Aversive Form of Racism." In *Prejudice, Discrimination, and Racism*, ed. John F. Dovidio and Samuel L. Gaertner. Orlando, Fla.: Academic Press.

Galston, William A. 1980. *Justice and the Human Good*. Chicago: University of Chicago Press.

———. 1982. "Defending Liberalism." *American Political Science Review* 76:621–629.

———. 1988. "Liberal Virtues." *American Political Science Review* 82:1277–1290.

———. 1991. *Liberal Purposes: Goods, Virtues, and Diversity in the Liberal State*. Cambridge: Cambridge University Press.

———. 1995. "Two Concepts of Liberalism." *Ethics* 105:516–534.

Geertz, Clifford. 1973. *The Interpretation of Cultures: Selected Essays*. New York: Basic Books.

Gibbs, Jewelle Taylor. 1988a. "Young Black Males in America: Endangered, Embittered, and Embattled." In *Young, Black, and Male in America: An Endangered Species*, ed. Jewelle Taylor Gibbs. New York: Auburn House.

———, ed. 1988b. *Young, Black, and Male in America: An Endangered Species*. New York: Auburn House.

Gite, Lloyd. 1993. "The New Agenda of the Black Church: Economic Development for Black America." *Black Enterprise* 24:5, 54–59.

Glendon, Mary Ann. 1991. *Rights Talk: The Impoverishment of Political Discourse*. New York: Free Press.

Goldstein, Herman. 1990. *Problem-Oriented Policing*. Philadelphia: Temple University Press.

Gould, Carol C. 1993. "Diversity and Democracy: Representing Differences." Paper prepared for presentation at the 1993 Conference for the Study of Political Thought, Yale University, New Haven, Conn., April 16–18, 1993.

Graber, Mark A. 1991. *Transforming Free Speech: The Ambiguous Legacy of Civil Libertarianism*. Berkeley: University of California Press.

Graham, Lawrence Otis. 1995. *Member of the Club: Reflections on Life in a Racially Polarized World*. New York: HarperCollins.

Gray, John. 1986. *Liberalism*. Minneapolis: University of Minnesota Press.

Greider, William. 1992. "Stand and Deliver." *Utne Reader* 54:73–79.

Guest, Stephen. 1991. *Ronald Dworkin*. Stanford, Calif.: Stanford University Press.

Guinier, Lani. 1994. *The Tyranny of the Majority: Fundamental Fairness in Representative Democracy*. New York: Free Press.

Hacker, Andrew. 1992. *Two Nations: Black and White, Separate, Hostile, Unequal.* New York: Charles Scribner's Sons.

Haines, Herbert H. 1988. *Black Radicals and the Civil Rights Mainstream, 1954–1970.* Knoxville: University of Tennessee Press.

Hale-Benson, Janice E. 1986. *Black Children: Their Roots, Culture, and Learning Styles.* Rev. ed. Baltimore: Johns Hopkins University Press.

Halpern, Robert. 1995. *Rebuilding the Inner City: A History of Neighborhood Initiatives to Address Poverty in the United States.* New York: Columbia University Press.

Hamilton, Charles V. 1976. "Public Policy and Some Political Consequences." In *Public Policy for the Black Community: Strategies and Perspectives,* ed. Marguerite Ross Barnett and James A. Hefner. New York: Alfred Publishing.

Haney-Lopez, Ian. 1996. *White by Law: The Legal Construction of Race.* New York: New York University Press.

Harris, Forrest E. 1993. *Ministry for Social Crisis: Theology and Praxis in the Black Church Tradition.* Macon, Ga.: Mercer University Press.

Hartz, Louis. 1955. *The Liberal Tradition in America.* New York: Harcourt Brace.

Hatch, John, and Steve Derthick. 1992. "Empowering Black Churches for Health Promotion." *Health Values* 16(5):3–9.

Heisler, Martin O. 1991. "Ethnicity and Ethnic Relations in the Modern West." In *Conflict and Peacemaking in Multiethnic Societies,* ed. Joseph V. Montville. New York: Lexington Books.

Henderson, Lenneal J. Jr. 1984. "Black Business Enterprise and Public Policy." In *Contemporary Public Policy Perspectives and Black Americans,* ed. Mitchell F. Rice and Woodrow Jones Jr. Westport, Conn.: Greenwood Press.

Herring, Cedric. 1994. "Who Represents the People? African Americans, Public Policy, and Political Alienation during the Reagan-Bush Years." In *African Americans and the New Policy Consensus: Retreat of the Liberal State?* ed. Marilyn E. Lashley and Melanie Njeri Jackson. Westport, Conn.: Greenwood Press.

Hirshman, Linda R. 1992. "The Rape of Locke: Race, Gender, and the Loss of Liberal Virtue." *Stanford Law Review* 44:1133–1162.

Hirshmann, Nancy J. 1996. "Toward a Feminist Theory of Freedom." *Political Theory* 24:46–67.

Hochschild, Jennifer L. 1995. *Facing Up to the American Dream: Race, Class, and the Soul of the Nation.* Princeton, N.J.: Princeton University Press.

Holmstrom, David. 1995. "Seeking Solutions for the Hand-Gun Generation." *The Christian Science Monitor,* 5 June, 13.

Houppert, Karen. 1994. "Establish Afrocentric All-Male Academies." *Utne Reader* 61:83–85.

Hoy, Terry. 1990. "The Moral Ontology of Charles Taylor: Contra Deconstructivism." *Philosophy and Social Criticism* 16:207–225.

Ignatiev, Noel. 1995. *How the Irish Became White.* New York: Routledge.

Jackson, Walter A. 1990. *Gunnar Myrdal and America's Conscience: Social Engineering and Racial Liberalism, 1938–1987.* Chapel Hill: University of North Carolina Press.

Jacob, John E. 1994. "Black America, 1993: An Overview." In *The State of Black America 1994*, ed. Billy J. Tidwell. New York: National Urban League.

Jenks, Chris. 1993. *Culture*. London: Routledge.

Jenks, Christopher. 1992. *Rethinking Social Policy: Race, Poverty, and the Underclass*. Cambridge: Harvard University Press.

Jennings, James. 1992a. *The Politics of Black Empowerment: The Transformation of Black Activism in Urban America*. Detroit, Mich.: Wayne State University Press.

———. 1992b. Introduction to *Race, Politics, and Economic Development: Community Perspectives*, ed. James Jennings. London: Verso.

———. 1992c. "Blacks, Politics, and the Human Service Crisis." In *Race, Politics, and Economic Development: Community Perspectives*, ed. James Jennings. London: Verso.

Jennings, Keith. 1992. "Understanding the Persisting Crisis of Black Youth Unemployment." In *Race, Politics, and Economic Development: Community Perspectives*, ed. James Jennings. London: Verso.

Johnson, Lyndon B. 1992. "Address Before a Joint Session of Congress." In *Documentary History of the Modern Civil Rights Movement*, ed. Peter B. Levy. New York: Greenwood Press.

Jones, Dionne J., Eva W. Chunn, and Stephanie G. Robinson. 1988. "Education: In Search of Equity and Excellence." In *Black Americans and Public Policy: Perspectives of the National Urban League*. New York: National Urban League.

Jones, Mack. 1992. "The Black Underclass as Systemic Phenomenon." In *Race, Politics, and Economic Development: Community Perspectives*, ed. James Jennings. London: Verso.

Jones-Wilson, Faustine C., Nancy L. Arnez, and Charles A. Asbury. 1992. "Why Not Public Schools?" *The Journal of Negro Education* 61:125–137.

Kaggwa, Larry N. 1993. "Digging in to Fight Blight." *The Washington Post*, 5 August, DC3.

Katz, Michael B. 1986. *In the Shadow of the Poorhouse: A Social History of Welfare in America*. New York: Basic Books.

———. 1989. *The Undeserving Poor: From the War on Poverty to the War on Welfare*. New York: Pantheon Books.

Kaus, Mickey. 1992. *The End of Equality*. New York: Basic Books.

Keane, John. 1988a. *Democracy and Civil Society*. London: Verso.

———. 1988b. "Despotism and Democracy." In *Civil Society and The State: New European Perspectives*, ed. John Keane. London: Verso.

Kelley, Robin D. G. 1994. *Race Rebels: Culture, Politics, and the Black Working Class*. New York: Free Press.

Kennedy, John F. 1992. "Address." In *Documentary History of the Modern Civil Rights Movement*, ed. Peter B. Levy. New York: Greenwood Press.

King, Martin Luther Jr. 1970. "Letter from Birmingham Jail." In *What Country Have I? Political Writings by Black Americans*, ed. Herbert Storing. New York: St. Martin's Press.

———. 1992. "I Have a Dream." In *Documentary History of the Modern Civil Rights Movement*, ed. Peter B. Levy. New York: Greenwood Press.

Kirkland, Frank M. 1992. "Social Policy, Ethical Life, and the Urban Underclass." In *The Underclass Question*, ed. Bill E. Lawson. Philadelphia: Temple University Press.

Koprowicz, Connie, and Dianna Gordon. 1996. "A Charter for Change." *State Legislatures* 22(2):16–21.

Kozol, Jonathan. 1991. *Savage Inequalities: Children in America's Schools*. New York: Crown.

Kramer, Ralph M. 1981. *Voluntary Agencies in the Welfare State*. Berkeley: University of California Press.

Kukathas, Chandran. 1992. "Are There Any Cultural Rights?" *Political Theory* 20:105–139.

Kull, Andrew. 1992. *The Color-Blind Constitution*. Cambridge: Harvard University Press.

Kymlicka, Will. 1989. *Liberalism, Community, and Culture*. Oxford: Oxford University Press.

———. 1993. "Three Forms of Group-Differentiated Citizenship in Canada." Paper prepared for presentation at the 1993 Conference for the Study of Political Thought, Yale University, New Haven, Conn., April 16–18, 1993.

———. 1995a. *Multicultural Citizenship: A Liberal Theory of Minority Rights*. New York: Oxford University Press.

———, ed. 1995b. *The Rights of Minority Cultures*. New York: Oxford University Press.

Larson, Tom E. 1988. "Employment and Unemployment of Young Black Males." In *Young, Black, and Male in America: An Endangered Species*, ed. Jewelle Taylor Gibbs. New York: Auburn House.

Lawrence, Charles R. 1987. "The Id, the Ego, and Equal Protection: Reckoning with Unconscious Racism." *Stanford Law Review* 39:317–388.

Lawson, Bill E., ed. 1992. *The Underclass Question*. Philadelphia: Temple University Press.

Leake, Donald O., and Christine J. Faltz. 1993. "Do We Need to Desegregate All of Our Black Schools?" *Educational Policy* 7:370–387.

Lee, Carol D. 1992. "Profile of an Independent Black Institution: African-Centered Education at Work." *The Journal of Negro Education* 61:160–177.

Leinen, Stephen. 1984. *Black Police, White Society*. New York: New York University Press.

Lester, Julius. 1992. "The Angry Children of Malcolm X." In *Documentary History of the Modern Civil Rights Movement*, ed. Peter B. Levy. New York: Greenwood Press.

Lincoln, C. Eric. 1983. Forward to *Black Religion and Black Radicalism: An Interpretation of the Religious History of Afro-American People*, by Gayraud S. Wilmore. 2nd ed. Maryknoll, N.Y.: Orbis Books.

———. 1994. *The Black Muslims in America*. 3rd ed. Grand Rapids, Mich.: William B. Eerdmans.

Lincoln, C. Eric, and Lawrence H. Mamiya. 1990. *The Black Church in the African American Experience*. Durham, N.C.: Duke University Press.

Litt, Edgar. 1970. *Beyond Pluralism: Ethnic Politics in America*. Glenview, Ill.: Scott, Foresman and Company.

Littlejohn-Blake, Sheila M., and Carol Anderson Darling. 1993. "Understanding the Strengths of African American Families." *Journal of Black Studies* 23:460–471.

Lively, Donald E. 1992. *The Constitution and Race*. New York: Praeger.

Locke, John. 1975. *An Essay Concerning Human Understanding*, ed. Peter H. Nidditch. London: Oxford University Press.

———. 1982. *Second Treatise of Government*, ed. Richard Cox. Arlington Heights, Ill.: Harlan Davidson.

London, Bruce. 1975. "Racial Differences in Social and Political Participation: Not Simply a Matter of Black and White." *Social Science Quarterly* 56:274–286.

London, Bruce, and Michael Giles. 1987. "Black Participation: Compensation or Ethnic Identification." *Journal of Black Studies* 18:20–44.

Lott, Tommy. 1992. "Marooned in America: Black Urban Youth Culture and Social Pathology." In *The Underclass Question*, ed. Bill E. Lawson. Philadelphia: Temple University Press.

Loury, Glenn C. 1994. "The Role of Normative Values in Rescuing the Urban Ghetto." In *Building a Community of Citizens: Civil Society in the 21st Century*, ed. Don E. Eberly. Lanham, Md.: University Press of America.

Lowi, Theodore J. 1979. *The End of Liberalism: The Second Republic of the United States*. 2nd ed. New York: W.W. Norton.

Lustig, R. Jeffrey. 1982. *Corporate Liberalism: The Origins of Modern American Political Theory, 1890–1920*. Berkeley: University of California Press.

Lyman, Stanford M. 1991. "The Race Question and Liberalism: Casuistries in American Constitutional Law." *International Journal of Politics, Culture, and Society* 5:183–247.

MacIntyre, Alasdair. 1984. *After Virtue: A Study in Moral Theory*. 2nd ed. Notre Dame, Ind.: University of Notre Dame Press.

MacKinnon, Catherine A. 1989. *Toward a Feminist Theory of the State*. Cambridge: Harvard University Press.

Majors, Richard, and Janet Mancini Billson. 1992. *Cool Pose: The Dilemmas of Black Manhood in America*. New York: Lexington Books.

Malcolm X. 1970. "The Ballot or the Bullet." In *What Country Have I? Political Writings by Black Americans*, ed. Herbert Storing. New York: St. Martin's Press.

Mann, Coramae Richey. 1993. *Unequal Justice: A Question of Color*. Bloomington: Indiana University Press.

Marable, Manning. 1986. "Black History and the Vision of Democracy." In *The New Populism: The Politics of Empowerment*, ed. Harry C. Boyte and Frank Riessman. Philadelphia: Temple University Press.

———. 1991a. *Race, Reform, and Rebellion: The Second Reconstruction in Black America, 1945–1990*. 2nd ed. Jackson: University Press of Mississippi.

———. 1991b. "The Black Male: Searching Beyond Stereotypes." In *The Black Family: Essays and Studies*, ed. Robert Staples. 4th ed. Belmont, Calif.: Wadsworth.

Marable, Manning, and Leith Mullings. 1994. "The Divided Mind of Black America: Race, Ideology, and Politics in the Post–Civil Rights Era." *Race & Class* 36(1):61–72.

Marx, Karl. 1963. "On the Jewish Question." In *Early Writings*, ed. and trans. T. B. Bottomore. New York: McGraw-Hill.

Massey, Douglass, and Nancy Denton. 1993. *American Apartheid: Segregation and the Making of the Underclass*. Cambridge: Harvard University Press.

Mastrofski, Stephen D., and Jack R. Greene. 1993. "Community Policing and the Rule of Law." In *Police Innovation and Control of the Police: Problems of Law, Order, and Community*, ed. David Weisburd and Craig Uchida. New York: Springer-Verlag.

McAlpine, Robert, Billy J. Tidwell, and Monica L. Jackson. 1988. "Civil Rights and Social Justice: From Progress to Regress." In *Black Americans and Public Policy: Perspectives of the National Urban League*. New York: National Urban League.

McCloud, Aminah Beverly. 1995. *African American Islam*. New York: Routledge.

McKean, Jerome. 1994. "Race, Ethnicity, and Criminal Justice." In *Multicultural Perspectives in Criminal Justice and Criminology*, ed. James E. Hendricks and Bryan Byers. Springfield, Ill.: Charles C. Thomas.

McLanahan, Sara, and Gary Sandefur. 1994. *Growing Up with a Single Parent: What Hurts, What Helps*. Cambridge: Harvard University Press.

McPherson, J. Miller. 1977. "Correlates of Social Participation: A Comparison of Ethnic Community and Compensatory Theories." *The Sociological Quarterly* 18:197–208.

Medler, Alex. 1996. "Promise and Progress." *The American School Board Journal* 183(3):26–28.

Meier, Kenneth J., Joseph Stewart Jr., and Robert E. England. 1989a. *Race, Class, and Education: The Politics of Second-Generation Discrimination*. Madison: University of Wisconsin Press.

———. 1989b. "Second-Generation Educational Discrimination and White Flight from Public Schools." *National Political Science Review* 1:76–90.

Meredith, James. 1992. "Statement." In *Documentary History of the Modern Civil Rights Movement*, ed. Peter B. Levy. New York: Greenwood Press.

Mill, John Stuart. 1896. *A System of Logic*. London: Longman, Green and Co.

———. 1984a. "Inaugural Address Delivered to the University of St. Andrews." In *Collected Works of John Stuart Mill*, vol. 21, ed. John M. Robson. Toronto: University of Toronto Press.

———. 1984b. "The Negro Question." In *Collected Works of John Stuart Mill*, vol. 21, ed. John M. Robson. Toronto: University of Toronto Press.

———. 1989a. "On Liberty." In *On Liberty and Other Writings*, ed. Stefan Collini. Cambridge: Cambridge University Press.

———. 1989b. "The Subjection of Women." In *On Liberty and Other Writings*, ed. Stefan Collini. Cambridge: Cambridge University Press.

Miller, Arthur H., et al. 1981. "Group Consciousness and Political Participation." *American Journal of Political Science* 25:494–511.

Mitchell, Mozella G. 1994. *New Africa in America: The Blending of African and American Religious and Social Traditions Among Black People in Meridian, Mississippi and Surrounding Counties*. New York: Peter Lang.

Morrison, John D. 1991. "The Black Church as a Support System for Black Elderly." *Journal of Gerontological Social Work* 17(1/2):105–120.

Mukenge, Ida Rousseau. 1983. *The Black Church in Urban America*. Lanham, Md.: University Press of America.

Murray, Charles. 1984. *Losing Ground: American Social Policy, 1950–1980*. New York: Basic Books.

Myrdal, Gunnar, et al. 1944. *An American Dilemma: The Negro Problem and Modern Democracy*. New York: Harper & Brothers.

National Urban League. 1988. *Black Americans and Public Policy: Perspectives of the National Urban League*. New York: National Urban League.

Nord, Warren A. 1995. *Religion & American Education: Rethinking a National Dilemma*. Chapel Hill: University of North Carolina Press.

Nozick, Robert. 1974. *Anarchy, State, and Utopia*. New York: Basic Books.

Okin, Susan Moller. 1989. *Justice, Gender, and the Family*. New York: Basic Books.

———. 1991. "John Rawls: Justice as Fairness–For Whom?" In *Feminist Interpretations of Political Theory*, ed. Mary Lyndon Shanley and Carole Pateman. University Park: Pennsylvania State University Press.

Oliver, Melvin L., and Thomas M. Shapiro. 1995. *Black Wealth/White Wealth: A New Perspective on Racial Inequality*. New York: Routledge.

Oliver, William. 1989. "Black Males and Social Problems: Prevention through Afrocentric Socialization." *Journal of Black Studies* 20:15–39.

———. 1994. *The Violent Social World of Black Men*. New York: Lexington Books.

Olsen, Marvin E. 1970. "Social and Political Participation of Blacks." *American Sociological Review* 35:682–697.

Omi, Michael, and Howard Winant. 1994. *Racial Formation in the United States: From the 1960s to the 1990s*. 2nd ed. New York: Routledge.

Orfield, Gary. 1986. "The Movement for Housing Integration: Rationale and the Nature of the Challenge." In *Housing Desegregation and Federal Policy*, ed. John M. Goering. Chapel Hill: University of North Carolina Press.

———. 1988. "Race and the Liberal Agenda: The Loss of the Integrationist Dream, 1965–1974." In *The Politics of Social Policy in the United States*, ed. Margaret Weir, Ann Shola Orloff, and Theda Skocpol. Princeton, N.J.: Princeton University Press.

Orloff, Ann Shola. 1988. "The Political Origins of America's Belated Welfare State." In *The Politics of Social Policy in the United States*, ed. Margaret Weir, Ann Shola Orloff, and Theda Skocpol. Princeton, N.J.: Princeton University Press.

Oser, Alan S. 1994. "When Housing Comes, Can Stores Be Far Behind." *The New York Times*, 9 October, R7.

Page, Benjamin I., and Robert Y. Shapiro. 1992. *The Rational Public: Fifty Years of Trends in Americans' Policy Preferences*. Chicago: University of Chicago Press.

Pateman, Carole. 1991. "Feminist Critiques of the Public-Private Dichotomy." In *Contemporary Political Theory*, ed. Philip Pettit. New York: Macmillan.

Paul, Jeffrey. 1984. "Rawls on Liberty." In *Conceptions of Liberty in Political Philosophy*, ed. Zbigniew Pelczynski and John Gray. London: Athlone Press.

Peak, Kenneth J., and Ronald W. Glensor. 1996. *Community Policing and Problem Solving: Strategies and Practices.* Upper Saddle River, N.J.: Prentice Hall.

Pennick, Edward J. 1990. "Land Ownership and Black Economic Development." *The Black Scholar* 21(1):43–46.

Piven, Francis Fox, and Richard A. Cloward. 1977. *Poor People's Movements: Why They Succeed, How They Fail.* New York: Vintage Books.

Pocock, J.G.A. 1975. *The Machiavellian Moment: Florentine Political Thought and the Atlantic Republican Tradition.* Princeton, N.J.: Princeton University Press.

Polite, Vernon C. 1992. "Getting the Job Done Well: African American Students and Catholic Schools." *The Journal of Negro Education* 61:211–222.

———. 1994. "Reproduction and Resistance: An Analysis of African-American Males' Responses to Schooling." In *Too Much Schooling, Too Little Education: A Paradox of Black Life in White Societies*, ed. Mwalimu J. Shujaa. Trenton, N.J.: Africa World Press.

Pope, Jacqueline. 1992. "The Colonizing Impact of Public Service Bureaucracies in Black Communities." In *Race, Politics, and Economic Development: Community Perspectives*, ed. James Jennings. London: Verso.

Prokesch, Steven. 1992. "Housing Pact is Reached for Brooklyn." *The New York Times*, 6 October, B1,4.

Putnam, Robert D. 1995a. "Bowling Alone: America's Declining Social Capital." *Journal of Democracy* 6:65–78.

———. 1995b. "Bowling Alone: Revisited." *The Responsive Community* 5(2):18–33.

———. 1995c. "Tuning In, Tuning Out: The Strange Disappearance of Social Capital in America." *PS: Political Science and Politics* 28:664–683.

Quant, Jean B. 1970. *From the Small Town to the Great Community: The Social Thought of Progressive Intellectuals.* Brunswick, N.J.: Rutgers University Press.

Raspberry, William. 1995. ". . . But Keep it in Perspective." *The Washington Post*, 16 June, A25.

Ratteray, Joan Davis. 1992. "Independent Neighborhood Schools: A Framework for the Education of African Americans." *The Journal of Negro Education* 61:138–147.

———. 1994. "The Search for Access and Content in the Education of African-Americans." In *Too Much Schooling, Too Little Education: A Paradox of Black Life in White Societies*, ed. Mwalimu J. Shujaa. Trenton, N.J.: Africa World Press.

Rawls, John. 1971. *A Theory of Justice.* Cambridge: Harvard University Press.

Raz, Joseph. 1986. *The Morality of Freedom.* Oxford: Oxford University Press.

———. 1990. "Facing Diversity: The Case of Epistemic Abstinence." *Philosophy and Public Affairs* 19:3–46.

———. 1992. "Liberalism, Skepticism, and Democracy." In *Democracy: Theory and Practice*, ed. John Arthur. Belmont, Calif.: Wadsworth.

———. 1994. "Multiculturalism: A Liberal Perspective." *Dissent* (Winter 1994):67–79.

Reed, Rodney J. 1988. "Education and Achievement of Young Black Males." In *Young, Black, and Male in America: An Endangered Species*, ed. Jewelle Taylor Gibbs. New York: Auburn House.

Rice, Mitchell F., and Woodrow Jones Jr. 1994. *Public Policy and the Black Hospital: From Slavery to Segregation to Integration.* Westport, Conn.: Greenwood Press.

Richardson, W. Franklyn. 1994. "Mission to Mandate: Self-Development through the Black Church." In *The State of Black America 1994*, ed. Billy J. Tidwell. New York: National Urban League.

Rickard, Maurice. 1994. "Liberalism, Multiculturalism, and Minority Protection." *Social Theory and Practice* 20:143–170.

Riessman, Frank. 1986. "The New Populism and the Empowerment Ethos." In *The New Populism: The Politics of Empowerment*, ed. Harry C. Boyte and Frank Riessman. Philadelphia: Temple University Press.

Roediger, David R. 1991. *The Wages of Whiteness: Race and the Making of the American Working Class.* London: Verso.

———. 1992. "The Racial Crisis of American Liberalism." *New Left Review* 196:114–119.

———. 1994. *Towards the Abolition of Whiteness: Essays on Race, Politics, and Working Class History.* London: Verso.

Rorty, Amelie Oksenberg. 1994. "The Hidden Politics of Cultural Identification." *Political Theory* 22:152–166.

Rose, David L. 1994. "Twenty-Five Years Later: Where Do We Stand on Equal Employment Opportunity Law Enforcement." In *Equal Employment Opportunity: Labor Market Discrimination and Public Policy*, ed. Paul Berstein. New York: Aldine De Gruyter.

Rosenberg, Gerald N. 1991. *The Hollow Hope: Can the Courts Bring about Social Change?* Chicago: University of Chicago Press.

Rosentraub, Mark S., and Karen Harlow. 1984. "Police Policies and the Black Community: Attitudes toward the Police." In *Contemporary Public Policy Perspectives and Black Americans*, ed. Mitchell F. Rice and Woodrow Jones Jr. Westport, Conn.: Greenwood Press.

Russell, Kathy, Midge Wilson, and Ronald Hall. 1993. *The Color Complex: The Politics of Skin Color among African Americans.* New York: Anchor Books.

Salamon, Lester M. 1995. *Partners in Public Service: Government-Nonprofit Relations in the Modern Welfare State.* Baltimore: Johns Hopkins University Press.

Samuelson, Robert J. 1995. "Affirmative Action: Theatrics . . ." *The Washington Post*, 9 August, A19.

Sandel, Michael J. 1982. *Liberalism and the Limits of Justice.* Cambridge: Cambridge University Press.

———. 1984a. "The Procedural Republic and the Unencumbered Self." *Political Theory* 12:81–96.

———. 1984b. Introduction to *Liberalism and Its Critics*. Oxford: Basil Blackwell.

———. 1996. *Democracy's Discontent: America in Search of a Public Philosophy.* Cambridge: Belknap Press of Harvard University Press.

Sawyer, Mary R. 1994. *Black Ecumenism: Implementing the Demands of Justice*. Valley Forge, Pa.: Trinity Press International.

Schaar, John H. 1967. "Equality of Opportunity, and Beyond." In *Nomos IX: Equality*, ed. J. Roland Pennock and John W. Chapman. New York: Athorton Press.

Schofield, Janet Ward. 1986. "Causes and Consequences of the Color-Blind Perspective." In *Prejudice, Discrimination, and Racism*, ed. John F. Dovidio and Samuel Gaertner. Orlando, Fla.: Academic Press.

Scott, Joseph W., and Albert Black. 1991. "Deep Structures of African American Family Life: Female and Male Kin Networks." In *The Black Family: Essays and Studies*, ed. Robert Staples. 4th ed. Belmont, Calif.: Wadsworth.

Seligman, Adam B. 1992. *The Idea of Civil Society*. New York: Free Press.

Sewell, William H. Jr. 1992. "A Theory of Structure: Duality, Agency, and Transformation." *American Journal of Sociology* 98:1–29.

Shingles, Richard D. 1981. "Black Consciousness and Political Participation: The Missing Link." *American Political Science Review* 75:76–91.

Shklar, Judith. 1989. "The Liberalism of Fear." In *Liberalism and the Moral Life*, ed. Nancy Rosenblum. Cambridge: Harvard University Press.

Shujaa, Mwalimu J., ed. 1994a. *Too Much Schooling, Too Little Education: A Paradox of Black Life in White Societies*. Trenton, N.J.: Africa World Press.

———. 1994b. "Afrocentric Transformation and Parental Choice in African-American Independent Schools." In *Too Much Schooling, Too Little Education: A Paradox of Black Life in White Societies*, ed. Mwalimu J. Shujaa. Trenton, N.J.: Africa World Press.

Shull, Steven A. 1993. *A Kinder, Gentler Racism? The Reagan-Bush Civil Rights Legacy*. Armonk, N.Y.: M.E. Sharpe.

Sigelman, Lee, and Susan Welch. 1991. *Black Americans' Views of Racial Inequality: The Dream Deferred*. Cambridge: Cambridge University Press.

Sitkoff, Harvard. 1993. *The Struggle for Black Equality, 1954–1992*. Rev. ed. New York: Hill and Wang.

Skocpol, Theda. 1992. *Protecting Soldiers and Mothers: The Political Origins of Social Policy in the United States*. Cambridge: Belknap Press of Harvard University Press.

Smedley, Audrey. 1993. *Race in North America: Origin and Evolution of a Worldview*. Boulder, Colo.: Westview Press.

Smith, Robert C. 1995. *Racism in the Post–Civil Rights Era: Now You See It, Now You Don't*. Albany, N.Y.: State University of New York Press.

Smith, Rogers M. 1993. "Beyond Tocqueville, Myrdal, and Hartz: The Multiple Traditions in America." *American Political Science Review* 87:549–566.

Smith, Steven Rathgeb, and Michael Lipsky. 1993. *Nonprofits for Hire: The Welfare State in the Age of Contracting*. Cambridge: Harvard University Press.

Sniderman, Paul M., and Michael Gray Hagen. 1985. *Race and Inequality: A Study in American Values*. Chatham, N.J.: Chatham House Publishers.

Sniderman, Paul M., Philip E. Tetlock, and Edward G. Carmines, eds. 1993. *Prejudice, Politics, and the American Dilemma*. Stanford, Calif.: Stanford University Press.

Sniderman, Paul M., and Thomas Piazza. 1993. *The Scar of Race*. Cambridge: Harvard University Press.

Solomon, Barbara. 1988. "The Impact of Public Policy on the Status of Young Black Males." In *Young, Black, and Male in America: An Endangered Species*, ed. Jewelle Taylor Gibbs. New York: Auburn House.

Southern, David W. 1987. *Gunnar Myrdal and Black-White Relations: The Use and Abuse of* an American Dilemma, *1944–1969*. Baton Rouge: Louisiana State University Press.

Spann, Girardeau A. 1993. *Race against the Court: The Supreme Court and Minorities in Contemporary America*. New York: New York University Press.

Spinner, Jeff. 1994. *The Boundaries of Citizenship: Race, Ethnicity, and Nationality in the Liberal State*. Baltimore: Johns Hopkins University Press.

Stack, Carol B. 1991. "Sex Roles and Survival Strategies in an Urban Black Community." In *The Black Family: Essays and Studies*, ed. Robert Staples. 4th ed. Belmont, Calif.: Wadsworth.

Staples, Robert. 1991. "The Political Economy of Black Family Life." In *The Black Family: Essays and Studies*, ed. Robert Staples. 4th ed. Belmont, Calif.: Wadsworth.

Steele, Shelby. 1991. "The Recoloring of Campus Life." In *Second Thoughts about Race in America*, ed. Peter Collier and David Horowitz. Lanham, Md.: Madison Books.

Stevenson, Howard C. 1990. "The Role of the African-American Church in Education about Teenage Pregnancy." *Counseling and Values* 34:130–133.

Stewart, Jill. 1990. "Nehemiah West Backers Face First Key Test." *The Los Angeles Times*, 14 May, B1, 8.

Svensson, Frances. 1979. "Liberal Democracy and Group Rights: The Legacy of Individualism and its Impact on American Indian Tribes." *Political Studies* 27:421–439.

Takaki, Ronald. 1987a. "Reflections on Racial Patterns in America." In *From Different Shores: Perspectives on Race and Ethnicity in America*, ed. Ronald Takaki. New York: Oxford University Press.

———. 1987b. "To Count or Not to Count by Race and Gender?" In *From Different Shores: Perspectives on Race and Ethnicity in America*, ed. Ronald Takaki. New York: Oxford University Press.

Taylor, Charles. 1976. "Responsibility for Self." In *The Identities of Persons*, ed. Amelie O. Rorty. Berkeley: University of California Press.

———. 1985a. *Human Agency and Language: Philosophical Papers*, vol. 1. Cambridge: Cambridge University Press.

———. 1985b. *Philosophy and the Human Sciences: Philosophical Papers*, vol. 2. Cambridge: Cambridge University Press.

———. 1985c. "The Person." In *The Category of the Person*, ed. Michael Carrithers, Steven Collins, and Steven Lukes. Cambridge: Cambridge University Press.

———. 1989a. *Sources of the Self: The Making of the Modern Identity*. Cambridge: Harvard University Press.

————. 1989b. "Cross-Purposes: The Liberal-Communitarian Debate." In *Liberalism and the Moral Life*, ed. Nancy L. Rosenblum. Cambridge: Harvard University Press.

————. 1991. *The Ethics of Authenticity*. Cambridge: Harvard University Press.

————. 1992. *Multiculturalism and the "Politics of Recognition,"* ed. Amy Gutman. Princeton, N.J.: Princeton University Press.

————. 1993. "The Motivation Behind a Procedural Ethics." In *Kant & Political Philosophy: The Contemporary Legacy*, ed. Ronald Beiner and William James Booth. New Haven, Conn.: Yale University Press.

————. 1995. *Philosophical Arguments*. Cambridge: Harvard University Press.

Taylor, Clarence. 1994. *The Black Churches of Brooklyn*. New York: Columbia University Press.

Terchek, Ronald J. 1986. "The Fruits of Success and the Crisis of Liberalism." In *Liberals on Liberalism*, ed. Alfonso J. Damico. Totowa, N.J.: Rowman and Littlefield.

Thomas, Stephen B., et al. 1994. "The Characteristics of Northern Black Churches with Community Health Outreach Programs." *American Journal of Public Health* 84:575–579.

Tidwell, Billy J., ed. 1994. *The State of Black America 1994*. New York: National Urban League.

Tidwell, Billy J., Karen V. Hill, and Lisa Bland Malone. 1988. "Black Economic Development: Still on the Margin." In *Black Americans and Public Policy: Perspectives of the National Urban League*. New York: National Urban League.

Turner, Margery Austin, Michael Fix, and Raymond J. Struyk. 1991. *Opportunities Denied, Opportunities Diminished: Racial Discrimination in Hiring*. Washington, D.C.: Urban Institute Press.

Volkomer, Walter E. 1969. Introduction to *The Liberal Tradition in American Thought*. New York: Capricorn Books.

Waldinger, Roger, and Thomas Bailey. 1991. "The Continuing Significance of Race: Racial Conflict and Racial Discrimination in Construction." *Politics & Society* 19:291–323.

Waligorski, Conrad. 1981. "Anglo-American Political-Economic Liberalism." Introduction to *Anglo-American Liberalism: Readings in Normative Political Economy*, ed. Conrad Waligorski and Thomas Hone. Chicago: Nelson-Hall.

Walker, Samuel, Cassia Spohn, and Miriam DeLone. 1996. *The Color of Justice: Race, Ethnicity, and Crime in America*. Belmont, Calif.: Wadsworth.

Wallace-Benjamin, Joan. 1994. "Organizing African-American Self-Development: The Role of Community-Based Organizations." In *The State of Black America 1994*, ed. Billy J. Tidwell. New York: National Urban League.

Walzer, Michael. 1982. "Pluralism in Political Perspective." In Michael Walzer et al., *The Politics of Ethnicity*. Cambridge: Harvard University Press.

————. 1983. *Spheres of Justice: A Defense of Pluralism and Equality*. New York: Basic Books.

————. 1984. "Liberalism and the Art of Separation." *Political Theory* 12:315–330.

————. 1990. "The Communitarian Critique of Liberalism." *Political Theory* 18:6–23.

———. 1992a. *What it Means to be an American*. New York: Marsilio.

———. 1992b. "The Civil Society Argument." In *Dimensions of Radical Democracy: Pluralism, Citizenship, Community*, ed. Chantal Mouffe. London: Verso.

———. 1994. "Multiculturalism and Individualism." *Dissent* (Spring 1994):185–191.

Ward, Janie V. 1995. "Cultivating a Morality of Care in African American Adolescents: A Culture-Based Model of Violence Prevention." *Harvard Educational Review* 65:175–188.

Watson, Betty Collier, Vincent Austin, and James Reed. 1988. "Employment and Training: Toward the Year 2000." In *Black Americans and Public Policy: Perspectives of the National Urban League*. New York: National Urban League.

Webb, Vincent J., and Chris E. Marshall. 1995. "The Relative Importance of Race and Ethnicity on Citizen Attitudes toward the Police." *American Journal of Police* 14(2):45–66.

Weir, Margaret, and Theda Skocpol. 1985. "State Structures and the Possibilities for 'Keynesian' Responses to the Great Depression in Sweden, Britain, and the United States." In *Bringing the State Back In*, ed. Peter B. Evans, Dietrich Rueschemeyer, and Theda Skocpol. Cambridge: Cambridge University Press.

West, Cornel. 1993. *Race Matters*. New York: Vintage Books.

Whittler, Tommy E., Roger J. Calantone, and Mark R. Young. 1991. "Strength of Ethnic Affiliation: Examining Black Identification with Black Culture." *The Journal of Social Psychology* 131:461–467.

Williams, Juan. 1991. "The Movement Continues." In *Second Thoughts about Race in America*, ed. Peter Collier and David Horowitz. Lahman, Md.: Madison Books.

Williams, Melissa S. 1995. "Justice toward Groups: Political Not Juridical." *Political Theory* 23:67–91.

Williams, Patricia J. 1991. *The Alchemy of Race and Rights*. Cambridge: Harvard University Press.

Wilmore, Gayraud S. 1983. *Black Religion and Black Radicalism: An Interpretation of the Religious History of Afro-American People*. 2nd ed. Maryknoll, N.Y.: Orbis Books.

Wilson, James Q. 1994. "Culture, Incentives, and the Underclass." In *Values and Public Policy*, ed. Henry J. Aaron, Thomas E. Mann, and Timothy Taylor. Washington, D.C.: Brookings.

Wilson, William Julius. 1987. *The Truly Disadvantaged: The Inner City, the Underclass, and Public Policy*. Chicago: University of Chicago Press.

———. 1996. *When Work Disappears: The World of the New Urban Poor*. New York: Knopf.

Wohlstetter, Priscilla, Richard Wenning, and Kerri L. Briggs. 1995. "Charter Schools in the United States: The Question of Autonomy." *Educational Policy* 9:331–358.

Wolfinger, Raymond E. 1966. "Some Consequences of Ethnic Politics." In *The Electoral Process*, ed. M. Kent Jennings and L. Harmon Zeigler. Englewood Cliffs, N.J.: Prentice Hall.

Wood, Gordon S. 1969. *The Creation of the American Republic, 1776–1787.* New York: W.W. Norton.

Yates, Donald L., and Vijayan K. Pillai. 1992–93. "Race and Police Commitment to Community Policing." *Journal of Intergroup Relations* 19(4):14–23.

Young, Iris Marion. 1989. "Polity and Group Difference: A Critique of the Ideal of Universal Citizenship." *Ethics* 99:250–274.

———. 1990. *Justice and the Politics of Difference.* Princeton, N.J.: Princeton University Press.

Young, James P. 1996. *Reconsidering American Liberalism: The Troubled Odyssey of the Liberal Idea.* Boulder, Colo.: Westview Press.

# INDEX